Number 129

Centennial Series of the Association of Former Students,
Texas A&M University

The Fightin' Texas Aggie Band

With gratitude for his leadership as chairman from 2012 to 2017, the Advancement Board of Texas A&M University Press sponsors this book in appreciation and honor of Gary J. Martin '71, a proud former member and loyal supporter of the Fightin' Texas Aggie Band.

The Fightin' Texas Aggie Band

125th Anniversary Edition

Mary Jo Powell

TEXAS A&M UNIVERSITY PRESS

College Station

This paper meets the requirements of ANSI/NISO Z39.48–1992 (Permanence of Paper).
Binding materials have been chosen for durability.
Manufactured in China through Four Colour Print Group

Library of Congress Cataloging-in-Publication Data

Names: Powell, Mary Jo, 1953– author.
Title: The Fightin' Texas Aggie Band : 125th anniversary edition / Mary Jo Powell.
Other titles: Fighting Texas Aggie Band | Centennial series of the Association
    of Former Students, Texas A&M University ; no. 129.
Description: Revised edition. | College Station : Texas A&M University Press,
    [2019] | Series: Centennial series of the Association of Former Students,
    Texas A&M University ; Number 129 | Includes bibliographical references
    and index. | First edition by Donald B. Powell and Mary Jo Powell.
Identifiers: LCCN 2019017465| ISBN 9781623498238 (book/cloth : alk. paper) |
    ISBN 9781623498245 (e-book)
Subjects: LCSH: Fightin' Texas Aggie Band—History. | Marching
    bands—Texas—College Station—History. | Agricultural and Mechanical
    College of Texas. Corps of Cadets—Bands—History. | Texas A & M
    University. Corps of Cadets—Bands—History.
Classification: LCC ML28.C64 F546 2019 | DDC 784.8/3060764242—dc23
LC record available at https://lccn.loc.gov/2019017465

This book is dedicated to the members of the Fightin' Texas Aggie Band—past, present, and future. For 125 years they have stepped off with a special marching magic that turned the heads and stirred the hearts of all who watched. May they march ever onward. In addition to celebrating the quasquicentennial of the band, this revised edition also commemorates the golden anniversary of the Texas Aggie Band Association, a group of band alumni and friends dedicated to seeing that the band marches on forever.

Contents

Acknowledgments   xi

Introduction   xiii

Chapters

1. Joseph Holick and the Early Bandmasters, 1894–1924   1

2. The Tradition Begins: Lieutenant Colonel Richard J. Dunn, 1924–46   15

3. The Military Precision: Lieutenant Colonel E. V. Adams '29, 1946–73   30

4. The Big Bold Sound: Colonel Joe T. Haney, 1973–89   54

5. The Legend Continues: Lieutenant Colonel Ray E. Toler, 1989–2001   94

6. The Expanding Music Program: Dr. Timothy B. Rhea, 2002   121

7. "On the Road Again . . ."   137

8. The Definitive Aggie Bandsman: Colonel Jay O. Brewer '81, 1977–   147

Appendixes

A. Band Leadership   157

B. Rosters of Aggie Band Members   171

Notes   243

Acknowledgments from the 1994 Edition

While we are indebted to the Fightin' Texas Aggie Band for providing the inspiration and subject matter for this book, special thanks also are due to a large group of individuals without whose assistance the actual text, accompanying photographs, and various lists and rosters would not have been possible.

Leading the research team for the 1994 edition was Robert E. Lang of the Class of 1949, who served as our chief researcher; his wife, Patricia Lang; Robert C. Barker '71, photographic research; Joe Fenton '58, then curator of the Sam Houston Sanders Corps of Cadets Center at Texas A&M University; his wife, Pat, staff assistant at the Corps Center; and John E. West '57. Sadly, Bob Lang, Joe Fenton, and John West are no longer with us. All provided invaluable assistance and support throughout this project.

Research associates who were especially helpful in compiling the roster of present and former band members include the late Jean S. Stanley, Edward Broussard '94, Pamela Netzinger Burleigh '92, and Carolyn M. Skopik.

While many band members and fans of the band contributed anecdotes and information, the following provided special help: Mrs. E. V. (Belle) Adams, Edward V. Adams Jr. '61, Paul Allen Jr. '47, R. William Barzak '48, Searcy Bracewell '38, Jay O. Brewer '81, William G. Caughlin '49, Edwin H. Cooper '53, Gerald Cunningham '48, Richard Dockum '30, Robert Drago Jr. '49, I. E. Elkins '47, Tull Gearreald '34, Joseph Gordon '43, Don Hackney '44, Joe T. Haney '48, Bedford "Scoot" Harrison '48, Donald R. "Buck" Henderson '62, Gus Herzik Jr. '34, Dorothy Hopkins, Earl Horn '33, George Humble '48, Thomas Knox '48, Roger Kret '82, Paul Laroche '45, Earl Patterson '25, John M. Percifield Jr. '91, Henry Qualtrough '36, Vic Russek Jr. '52, Ben Schleider '43, Don Simpson '49, Ernest Slaughter Jr. '47, Sidney Smith '44, G. C. "Pete" Stanley '46, Thomas Terrell '34, and Ray E. Toler. Many of these individuals have also died since the original publication of this book. Information made available by the Sam Houston Sanders Corps of Cadets Center at Texas A&M University, the Cushing Memorial Library & Archives at Texas A&M University, and the Texas Aggie Band Association was also used extensively.

In addition, we received literally hundreds of photographs beyond the ones that appear here. Those photographs were contributed by Chandler W. Arden, Robert C. Barker '71, Mauris Barton '32, Wayne Bertrand '88, W. Mack Bradford, Michelle Brenckman '79, Olin Brown '60, William G. Caughlin '49, Jerry C. Cooper '63, Richard E. Ferguson, Brad Garrett '78, Paul Glenn, Jim Hall '69, J. Harold Hughes '52, Homer A. Hunter '25, Glen Johnson '78, R. Doyle Johnson '65, Carol E. Jordan '80, Phyllis P. Keller '80, Michael R. Kellett '92, Michael A. Kelley '89, William R. Ledbetter '40, James W. Lyle, Michael McKnight '89, John C. Otto '70, Buddy D. Patterson '56, P. T. "Pete"

Rathbone '55, Jill Raupe '88, O. L. Richardson Jr. '45, Ken Roberson '57, Vernon Roberts '53, Bob Russell '42, Edwin Rydell '86, Christian Schnitger '91, Richard W. Smith '75, Samuel Don Smith '68, Don B. Sparks '50, Karl Stephens '57, J. H. Thomas '53, Sylvia Ann Tijerina, John E. West '57, Texas A&M University Photographic Services, the Texas A&M University Archives, and the Sam Houston Sanders Corps of Cadets Center. Several of these individuals have also passed away.

There are others, too numerous to name here, who have contributed to the magic that is the Fightin' Texas Aggie Band. In addition to those named here, we thank all of them as well.

Acknowledgments for the 125th Anniversary Edition

When I worked on the original edition of *The Fightin' Texas Aggie Band* in 1993, it was a joint project with my husband (former Aggie Band member Donald B. Powell '56). We received help from an enormous number of people, many of whose names are listed in the acknowledgments that appear above.

There were, of course, new helpers for the revision. Band members who have marched since 1994 have continued to inspire me with their dedication, but this revision couldn't have been accomplished without the assistance of the following individuals from the current band staff; director of bands and musical activities Timothy B. Rhea, senior associate director of the Aggie Band Jay O. Brewer, and administrative assistant Susan Haven, who with the help of student workers Russell Bodeker 2017, Amber Macha 2019, and Dylan Bradshaw 2018 helped compile the Second Century Roster of Band Members. Chris Sullivan '98 and a group of his bandmates also provided invaluable assistance on the Second Century Roster, which includes those who have marched in the band since the publication of the first book. Please note that the two rosters are in slightly different formats. The pre-1994 list gives the year each person is believed to have entered the Aggie Band. This is because, during its first century, students marched during the Great Depression, two world wars, and numerous other military conflicts. These students often left and then returned to the band, either semesters or years later, and some never returned at all. The Second Century Roster gives the class years instead of the starting year, which is the way most Aggies list their affiliation with the university.

Special thanks go out to Robert C. Barker '71, who worked with my husband and me on a variety of projects related to the Aggie Band. I would have been lost without his institutional memory of the Aggie Band, the Texas Aggie Band Association, and *The Texas Aggie Band Show* and the literally hundreds of photographs he submitted for the first book. In addition to Barker, I offer my personal thanks to Bruce Bockhorn '74, Don's successor as host of the band show and the band's unofficial statistician. No one works with numbers quite like Bruce. And finally, although they are acknowledged above, both Jay Brewer and Tim Rhea have, without complaining, put up with—and answered—what must have seemed like countless emails seeking the details that fill this book. David Marion '65 and Harvey Schulz '69 also helped in many ways. Patricia Clabaugh of Texas A&M University Press and freelance copyeditor Laurel Anderton also helped provide the finished book you have before you.

My friends and family also deserve special thanks for their continuing support during these revisions. I love you all and can't thank you enough.

And last, but certainly not least, I must praise Thom Lemmons, senior editor at Texas A&M University Press. As a skillful editor, he always knew just what to say and how to provide encouragement when it was needed. In the years prior to my retirement, I was a writer, editor, and associate director of what was then called the Office of University Relations, A&M's main public relations operation. In that role I dealt with many writers and editors. I hope I did it with the skill and finesse that Thom has shown me.

Mary Jo Powell
July 29, 2018

Introduction

"Ladies and gentlemen! Now forming at the north end of Kyle Field, the nationally famous Fightin' Texas Aggie Band!" The spectators gathered in that venerable stadium join the announcer in repeating the last words of that equally famous introduction. A loud cheer erupts and then an eerie silence as the crowd listens for the drum major's command.

A lone figure strides forward and turns to face the assembled military unit. In a voice both loud and clear the command rings out, "Band, attention! Recall, step off on Hullabaloo!" Each word of the command is drawn out for full effect. The crowd cheers in anticipation. The drum major's whistle blows; the baton rises. Four hundred instruments snap to playing position and twelve silver bugles with maroon and white banners flash in the light. The baton moves and the traditional bugle herald known as "Recall" echoes across the playing field as a prelude to another performance of the largest and most outstanding military marching band in the nation.

Hullabaloo, the first word of "The Aggie War Hymn," moves the band down the field at a deliberate 104 beats per minute. Sharp turns and smooth countermarches are greeted with ever-increasing cheers. The precision is unbelievable. The marching is perfect and the cavalry boots on the senior band members move as one. With no break in the music, the "War Hymn" ends and the band moves directly into a stirring and patriotic military march. The music is bold, brassy, and beautiful.

Another march, another impossible maneuver, another loud response from one hundred thousand spectators. Now even the fans who came to root for the other team are cheering and applauding the Fightin' Texas Aggie Band.

The sound of the "War Hymn" is heard again as parts of the band flank left and right and a huge moving "T," the signature of the band, appears on the field. The "T" moves down the field and countermarches in the opposite direction. Suddenly the music stops, but the band continues marching at the same deliberate pace. Finally, on the drum major's signal, the musicians break the precise military march and run from the field. The crowd is on its feet. The nationally famous Fightin' Texas Aggie Band has won another halftime.

It wasn't easy, though. It took the determination, discipline, and enduring pride of bandmasters and band members to achieve that reputation. This is the story of those who made the Fightin' Texas Aggie Band the pulse of the spirit of Aggieland. It is a 125-year story that pays tribute to the bandmasters who gave birth to the band, who developed its precision marching style, who wrote and arranged its stirring music, and who maintain the legend and the tradition as "The Colonel." It is a story told through the eyes and from the hearts of those young men and women who were tough enough and proud enough and good enough to be "The Noble Men of Kyle."

The Fightin'
Texas Aggie Band

1

Joseph Holick and the Early Bandmasters, 1894–1924

I was a small boy and couldn't do lumbering work.

—Joseph Holick

Joseph Holick and his older brother Louis had spent two years working as farmhands in Kansas. It was hard work and not exactly what they had in mind when they came to America from Czechoslovakia in 1885. Joseph had been an apprentice cobbler in his native land, but Louis had told him he would have a better life in America. The younger Holick wasn't so sure now. In Europe, Joseph had heard Johann Strauss conduct concerts in Vienna. The experience was wonderful and inspired him to teach himself to play the clarinet. Sunup to sundown farmwork, however, gave the young man little time for his music.

One day Louis told Joseph that he had heard there were good jobs—at good wages—available in the lumber mills near Orange, Texas. Believing any job would be better than farmwork, Joseph, then twenty-two, quickly agreed to go with his brother. Because the pair had no money for transportation, they climbed aboard an empty boxcar on a southbound freight train early the next day.

When they awoke the following morning, the train was not moving. As the older brother, Lou-

is was probably the one who first ventured outside to explore. The boxcar was standing alone on a railroad siding near a small-town depot; the rest of the train was nowhere to be seen. The two young men jumped down from the boxcar and walked toward the depot. As they approached, they could read the sign: Bryan, Texas. They were still a long way from their destination, but luck was with them. They had an uncle who lived in Bryan. They could stay with him until they found a way to continue their journey to Orange.[1]

Joseph, however, was having second thoughts about the lumber mills. Seventy-five years later, he would remember his reluctance to continue the journey. "I was a small boy and couldn't do lumbering work," he said.[2] During his first days in Bryan he had met Raymond Blatherwick, who owned a boot shop on the town's main street. Upon learning that the young man had trained to be a cobbler, Blatherwick offered him the chance to remain in Bryan and work in his shop. That sounded better than farming or lumber mill work to Joseph, so he stayed, while his older brother went on to seek his fortune elsewhere.

Holick became a fine cobbler under Blatherwick. Some of the work he did was for members of the faculty at the military college a few miles south of Bryan. It was the Agricultural and Mechanical College of Texas, a land-grant school still struggling to emerge from its infancy. By the early 1890s, the school was finally making some progress under its new president, Lawrence Sullivan Ross, a former governor of Texas.

According to one story recounted by the Holick family, President Ross himself came into the Blatherwick Boot Shop one day to have a pair of boots repaired. As Holick was working on the boots, the president mentioned that it was difficult for the cadets at the college to get to Bryan to have their boots repaired. Ross reportedly added that it would certainly be a great help if a cobbler could be located at the college. He asked whether Holick would be interested in moving to the campus, promising that the school would provide a room in the dormitory and there would be plenty of work for someone who knew how to repair boots.

The young cobbler was still single, and this sounded like a wonderful opportunity. Holick moved to the college and set up his shop in the dormitory. As promised, there was plenty of work and he enjoyed it. In the evenings he had time to pursue his love of music, playing his clarinet to entertain himself—and, as it turned out, others on campus.

When the school's commandant, Lieutenant Ben Morris, learned of Holick's musical talents he approached the young cobbler with a new opportunity: In addition to his duties as the campus cobbler, would he be interested in becoming the college bugler? Lieutenant Morris suggested a salary of sixty-five dollars per year, and Holick agreed to add the playing of "Reveille" and "Taps" to his duties as a cobbler just as soon as he could teach himself to play the bugle. Learning the bugle calls and how to play them proved to be even easier than learning the clarinet. Soon he was beginning each day by awakening the cadets with "Reveille" and ending their day with "Taps"—and receiving sixty-five dollars per year.

It was more money than Holick had seen before. He figured the college ought to get more than just two tunes for its money, and when he had established himself as the bugler, he asked the commandant for permission to start a cadet band. He knew the interest was there, as cadets had often come to his room at night to listen to him play his clarinet, and he knew that several of them wanted to learn to play an instrument as well.[3]

Perhaps he had read a letter on October 1, 1893, to the campus newspaper, the *Battalion*, written by a student at the college:

> We have for the past four or five years been entirely without music and it is just as necessary to have an orchestra as it is to have a glee club, societies, baseball or football teams, or a gymnasium, for it not only refreshes the body, but the mind also. It has been the custom in all the institutions in the United States to form musical clubs first, for without music no public meeting can be successfully held. The A. and M. is greatly deficient in this line, and to make us equal to any of the other institutions we must start on this one particular and important point at once. We have any amount of talent, which if properly trained by constant practice, would reflect not only credit upon ourselves, but our college also. There is not a student here who does not love music, and it would make him feel proud to think that we could make fine music, and he would come to hear us wherever we might play; for there is nothing that can produce the same effect that music can. The societies would grow, and they can find nothing which will excite enthusiasm better than to have music at each meeting. As it is now, the new cadets go up to the societies to see what is going on, and they find they have a few orations, and a debate, and no matter how interesting it is there is nothing to break up the monotony, and the same thing is repeated. The result is they leave disgusted declaring that they will never go to societies again; where, on the other hand, they go up and hear good music and would become enthusiastic as they never have before. Hoping to see that this organization is soon enrolled among the others I remain,
>
> R. L. Dinwiddie

What influence Dinwiddie's letter had on the decision to start a band at the Agricultural and Mechanical College of Texas is not clear, but shortly after the letter appeared, President Ross agreed to let Joseph Holick solicit membership for a cadet band.[4]

With the help of a student named Arthur Jenkins, Holick found thirteen cadets who were interested in being in the new band. There was much enthusiasm, but little money available for instruments. One of the cadets, J. K. Woods, knew of a band that was no longer in operation in his hometown, Del Rio, where they could borrow some instruments. A mathematics professor named Robert F. Smith was sympathetic to their cause and donated one hundred dollars to get the organization started. With this help, Holick was able to properly equip the band with both instruments and uniforms.[5]

Those early uniforms were just embellished versions of the standard gray cadet uniforms. The band members added the emblem of a chas-

Joseph Holick, the first bandmaster, circa 1893. Courtesy Holick family.

seur horn to their caps, with the letters "AMC" above the horn. This emblem was a curved horn or bugle that had historically been used by military musicians in rifle or light infantry units to relay commands in battle. Actually, the proper emblem for band musicians should have been the lyre, which has been used by the band since 1903. The chasseur horn emblem was probably used by the first cadet band because it was the emblem Holick wore on the front of his Texas Militia cap. An additional change in the band members' uniforms was the addition of a double black stripe on the trousers, a custom among army musicians. Cadets not in the band wore a single stripe. A short time later, the band would add a white cork helmet of the type made famous by the British Army in India. The band also had an allwhite cotton duck uniform and often wore the white trousers of that uniform with their gray tunics and the white helmet around 19. By 1904 they had added white duck caps for their all-white uniforms.[6]

The original thirteen bandsmen wearing those uniforms in 1894 were Texans J. K. Woods of Del Rio, T. B. Duggan of San Saba, A. W. Amthor of Pleasant Hill, P. B. Bittle of College Station, Arthur Jenkins of Bryan, W. Bretchneider of Cat Springs, W. C. Carothers of Sulphur Springs, S. Cohn (spelled Kohn in later band records) of Waco, W. M. Mathis of Rockport, H. L. Williams of Austin, and O. Gersteman of Houston, along with H. D'Echaux of Gibson, Louisiana. As was the custom of bandmasters in small bands of that time, Holick played his clarinet in addition to directing.

The drum major of the first Aggie Band was H. A. "California" Morse. There is some evidence that Cadet Morse did not last the year in this leadership role, and tradition holds that he was asked to leave the college because of fighting.[7] Some believe that the early drum majors were chosen in physical combat, with the best fighter being named to the coveted position. Many current band members believe this to be the origin of the name "Fightin' Texas Aggie

Band." Most band musicians, however, believe the name more properly refers to the Fightin' Texas Aggie athletic teams, as in the Fighting Illini or the Fighting Irish.

The band was successful from its earliest days. In referring to the band, the college's inaugural yearbook, the 1895 *Olio*, stated: "We are all proud of our band. And we have reason to be; for though as yet not one year old, the organization is one which will reflect credit on the college anywhere, and its members may rest assured that their earnest efforts are fully appreciated, both by the Corps and the campus." In the Class of 1897 history in that same 1895 *Olio*, the following is included: "This article were hardly complete without a mention of the college band. Our class affords the greater part of talent and enjoys the honor of giving to the band a competent and fine drum major. We are inspired with pride when 'sweet melody swells the breeze,' for it is then we are reminded that the college has one of the best amateur bands in Texas."

The band's reputation began to develop early. Apparently Cadet Dinwiddie was right—the cadets did wish for music on campus. Dinwiddie was allowed to start an orchestra at about the same time Holick was starting the band, but the 1895 *Olio* contains no favorable comments about that organization.

After getting the band started, Holick returned to his cobbler's bench, and band member Arthur Jenkins became its leader for a year. A barber named George W. Gross directed the band until sometime in 1897, when he resigned. Joe Wrenn directed for the balance of the term, and then the college hired F. M. Miller. Miller left in late 1902, and on January 12, 1903, George W. Tyrrell arrived to take his place. Tyrrell was a nationally known musician from Pennsylvania. He was a euphonium soloist, but like his predecessors he did not last long at the college, returning to Pennsylvania the following year.

According to Joseph Holick's son John, his father was called back to direct the band each time a new bandmaster left abruptly. John Holick speculates that some of those early bandmasters were

fond of the bottle and did not set a good example for the cadets. When Tyrrell left in the middle of the semester, Holick was loaded down with work, but the college president, David Franklin Houston, convinced him to once again take up the baton when Houston could not find anyone to come to the college to be bandmaster. It is interesting to note that the college was going through presidents about as fast as bandmasters during this period. Houston had been the third president since Lawrence Sullivan Ross's death in 1898.

Anxious to get back to his real duties as a cobbler, Holick contacted Bradford Pier Day of Brenham, Texas, about the open bandmaster's position. Day was a member of the Second Texas Infantry Band and seemed well qualified to direct the cadet musicians. He agreed to come to the college, and he liked what he saw. Finally the college had a bandmaster who was determined to stay and—with that commitment—give some stability to the still young organization.

With so many changes in bandmasters, it had been difficult to maintain the initial enthusiasm

Bradford Pier Day, bandmaster 1904–17. Courtesy of Cushing Memorial Library & Archives, Texas A&M University

for a cadet band. With the arrival of Day, the band began to become an even more important part of life at the college. According to Edward Holick, another son of the founding director and a member of the band in the Class of 1915, Day started improving the music of the band, and it was Day who made the cadet band a permanent part of the Agricultural and Mechanical College of Texas.[8]

In addition to directing the band, Day also took over the duties of the campus bugler. By this time, the bugler sounded not only "Reveille" and "Taps" but also a "call to classes" and, when classes were over, a "recall," the same bugle call that begins each band performance today.[9]

By 1915 Day had been bandmaster for eleven years, longer than all the previous bandmasters combined. Through his leadership the band became an important part of campus life at the A&M College. The 1915 *Longhorn*, the college yearbook, on page 129 describes the band and the feeling the cadets had for the organization. Included was this comment: "Without its band the A&M College would lack the most pleasant feature of its life. Too much praise cannot be given to the officers and members of this organization for lightening the daily routine of our college life."

The oldest living former member of the Texas Aggie Band at the time this book was originally written, Ossie Greene of San Angelo, Texas, was captain of that 1915 band, and before his death he recalled his days of playing the baritone horn while living in Pfeuffer Hall, the band dormitory at that time. Pfeuffer Hall was built in 1887 for $11.50 and was razed in 1954. Greene also played in the orchestra mentioned in the yearbook and confirms that its members were paid. "Everyone got $4 per month," he says, "but first chair players were paid $6 and soloists were paid $8 per month." Greene must have been a popular and handsome cadet because the editor of the 1915 *Longhorn* included this explanation of his nickname under his picture in the yearbook: "Ossie gets the name of 'Browneyes' from the Glee Club trip, as all the girls ask about the pretty brown eyed boy in the orchestra." Greene said the band was limited to thirty members during the early part of this century, but it was somewhat difficult to find that many musicians to be in the organization. During his first year in the band there were only twenty-eight members.[10]

With Day firmly established as both bandmaster and bugler, Joseph Holick could return to full-time cobbling, and in doing so, make his second major contribution to the history of Texas A&M. As a full-time cobbler, he built his own building on campus. It was a small wooden structure behind Gathright Hall, one of the original buildings at the college. Holick continued to work on campus until 1929. That year, in order to expand his business, he moved Holick's Boot Shop to an off-campus location at 106 College Main in the area now known as Northgate. Instead of just repairing boots and shoes there, Holick began to make the knee-high, form-fitting riding boots that had been worn by senior cadets since World War I. Until 1930, cadets had to order their boots from a firm in San Antonio, with Holick handling any special requests himself to ensure a perfect fit. Today's cadets pay upward of $1,600 for a pair of senior boots, but as the first Aggie boot maker, Joseph Holick sold many pairs for $32.50 prior to World War II.

Holick gave birth to the band that became the nation's largest military marching band, but he also operated the boot shop that has made more than thirty thousand pairs of Aggie senior boots. From the day a cadet enters Texas A&M, the dream of wearing senior boots begins. For many cadets, Joseph Holick made that dream come true. When Holick died in 1971 at the age of 103, Aggie Band members in their senior boots carried the first Aggie bandmaster to his final resting place in the Mount Calvary Cemetery in Bryan. Holick's is still in operation today, although no longer owned by a member of the original Holick family. The store, located at 4315 Wellborn Road in College Station, still sells custom-made senior boots as well as custom wallets, sabers, name tags, and other related Corps of Cadets items. Leo Belovoski, an employee of Holick's since 1991, purchased the shop and its name in August 2006, thus carrying on the tradition started by the Aggie Band's first bandmaster.[11]

Bradford Pier Day continued to improve the band throughout his career as bandmaster. He remained in that position for thirteen years, until his death in November 1917. Once again, the college had to find a new bandmaster on short notice. Alois Slovacek, a cornet player and a former band leader for the Fourth Infantry Band, was available. It was reported that Slovacek was an excellent musician, but apparently he had a heavy accent that made it difficult for the cadets to understand him. He left the following year to open a music store and eventually to direct a boy's band for the city of Bryan. Included in that band were the sons of Joseph Holick as well as many future members of the Aggie Band, including a future director who would hold that position longer than anyone else—E. V. Adams.[12]

The September 30, 1920, edition of the *Battalion* mentions Howell Nolte's appointment as director of the band for the fall of 1920, but there is no further reference to Nolte, and the next bandmaster arrived sometime during the 1920–21 school year. He was George Fairleigh, a dapper little Englishman called "The Duke." Fairleigh was a retired army bandmaster who played cornet and piano.[13]

By this time, the band was becoming well known in many parts of the state and was traveling to football games and concerts. The group was also increasing in size as the college grew after the end of World War I. The band's limit of thirty members was discontinued after the war, and in 1920 there were forty-five cadets in the band, enough that the musicians felt they could challenge the one-hundred-piece band from the University of Texas—thus beginning a long-standing rivalry. The following notice appeared in the *Battalion* on November 20, 1920: "It is said that the T. U. Band is coming out 100 strong this year with new uniforms and new drills 'n everything prepared to outplay ours when we go over and beat them Thanksgiving Day. They don't expect to win the football game, but they do think their band can outplay ours. All we can see in store for them is bitter disappointment on this score because our band is going to do the same thing to their band as our team is going to do to their team—beat them badly. Our forty-five pieces can, and will, make their hundred pieces sound like a bad headache." Perhaps the Aggie Band did give the University of Texas Band a bad headache, but the Aggie football team suffered their only loss of the season that Thanksgiving Day by failing to score a touchdown against the Longhorn varsity.

It was under the direction of Fairleigh that the band gave its first radio performance, in 1923 on a Fort Worth radio station. The station must have had a far-reaching signal, because messages of congratulations came in from all over the United States as well as from Canada, Mexico, and Cuba. From Pennsylvania: "Your splendid concert came in fine through a heavy snow storm." From New Jersey: "Saxophone sextet and cornet duet especially enjoyed." From Canada: "Fine music, could be plainly heard here." And from Cuba, a letter in Spanish arrived that expressed a preference for "the Aggie War Song."[14]

The writer was referring, of course, to the new tune being played by the band, "The Aggie War Hymn." By 1923, the song was already becoming the band's most frequently played tune. The "War Hymn" was written by a former student while standing guard in France during World War I. According to Aggie legend, James V. "Pinky" Wilson was posted in a mud-filled trench in northern France when he began to think about his home and his alma mater, to which he hoped to return when the fighting was over. He took a recently received letter out of his pocket and used its back to begin to write the words and notes of a song that he would dedicate to Texas A&M if he survived the war and made it back to the college. The words were based on familiar Aggie yells—"Hullabaloo, Caneck, Caneck!" and "Chig-gar-roo-garrem! Chig-gar-roo-gar-rem! Rough! Tough! Real Stuff! Texas A&M!"

Wilson did make it back to Texas A&M to graduate in 1920, and he brought the song back with him. It was first played by the band at a football game in 1921 and was an immediate success. Today it is one of the nation's most recognized college fight songs. On his eighty-first birthday,

Pinky Wilson said, "It simply never occurred to me that this song would ever be what it has become. . . . I made no effort to keep the letter on which I had written it."[15] Pinky Wilson wrote the music, George Fairleigh arranged it for the band, and the band made it famous.

Although Fairleigh was a fine musician and an excellent director, he also favored a drink of whiskey once too often, and he left the college in 1924. The band was thirty years old by that time and had seen nine different directors. There had been successes, including a fifty-dollar first prize in a competition as early as 1899, a well-received concert before a Confederate Veterans convention in Houston, many popular concerts on campus through the years, and parades and football games at other locations.[16] But the stability found under Day was about to be lost. The early bandmasters had come and gone too quickly. If there was ever going to be anything special about the band from the A&M College of Texas, it would need a strong and effective leader who was willing to devote a long period of time to making it special.

In 1924, the Aggie Band was at a crossroads.[17]

Members of the first Aggie Band, shown in formation on campus in 1894, were, *from left*, S. Cohn (spelled Kohn in later band records), Arthur Jenkins, J. K. Woods, W. M. Mathis, H. D'Echaux, T. B. Duggan, H. L. Williams, W. Bretchneider, A. W. Amthor, O. Gersteman, H. A. "California" Morse, W. C. Carothers, and P. B. Bittle. Courtesy of Cushing Memorial Library & Archives, Texas A&M University.

Band members began wearing a distinctive white cork helmet with their uniforms in the late 1890s. Courtesy of Cushing Memorial Library & Archives, Texas A&M University.

The demand for music led to the formation of the college's first orchestra in 1895. Courtesy of Cushing Memorial Library & Archives, Texas A&M University.

The 1899 Aggie Band. Courtesy of Cushing Memorial Library & Archives, Texas A&M University.

The 1905–06 Band in concert dress white uniforms. 1906 *Long Horn* yearbook, courtesy of Cushing Memorial Library & Archives, Texas A&M University.

The 1905 band leads the Corps to "chow" at the mess hall. Courtesy of Cushing Memorial Library & Archives, Texas A&M University.

Smaller ensembles, including this 1908 brass quintet, were a popular feature of the early bands. Courtesy of Cushing Memorial Library & Archives, Texas A&M University.

The 1911 Bugle Corps, a separate part of the band, had the duty of calling cadets to formations and other campus activities, including classes. 1911 *Long Horn* yearbook, courtesy of Cushing Memorial Library & Archives, Texas A&M University.

The 1914–15 band, wearing West Point–style uniforms, assembled in front of the Academic Building with Bandmaster Day at right. The oldest living former band member at the time the original edition was written, Ossie Greene '15, is at the far left. Courtesy Stormy Kimbrey '58.

The Aggie Band prepares to lead the Corps of Cadets down Military Walk in 1915. Courtesy of Cushing Memorial Library & Archives, Texas A&M University.

From 1916 through 1926, the Corps of Cadets traveled to Waco each year for the football game between Texas A&M and Baylor University. The band painted its drum to show what should be done to the Baylor Bears. Courtesy of Cushing Memorial Library & Archives, Texas A&M University.

The 1919 Aggie Band led the Cadet Corps to Bryan for a joyous celebration of Armistice Day in 1919. Courtesy of Cushing Memorial Library & Archives, Texas A&M University.

George Fairleigh, *left*, is shown with the 1920–21 Aggie Band during his first year as bandmaster. Courtesy of Cushing Memorial Library & Archives, Texas A&M University.

In addition to starting the Aggie Band, Joseph Holick established the boot shop that made more than 30,000 pairs of Aggie senior boots. When he died at the age of 103, Aggie Band members in their senior boots carried him to his final resting place. Courtesy Holick family.

2

The Tradition Begins
Lieutenant Colonel Richard J. Dunn, 1924–46

*Before I came here the Bandmaster was also the bugler. I changed that.
I told them I had blown enough bugles; I am the Bandmaster.
Someone else can blow the bugle calls.*

—RICHARD J. DUNN

Richard J. Dunn learned to play the piano and the violin as a boy, and at seventeen joined the army to be in a military band. It was the time of the Spanish-American War. He knew little about marching band instruments but quickly learned to play the bugle and then the clarinet while serving in Cuba and the Philippines. After the war, he was stationed in New York City and took the time to study music at the Grand Conservatory. Dunn was such a good musician that he was offered the opportunity to join the Marine Band that John Philip Sousa had made so famous. He declined the offer, however, because he wanted to be an army bandmaster, a goal he reached in 1911 when he became bandmaster for the U.S. Army's 11th Infantry Band.

By 1924, when he was contacted by the A&M College of Texas about its vacant bandmaster's position, he was a well-respected musician and bandmaster who had twenty-six years of experience with military bands. He was well qualified to conduct a cadet band in what was considered a military college. Dunn resigned from the army and accepted a commission as a major in the Texas State Guard in order to become the eleventh bandmaster of the Texas A&M College Band.

When Dunn arrived, he was informed that the bandmaster had always had the additional duty of being the college bugler. He told the college officials that he had blown enough bugles. "I am the Bandmaster. Someone else can blow the bugle calls," was Dunn's response to the college. Soon the bandmaster title was changed to director. Those were the first of many changes Dunn would bring to the Fightin' Texas Aggie Band.[1]

Before World War I, the band had been limited to thirty members. After the war, it was allowed to increase in size, as there were more students and more interest in the band. When Dunn became director he was told that he should expect to direct a group of seventy-five musicians.[2] By the end of his first year, however, the band had grown to

Colonel Richard J. Dunn, director 1924–26. Courtesy Texas Aggie Band.

one hundred pieces. "We accepted all who knew which end of an instrument to blow in," Dunn responded when asked about the increase in size.[3] He accepted them all and made them musicians. Under Dunn's leadership, the A&M Band became the nation's largest military marching band. By 1942, he was conducting a 250-piece band. The increase in size resulted in part from the reputation of the director and a growing respect for the band as a musical organization.

Dunn improved more than just the size of the band; he also improved its look. The band wore the same uniform as the other cadets, and senior cadets had different uniform privileges—for example, wearing senior boots—so there was no uniformity in the band's appearance and no special look that set the band apart from the rest of the Cadet Corps.[4]

The Corps had changed from the original gray West Point–style uniforms just before World War I. When Dunn arrived, the students wore olive drab uniforms that included breeches with woolen wrap leggings. The seniors wore the same uniform with their knee-high leather boots. Dunn changed the band's appearance by adding white cross belts made of cotton webbing and based on the simulated cartridge belts worn by West Point cadets. The belts crossed the chest in an "X," with a brass breastplate at the center of the "X." The white webbing also formed a belt at the band member's waist. Dunn also replaced the woolen leg wrappings with canvas mounted leggings, which were a version of the side-lace, spat-type leggings worn by mounted army troops. The inside of the calf was leather to protect the leg when riding a horse. In the A&M Band version, the canvas was white and the leather was cordovan, resulting in a marching unit with flashes of maroon and white, the school's colors.[5]

In 1931, Dunn attempted to make further refinements in the band uniforms, but these were only partially accepted. The white web cross belts were replaced by white Sam Browne belts—wide leather belts with a narrow strap passing over the right shoulder. A white chin strap was added to the cap. The band introduced this innovation at a football game against Texas Christian University in October 1931. The white Sam Browne belts were worn for the next twenty-six years; the white chin straps lasted less than twelve months.[6]

The other uniform change advocated by Dunn and approved by the band's Class of 1932 was the replacement of the breeches with trousers, or "slacks" as they were referred to in 1931.[7] The October 21, 1931, edition of the *Battalion* gives a favorable report on the band's appearance in the new white Sam Browne belts but adds, "It is indeed regrettable that the slacks which were adopted at the same time cannot be purchased also . . . we hope the day is not far off when the band members will discard their boots and leggings for a nice pair of well-tailored slacks with a small white stripe down the side." Given the strong feelings Aggies have for their senior boots, it is not surprising that the "well-tailored slacks" never appeared.

Dunn made one additional contribution to the appearance of the band in 1933 when the group traveled to New Orleans for a football game against Tulane. This was the first appearance of the bugle rank at the front of the band—actually two ranks at first. Dunn had purchased long French bugles, and each was decorated with a banner that displayed the block "T" symbol the band had begun to use as its signature.[8] The bugles with the banners gave the band a more formal appearance, and their flourishes at the beginning of the band's performance have become an Aggie tradition.

One uniform innovation that was not accepted occurred in 1933 when drum major T. H. "Tommy" Terrell surprised everyone by showing up at a football game in an unauthorized allwhite uniform. There is no record of what happened to the uniform, or what happened to Terrell for wearing it, but the 1934 *Longhorn* reported that the band was "chapped" at him.

It was during Dunn's tenure that the band began to earn its "nationally famous" status as cited in today's traditional introduction. Under Dunn the band was doing more than just marching down the football field at halftime. It was beginning to form interesting designs during its halftime drills. By 1929, the band's signature—the marching block "T"—was being used, and fans began to talk about the band "always winning the halftime" regardless of the football score.

The demand to see the band was so great that the college arranged for the musicians to make their first long trip. Recognizing that the band was an asset to the college, the administration arranged for a special train to take the band to Lincoln, Nebraska, for a football game pitting the Aggies against the University of Nebraska. The band paraded through the streets of Lincoln and gave an outstanding performance at the game. According to reports in the 1931 yearbook, the band "gained considerable commendations from the Northern press and from the University of Nebraska."

According to the December 9, 1931, edition of the *Battalion*, the 1931 football season was the band's most successful season up to that time. "This year the band has succeeded in putting on drills on the football field that have never before been attempted by any band in the conference,"

stated the paper. The drill executed at the Thanksgiving Day game against the University of Texas apparently impressed quite a few people. The Aggie Band spelled out the names of both teams and the Aggie coach's name, made a star, and then formed a longhorn steer.

The high regard for the band during the Dunn era is also shown in the 1933 edition of the yearbook:

> Here is the organization that brings prestige to A. and M., wherever it goes. The A. and M. Band, in addition to being perhaps the outstanding unit in the Cadet Corps, is well known over the entire country. The Band has won far more than its share of trophies and has never failed to bring back honors as the result of trips taken or contests entered. One of the most valuable features of the Band is its ability to act as a good-will ambassador. In this capacity it can either initiate or further cement friendly relations between A. & M. and other colleges in Texas and the Southwest. Due to its peculiar organization the Band is a uniting bond between the various units of the Cadet Corps. It is the Athletic Department's best friend. It is a living force in the life of the campus.

Both the band and its director were becoming important to the college. According to Earl Patterson, the drum major in 1926, one of Texas A&M's well-known traditions was started by band members in the fall of 1925, when two Aggie Band seniors walked out of the band dormitory the day of the annual Aggie bonfire playing a mournful tune on a bass horn and a piccolo. They began to wander around the campus, and as they did other cadets fell in behind them in single file, each placing his hand on the shoulder of the cadet in front of him. Patterson believes that this was the beginning of the annual "Elephant Walk" at Texas A&M.[9]

Elephant Walk was so named because of the belief that elephants, when they are about to die, wander off from the herd to some unknown elephant graveyard to die. The seniors, upon completion of the building of their last bonfire, supposedly believe their usefulness to the student body is over and therefore wander off to die. The ritual of the single-file Elephant Walk led by two band seniors continued into the 1970s, when the tradition began to change because the number of students became so large that the class could no longer walk single file. The seniors then began to walk several abreast, arm in arm, in ranks that seemed to go on forever. By this time, the leadership responsibility for building the bonfire had shifted to a group of students known as "red pots" because of the color of their helmets. These students began to lead the procession, and although band members continue to participate with their classmates, they no longer lead the walk. In recent years it has become customary for members of the junior class, armed with cans of shaving cream, to become "elephant hunters" who ambush the elephants along their route. The result is a messier trip to the seniors' demise.

In 1926, the band tried desperately to end a riot in Waco during halftime of the football game between Texas A&M and Baylor University. Since 1916 the band, the Corps, and the football team had traveled every year to Waco for a parade and the football game, a practice known as a "Corps Trip." Beginning in 1924, the Baylor cheering section began to ridicule the drills staged by the A&M cadets, and tension between the schools had increased to the point where the college did not send the Cadet Corps to Waco as a body in 1926. Many of the cadets went on their own, however.

When the ridicule started at halftime, a fight broke out that grew into a riot. To try to bring the crowd back to order, Dunn had the Aggie Band play "The Star-Spangled Banner." "I had them play it over twice—very slowly," Dunn later explained, "to give police time to get to their places and for firemen to bring a hose."[10] With the sound of the music, the A&M cadets came to attention and saluted. According to witnesses, many other people who had come onto the field continued to riot. Unfortunately, one of the cadets was struck and killed while the band played. Larry Byrd of A&M's Class of 1924 reported the incident this way: "I was standing right next to him when he was hit. We were sorta gathered around in a circle playing. We were not in the stands. Everyone was having to look out for themselves. We were playing the National Anthem when this young Baylor guy comes up and hit him. . . . So many were getting hurt, I didn't think too much about it—not knowing he was going to die."

Baylor won the football game 20 to 9, and that night several band instruments were stolen from the hotel where the Aggie Band was staying. Texas A&M and Baylor ended the practice of the Aggies traveling to Waco every year following the incident and, in fact, broke off all relations between the two schools for several years, even though the institutions were only ninety miles apart.[11] When the teams finally agreed to meet again in 1931, Baylor came to College Station—for the first time since 1913. Remembering the 1926 incident, the Aggies won the football game 33 to 7.[12]

Dunn made the Texas Aggie Band one of the best in the nation, and the other schools in the Southwest Conference responded by improving their bands. His influence was so great that he was one of the very few bandmasters in the South at that time to be elected to the American Bandmasters Association.[13]

Under Dunn's direction the band began to play spring concerts every Sunday afternoon. The members usually wore their white duck uniforms for these concerts, which began in the late afternoon and continued until dinner. Another important social event during Dunn's time was the annual spring concert in Guion Hall. According to Haynes W. Dugan's *The Great Class of 1934*, this was always a full-dress affair.

Colonel Dunn's efforts to improve the band were successful, but perhaps his greatest contribution to Texas A&M came in the role of composer. In 1925, a student named Marvin Mimms sent Dunn some lyrics for a suggested school song for the college. The band director was pleased to have the opportunity to write the music so that Texas A&M could have an original alma mater hymn. At the time, no Southwest Conference school had a school song with both original words and original music. Baylor's song was to the tune of "In the Good Old Summertime," and the University of Texas used "I've Been Working on the Levee" or, as most now know it, "I've Been Working on the Railroad." Both of those songs are still used by those institutions. Dunn believed he had an opportunity to do something special for Texas A&M.

Although he had been at A&M for only a year, Dunn was nonetheless enthusiastic about creating new music for the school. He considered "The Aggie War Hymn" an invitation to battle and thus unsuitable for solemn occasions like commencement exercises. Using his talents as a musician and Mimms's words for inspiration, he wrote the musical score for "The Spirit of Aggieland." He also rewrote a few of Mimms's lines and adjusted others to better fit the meter. Dunn conceived the idea of a series of Aggie yells for the second chorus. He also gave the song its name (Mimms had originally used the title "Texas Aggies").

Dunn's work on the song was completed in less than a week so it would be ready for College Night—a welcome-back yell practice—at the start of the 1925 fall semester. (Instead of pep rallies, Aggies have yell practice.) Although Dunn later claimed that he could have done a better job had he had more time, former students everywhere think he did just fine.[14]

In September 1952—six years after Dunn had retired—a representative of Broadcast Music, Inc. (BMI), which had acquired the assets of the original publisher of "The Spirit of Aggieland," wrote Dunn to inform him that the copyright would expire in October 1953 unless it was renewed before that date. Mimms received the same letter and wrote Dunn to ask what it was about and whether he had any royalties coming to him. Dunn had been trying to locate Mimms since 1945 about reprinting the song but had been unsuccessful. Mimms, as it turned out, was the principal of Manuel Guerra High School in the small Texas border town of Roma. Apparently Dunn did not like the tone of Mimms's letter after he had spent a great deal of time trying to locate him. Dunn wrote back saying, "Whenever you might have

any royalty due you, you will receive it without the asking."

Dunn then replied to BMI that his copyright on "The Spirit of Aggieland" would not expire until 1972. A year later, BMI wrote back to remind Dunn that the song was about to fall into the public domain. Dunn replied immediately, again saying that his copyright would not expire until 1972 because he had copyrighted a second version in 1945. BMI replied that his letter of the previous year had not been received, noting that in any event his 1945 copyright would be useless if he allowed the original copyright to expire—publishers would then use the first version of the song and have no obligation to pay any royalties. This letter was dated September 25, 1953.

On September 30, Dunn applied for a renewal of the copyright of the 1925 version of the song and included a money order for two dollars. His 1945 version had changed the tempo and had added the yells as the second chorus. The copyright office returned his money, stating that his renewal application was received on October 2, 1953, and that the original copyright had expired the previous day, October 1. Dunn immediately wrote a new band arrangement of "The Spirit of Aggieland" and sent it to the copyright office for registration. That copyright was granted on November 12, 1953.

Apparently there never was a copyright on the 1945 version, for when Dunn's widow applied for a renewal in 1973, she was told that there was no record of the 1945 copyright. As a result, neither the 1925 version nor the 1945 version is copyrighted. The copyright for the 1953 version, however, was renewed in 1981. This copyright will expire without renewal provisions in 2028.[15]

Dunn wrote other music for Texas A&M. In the early 1930s he published "There Shall Be No Regrets," and he later wrote a popular march called "Sabre and Plow."[16] But it will be "The Spirit of Aggieland" for which he is remembered.

During the band's history it had been housed in several dormitories, including Pfeuffer, Foster, Austin, Bizzell, and even Gathright, one of the original buildings on campus.[17] Living quarters started to become permanent with the construction of the so-called new area on the south side of campus in 1939; Dorm 11, Harrington Hall, was designated as the band hall, complete with a rehearsal hall on its fourth floor. Later, a second band hall, Crocker or Dorm 16, was opened on the north side of campus with similar rehearsal space on its fourth floor.[18] At this time the band was divided into two: the Infantry Band and the Field Artillery Band, with one band living in each area. The two bands were combined for football games and yell practices into what became known as the Combined or Consolidated Band. Each of the smaller units had a drum major, and the arrangement with three drum majors has continued to the present.

For a time, the band members were limited to the two military service branches of Infantry and Field Artillery, but this requirement was abolished in 1943 when it was announced that the band would again be housed together in one dormitory instead of in two dormitories at opposite ends of campus.[19]

By that time World War II had begun, and it was difficult to maintain the band at the standard Dunn had set. In 1942, the band had a great reputation and was the largest the college had ever had—250 members. The football team played the University of Alabama in the Cotton Bowl that year. The Alabama band was known as the "Million Dollar Band." After seeing the Alabama band the editors of the 1942 *Longhorn* included a photograph of the Aggie Band with a caption reading "Two Million Dollar Band." By the following year, with so many students being inducted into the armed services, the band had decreased to ninety members. All were freshmen, including the drum major.[20]

Fortunately, when the band was asked to be movie stars for a Universal Pictures film, *We've Never Been Licked*, the group was still at full strength. The film is about the son of a former Texas A&M cadet and military officer. The young man, raised in the Philippines, arrives on campus to join the Corps of Cadets in the early days of World War II. The film crew arrived on campus in November 1942 and completely disrupted classes and campus life. The band missed a lot of class time filming a scene marching into Sbisa Dining Hall and stayed up late to record the college songs and yells for use in the movie.[21] As compensation, the two female stars of the film, Anne Gwynne and Martha O'Driscoll, came over to sit with the band at the football game while they were on campus.[22] One good thing did come out of the film company's visit to campus. In the fall of 1942 it had appeared that equipment and fuel were not going to be available for the construction and lighting of the bonfire that year. But because the bonfire was critical to the movie's script, Universal Pictures paid for and obtained everything necessary for the cadets to build the 1942 bonfire.[23]

With Aggies leaving to fight in the war, the number of students continued to decline. The Corps of Cadets was virtually nonexistent. At one point, Dunn put out a call for volunteers to come and join the band just to carry the bugles that now adorned the front of the band. One person who answered the call was I. E. Elkins, who marched with the band carrying a bugle. Elkins eventually became drum major in the last of the bands directed by Dunn.[24]

The last few years that Dunn was at Texas A&M were difficult for everyone. It must have bothered him to see what he had built being pulled apart, but as an army man—and as some put it, "a crusty old army man"—he understood the need for what was happening. And he knew that when the war was over the Aggie Band would come back bigger and stronger than ever before.

Major Dunn had been promoted to Lieutenant Colonel Dunn prior to World War II. He had built the tradition of the Aggie Band—including "winning the halftime," playing "The Spirit of Aggieland" (which he had written), putting the bugles up front, and creating the arrangement with three drum majors. To his men he was "The Colonel," and he set the standard of excellence for the Aggie Band. Each director since then, in his own time, has maintained that excellence and earned the right to be called "The Colonel."

The editors of the 1943 *Longhorn* understood what Colonel Dunn had done for Aggieland:

One of the most memorable sights for every student is the first time to see the Aggie Band. This occasion is usually College Night, when the Band plays for the first yell practice. The drum major leads the Band to the "Y" with a blazing red flare at the tip of his baton, and the freshmen hear "The Spirit of Aggieland" and "Goodbye to Texas" for the first time. These are songs and sights that no real Aggie can ever forget.

Under the direction of Colonel R. J. Dunn, the Aggie Band has grown from a small, poorly equipped organization to one of the largest and best in the nation. It was through the efforts of Colonel Dunn that the Band was able to obtain certain needed instruments from the Quartermaster Corps. . . . We are grateful to Colonel Dunn and to every member of the Band for devoting their time and efforts to making the Aggie Band an outstanding musical organization that enjoys national recognition.

Colonel Dunn retired from Texas A&M in 1946 after twenty-two years of directing the band, but he remained active in College Station until his death in 1961.

In honor of Colonel Dunn, members of Texas A&M's Classes of 1935 through 1941 installed a bronze plaque in the University Center auditorium building near the site of Guion Hall, where rehearsals and concerts had taken place under his direction. The plaque reads:

RICHARD J. DUNN
1881–1961

In memory of Colonel Dunn who was Bandmaster of the Texas Aggie Band from 1924 to 1946, during which time he composed the music to the "Spirit of Aggieland." He was greatly beloved by those who served under him.

The earliest known version of the Aggie Band's signature block "T" was designed and performed in 1929.
Courtesy Mauris Barton '32.

Colonel Richard J. Dunn improved the band's appearance with white crossed belts and leggings, shown here on
the 1929–30 band. Courtesy of Cushing Memorial Library & Archives, Texas A&M University.

The band led 2,500 members of the Corps of Cadets to the train station to depart on the Texas Aggie Special for a 1930 football game in Lincoln, Nebraska. The Aggies were outscored 12–0, but the band won the halftime. 1931 *Long Horn* yearbook, courtesy of Cushing Memorial Library & Archives, Texas A&M University.

Drum Major T. H. "Tommy" Terrell surprised everyone by appearing in an all-white uniform at a football game in 1933. According to reports, the band was "chapped" and the uniform was never seen again. 1934 *Long Horn* yearbook, courtesy of Cushing Memorial Library & Archives, Texas A&M University.

Under Colonel Dunn's direction the band began to form patterns on the football field and formed a Texas Lone Star at the 1934 Thanksgiving game in Austin. Courtesy of Cushing Memorial Library & Archives, Texas A&M University.

Band members with the original Aggie mascot, Reveille, in 1936. Courtesy William R. Ledbetter '40.

The band plays while the cadets march to "chow" at Sbisa Dining Hall prior to the 1937 football game against Southern Methodist University. The Aggies won the game, 14–0. Courtesy of Cushing Memorial Library & Archives, Texas A&M University.

The Aggieland Orchestra played popular dance music on the campus and throughout the state during the 1930s and 1940s. Courtesy Texas Aggie Band.

The band marches across the Quad in the rain en route to the University of Texas football game in 1939. The national championship Aggie football team won the game 20–0. Courtesy William R. Ledbetter '40.

At Final Review in 1940, Drum Major William R. "Bill" Ledbetter '40 passed the baton to his younger brother, James P. "Pat" Ledbetter '41. It was the only time a cadet succeeded his brother as drum major. Courtesy William R. Ledbetter '40.

The band played before a packed house at the 1940 Sugar Bowl in New Orleans, forming the outline of the State of Texas with a "T" near College Station's location. The Aggies won the national championship with the 14–13 victory over Tulane. Courtesy Bob Russell '42.

In 1939, the Aggie Band was divided into two bands, the Infantry Band and the Field Artillery Band, which created double bugle ranks when the bands played together for certain events. 1941 *Long Horn* yearbook, courtesy of Cushing Memorial Library & Archives, Texas A&M University.

According to legend, the Aggie Band started the Elephant Walk tradition with a bass horn and a clarinet or piccolo leading the other seniors. In the Elephant Walk prior to their last Aggie Bonfire before graduation, seniors wander around the campus like elephants waiting to die. 1942 *Aggieland* yearbook, courtesy of Cushing Memorial Library & Archives, Texas A&M University.

Hollywood came to Aggieland in 1942 to make a patriotic World War II movie called *We've Never Been Licked*. In this scene from the film, the band leads the cadets to "chow" in Sbisa Dining Hall. 1943 *Longhorn* courtesy of Cushing Memorial Library & Archives, Texas A&M University.

Actress Anne Gwynne, one of the stars of *We've Never Been Licked*, helps Colonel Dunn direct the Aggie Band as her co-star, Martha O'Driscoll, seated center, looks on. The stars were on campus to film the movie and see the Aggies beat Washington State, 21–0. 1943 *Long Horn* yearbook, courtesy of Cushing Memorial Library & Archives, Texas A&M University.

Head Drum Major Eugene Fields '44, like the other members of his class, never got the opportunity to march in his senior boots. Because of World War II, the college's programs were accelerated, enabling cadets to finish in less than four years, depriving many of the chance to wear the coveted boots. 1944 *Long Horn* yearbook, courtesy of Cushing Memorial Library & Archives, Texas A&M University.

3

The Military Precision
Lieutenant Colonel E. V. Adams '29, 1946–73

*When I was a sophomore, Colonel Dunn used to tell me to keep up my work on the cornet.
He would say, "One day I want you to direct this band." I thought he was bulling me,
but I went to music school after graduation just in case he wasn't.*

—E. V. Adams

As the years became more difficult, Colonel Dunn wrote Edward Vergne Adams and said, "Come home, Adams, I'm tired."[1] Adams came home, and he stayed twenty-seven years—longer than anyone who had ever directed the Aggie Band. E. V. Adams, called Vergne by his friends, was a member of Texas A&M's Class of 1929. He was in the band under Colonel Dunn when the white cross belts were worn. He was Dunn's handpicked successor. In fact, he had been named assistant band director just before World War II began but had been unable to accept because he had been called to active duty.[2]

Dunn was not the only former director of the Aggie Band with a direct connection to Adams. When Adams was a boy, his father operated a barbershop in Bryan next door to the music store owned by Alois Slovacek, who had been bandmaster of the Aggie Band in 1918–19. It was Slovacek who taught young Vergne Adams to play the cornet. As Adams was growing up there was

no high school band program in Bryan, so the young man played in the community band—a boys' band—directed by Slovacek. Other members of that band included the sons of Joseph Holick, the first bandmaster at Texas A&M.[3]

As a boy Adams would ride the trolley from Bryan out to the college to watch the Aggie Band—and to dream of one day playing with the group. In 1925 he did. Soon the band director noticed his talents and encouraged the young musician. Dunn told Adams he wanted him to work hard so he could come back someday to direct the Aggie Band. Years later, Adams said, "I thought he was bulling me, but I went to music school after graduation just in case he wasn't."[4]

After graduating from Texas A&M in 1929 and becoming a high school teacher, he returned to the college to earn an advanced degree. His master's thesis was titled "The Place of Creative Music in Public Schools." Adams went on to study music at Northwestern University, the Cincinnati Conservatory, and the VanderCook School of Music in Chicago. By the time World War II broke out, he had served as an award-winning band director at several secondary schools, including the original Bryan high school, Stephen F. Austin.[5]

At the beginning of World War II, Adams was called to active duty and served as an officer in chemical warfare in the Pacific. He had no connection with band music during his four years in the army except for one impromptu performance. He later recalled: "At one camp I was part of the Regimental staff at an evening retreat ceremony. We were saluting and waiting for the bugler to play 'Retreat' and 'To the Colors.' The bugler was standing near us—just a kid who couldn't play anything on that plastic army bugle. Finally, without saying a word, I walked over to him, took the bugle and blew the calls, handed the bugle back to him, and walked back to my position in the staff. They all looked at me sort of funny but no one ever said anything. That was the extent of my musical career during World War II."[6] Adams never was tolerant of people who could not do their jobs.

When the war was over, Adams accepted Dunn's plea to come home and take the baton as director of the Fightin' Texas Aggie Band. In transferring the baton, Dunn made only one request of his successor—that Adams not change the way the Aggie Band played "The Star-Spangled Banner."[7] It was Dunn's own arrangement, and it had a strong, bold beginning, unlike other arrangements of the anthem. Adams honored the request as he set out to rebuild the Aggie Band and capture the glory that Dunn had achieved before the war. He began his task on February 1, 1946. Veterans of the war were returning, and enrollment at the college was growing. Adams was commissioned as a lieutenant colonel in the Texas State Guard when he accepted the position of director of the Fightin' Texas Aggie Band.[8]

Things were so confusing during the war years and Dunn's last years that discipline had declined by the time Adams arrived. It had become a senior privilege to miss band practice. When Adams learned of that tradition, he announced that everyone, with no exceptions, was required to be

Lieutenant Colonel E. V. Adams, director, 1946–73. Courtesy Texas Aggie Band.

at band practice. One cadet apparently did not believe the new director could change what the senior felt was his right. He missed the next practice. Adams gave the cadet a second chance, and when he didn't come to band practice the second time, the new director went to his room, personally collected the cadet's belongings, and placed them outside the band dormitory. The cadet was removed from the band. There was no further problem with cadets missing band practice.[9]

Adams quickly brought the band back to a level that most people agreed exceeded anything Dunn had ever achieved before the war. After only weeks on the job, Adams conducted the band in a spring concert. The Battalion praised the band and quoted an "elderly gentleman" as saying after the concert, "That's the best band we've had in a long time."[10]

By the following fall, Adams had an Aggie Band of 225 members. He announced that the band would start spelling out words in "long hand script" on the field instead of using the more familiar block letter style. Only one dim newspaper photograph of the band rehearsing such script writing has been found. Apparently that part of Adams's plan did not last very long. His other plans included adding maneuvers not previously seen in Southwest Conference halftime performances. He intended to do more precision movements on the field, but all individual marching would be strictly by the *Army Drill Manual* with the addition of the countermarch.[11] From the beginning of Adams's tenure the halftime performances became more spectacular, with sharp precision drills—all designed by Adams.

The only available books on marching bands at the time suggested drills that Adams felt were not appropriate for a military band. In dismissing the marching style described in those books, Adams said: "We wore a military uniform and were part of a Cadet Corps. If we appeared in a review at a fast clip with a short choppy step with our knees raised, we would look downright foolish."[12]

When he was first developing his method of designing band drills, he used small figurines on a scale-model football field. When Adams got an idea for a drill, he tested it out with the figurines and then transferred the concept to a chart marked with dots scaled to thirty-inch intervals so that he could accurately compute the number of steps each member of the band would take in the drill. He could then determine the number of bars of music it would take to get each member in place.[13] He later designed the drills on special paper that was lined like a football field but with additional lines to show two-step intervals between the yard lines. If the band took thirty-inch steps, each sixth step would be on a yard line.[14] That is the basic principle that makes the Aggie Band's halftime performances look so good. Even if an individual is a little out of place at any given time, the placement will always be correct at the yard line.

As he perfected his method, the schedule for drills became routine. After the basic design work was completed, he would meet with the band in the rehearsal room on Monday afternoon to explain the drill and announce what music would be used. The musicians would then move to the drill field adjacent to the band dormitory. No instruments would be carried on Monday except the drums, which were necessary to set the cadence. The band would go through the drill, and any rough spots would be worked out on the field. In a practice still maintained today, the band director supervised the routine from a fourth-floor dormitory window. With a public address "bullhorn," Adams would stop the drill if he saw a mistake. Anyone who ever marched for him can remember the words "Think-Thank-Thunk-Stink-Stank-Stunk!" coming from that bullhorn. Adams seldom criticized individuals, but he communicated effectively with statements like "OK. We're going to try that again. But if the bugle rank could lead this we'd have it down already." The next time through the bugle rank would lead. They wouldn't want to hear from Adams again.[15]

On Tuesday afternoon the band members repeated the procedure, still without instruments, to perfect the drill. On Wednesday they carried instruments, and the music was added to the drill. Adding the music for the first time was almost like starting over. Before the practice was over, however, the mistakes had been corrected. On Thursday the drill was polished, and both marching and playing improved. For an out-of-town game, Thursday was the last practice period. A home game gave Adams and the cadets an extra day. If the band had a particularly rough time with a drill, an early morning practice session would be added. By Saturday the routine was perfect.[16]

Adams's impact on the band was so great that after only two years as its director he was named as winner of one of nine faculty-staff achievement awards by the *Battalion*. The band continued to be divided into two units, but Adams changed the names from the Infantry and Field Artillery Bands to the Maroon and White Bands. The consolidated group was soon referred to as the Combined Band.

Soon after arriving, Adams was faced with having to direct not two but three bands, as the college made the decision to separate the freshmen from the rest of the students and move them to the old Bryan Air Base, an area northwest of campus that has subsequently been known as the Annex, Texas A&M's Riverside Campus, and now the RELLIS campus, which stands for the seven Aggie core values of respect, excellence, leadership, loyalty, integrity, and selfless service. There were two reasons for separating the groups at that time: first, the campus was crowded with veterans returning from World War II; and second, the hazing of freshmen by upperclassmen was becoming a problem. So many freshmen were either leaving school or getting off to a poor academic start that something had to be done.

The Basic Division was created to help the freshmen properly start their academic careers, and the Freshman Battalion was created to provide the military organization. Since the freshmen were so far from the main campus, a separate band was deemed necessary to play for them to march to meals and to give some sense of pride to the Freshman Battalion.

The first "fish band" was created in the fall of 1947, and the organization continued to exist through the spring of 1954, even though the Freshman Battalion moved back to the main campus in 1950.[17] The Freshman Band was led by a freshman drum major and a freshman bugle rank and played for all freshman functions that required a band. In a Corps Trip parade or a review, the Aggie Band would play for the upperclassmen to march by and then the Freshman Band would move into position to play for the freshmen to pass by. At football games, the freshmen sat and played with the upperclassmen's band but did not march at halftime.[18] With the Freshman Band so far from the main campus, Adams was spread pretty thin. The college helped with the logistics by providing a jeep for Adams to use to travel between the two locations. In remembering those days, his wife, who sometimes rode with her husband when he traveled to the air base to direct the Freshman Band, said, "I guess he could have gone in his own car, but I kind of think he liked to drive the jeep. I know I liked it."[19]

The concept of separating the freshmen may have had some merit, but in reality the practice only resulted in the creation of two fish years. When a cadet became a sophomore and moved in with the Aggie Band, he was treated as if he were still a fish and the hazing continued. In the fall of 1954 the freshmen were combined with the other band members, but they were still called fish.[20]

Apparently the term "fish" for a freshman in the band or in any unit of the Corps of Cadets has been around for a long time. Even when the band first began, its freshmen were already being called fish. The Class of 1898, which arrived in 1894, reported in its section of the 1895 *Olio* (the name of the school's earliest yearbooks), "How well we remember our arrival at College and the first few days following. How embarrassed we felt when we alighted from the train and saw so many old cadets around us, all crying 'Fish! Fish! Look at the Fish!'" Although the word is now always written in lower case, the experience of having few privileges and being treated differently has not changed.

"Congratulations! Well Done!" read the headline on an editorial in the December 9, 1947, edition of the *Battalion* in Adams's second year. The editorial called the band's performance at the University of Texas football game "one of the best performances ever." It continued: "Certainly the showing topped anything in the Southwest this year. The timing in the intricate crisscross was perfect and the marching letters proved an innovation which attracted wide-spread notice." The crisscross and its later variations would become the band's most anticipated maneuver.

Thanksgiving Day 1947 was the first time the Aggie Band performed the crisscross maneuver developed by Adams. In the original version of this movement, the band is split into two units that then march diagonally toward the center of the field, where they meet and pass through one another at right angles. Other band directors have said this maneuver is impossible because it requires two band members to be in the same place at the same time. In later years some who did not know of its early origin in 1947 would spread the rumor that the drill was developed by a computer.[21]

"It's all a matter of mathematics," Adams responded. "One man can take up only a certain amount of space at one time and moves in one direction at a predictable rate of speed." That predictable rate of speed is currently 104 beats per minute in thirty-inch steps.[22]

Recently Adams's son, Edward V. Adams Jr., who marched in his father's band from 1957 to 1961, said that his father claimed to have come up with drills like the crisscross from nightmares in his sleep. Adams himself once said, "Sometimes a drill just comes to me in my sleep. Everyone asks me how I think the drills up and I just can't explain."[23]

Another Southwest Conference band director of the era is reported to have said: "I dread going against the Aggie Band. . . . At least in our stadium there are friendly faces. What is so humiliating is to see the Aggie Band do things band directors talk about as being impossible, and do them perfectly. It takes two weeks to recover from the trauma."[24] According to an article in the *San Antonio Light* on September 17, 1960, the Aggie Band's reputation had reached the point that at least one band gave up without a fight. When the Texas Aggie football team went to San Antonio to play the Trinity Tigers, the Trinity band decided to just sit that one out and let the Aggie Band have the whole halftime. This time the football team won, too. It was the football team's only win of the year.

Even though his methods for coming up with the designs for the halftime drills may remain a mystery, one thing that is certain is that Adams was a man of precision. Time was an exact thing to him. When the band was on the field or in a parade, his stopwatch never left his hand. His rehearsals started at precise times. "Drill outside with instruments, ready to step off at 5:05," he would announce, and the band would step off at precisely 5:05. Adams's halftime shows were clocked to the second. It was not unusual for him to make an adjustment during rehearsal because he had already told the director of the opposing team's band that the Aggie Band performance would be exactly six minutes and seventeen seconds. When the band marched at that game, its performance would take exactly six minutes and seventeen seconds. Adams was a man of his word.[25]

He believed a good drill was one that challenged the band members, one that was more difficult than they thought they could perform but that in fact they could perform with perfection. "I judge a drill not by the audience applause," Adams insisted, "but by the looks of the men's faces when they come off the field. If they did their jobs well, I can feel the glow of their pride." Adams clearly preferred preparing the band for halftime drills rather than parades. "A good parade," he once said, "is one in which we march in front of the horses."[26]

Adams made further refinements in the appearance of the band, following up on actions that Dunn had taken. Beginning in 1946 and continuing until 1973, the band was issued white helmets while the other cadets had olive drab ones. These were actually helmet liners that the army wore under the steel helmets used in World War II. They were reminiscent of the white helmets worn by the band at the turn of the century, but they were worn instead as rain hats and on occasions when all of the Corps was in helmets.[27] Under Adams's direction the bugle banners instituted by Dunn were redesigned by two cadets, W. E. "Gene" Hollar of the Class of 1950 and Carl Whyte of the Class of 1949. The new banners replaced the block "T" with a treble clef superimposed on an open "T" with an "A and M" on the crossbar and the word "Band" on the base of the "T." The emblem was white with maroon letters and symbols on one side of the banner, and maroon with white letters and symbols on the other side.[28] The long French bugles were replaced with shorter ones at the same time. The white Sam Browne belts were continued but were not worn by members of the Freshman Band. In addition, Adams put only seniors on the bugle rank, thereby improving the look of the band with boots across the front and down the sides of the formations.

He also refined the band's traditional entrance, retaining the "Recall! Step Off on Hullabaloo!" concept but spreading the band out over the end zone, thus providing a more effective entry onto the field.[29] These changes came just in time. Television was beginning to cover college football games, and in the earliest days of television the cameras also covered the bands.

Television provided new opportunities for more people to see and hear the Aggie Band. In the 1950s it was a really big event to be on television. A headline in the *Bryan Daily Eagle* on September 15, 1957, read "Aggie Marching Band Prepares for TV Spot." The accompanying article reported that the band would be given ten minutes on television because the opposing band would not be there.[30] After each television appearance the band received an avalanche of mail praising its performance. Typical of such comments are the following:

"Got my usual case of goosebumps."

"Allow me to tip my hat to the finest marching band in the country."

"Thought it was some kind of illusion."

"Your boys put on a great drill."

"The college I attended had a fine band, but it never did anything to compare with the superb halftime performance you put on Thanksgiving Day."

"Yesterday I had the privilege of watching perhaps the finest demonstration of a college band it has been my pleasure to witness."

"Just out of this world. If God was to pick a marching band . . . of his own, he would pick yours."[31]

As the band began to grow, prospective students from all over the country were contacting Texas A&M about enrolling and joining the band. One such student from New Jersey had no doubt heard of the hot Texas weather. On his pre-enrollment card he indicated a preference for an air-conditioned dormitory room. At that time, in 1967, the band dormitory was not air conditioned, so Adams wrote the young man to inform him of that fact and asked whether he wished to have his name removed from the roster of new band members. The prospective student replied: "Do not remove my name from the band roster. I'd rather burn than switch."[32] The band had a new recruit.

By 1955 the band's fame had grown so much that there was a demand to send the group all the way to California for the opening game of the 1955 football season. There were now 250 band members, and transporting that many people to California and back would cost a lot of money— even in 1955. As it turned out, raising the money was no problem once the former students of Texas A&M learned that the band had a chance for the trip. More than $2500 was quickly raised to send the band by special train. Adams would later say the trip was one of the highlights of his career.[33]

Band members returned to College Station early that year for practice. The game between Texas A&M and the University of California at Los Angeles was to be played on the Friday night before school started on Monday. After a week of drill in the hot Texas sun of early September, Colonel Adams and the band boarded a special train at 10:30 p.m. on a Wednesday night and arrived in Los Angeles just before noon on Friday. Almost twenty years later, Adams talked about the band's trip to California. "Many of our kids had never been on a train before," he said. "There was a 'fancy' dining car with table clothes and napkins and good food."

On Friday night, September 16, 1955, the Fightin' Texas Aggie Band marched into the Los Angeles Coliseum and made history. It was the longest trip the band had ever made. The Aggie football team was outscored by UCLA, but the Aggie Band thrilled the sixty-five thousand fans, who had never seen anything quite like the group's halftime performance. The magazine *Marching Band* was there and covered the band's performance in two articles in its October 1955 edition. Fred Myers wrote: "One of the most spectacular halftime shows ever witnessed on a football field was the performance put on by the Marching Band of Texas A. & M. College at the Los Angeles Memorial Coliseum Friday, Sept. 15 [*sic*] when the Aggies were the grid guests of the Los Angeles Bruins of UCLA. . . . In mid-field the band treated the thousands of spectators to one of the finest exhibitions of precision maneuvers ever seen on the West Coast, crossing and crisscrossing the field and weaving intricate patterns which were almost unbelievable."

In commenting on the drum majors, Andy Feeley—editor of the "Drum Major" section of the magazine—wrote: "As the three men led their 240-piece unit through the tunnel and onto the floor of the huge stadium, I went cold to the thrill of so stirring an impression. With their batons in carry position, the heels of their heavy Army field boots thundering on the turf, I could only think of the powerful Roman legions and their leaders victoriously parading into the coliseum of that now lost civilization."

W. S. Duniway, publicity director for the University of Southern California, sent Adams the following clipping from the September 19, 1955, edition of the *Hollywood Citizen-News*:

> Here's a belated salute to Texas A. & M.'s 240-piece band. It's a lulu, being even superior to the vaunted Big Ten bands when it comes to precision marching.
>
> Ten minutes before kickoff time the great Aggie Band held the big crowd spellbound with a rendition of the "Star Spangled Banner" the likes of which they'd never heard. I still say the Aggie Band comes as close to playing it the way Francis Scott Key intended it to be played as any band I've ever heard.

Duniway sent a personal note to Adams with the clipping in which he also praised the Aggie Band, comparing it with bands from the Big 10 conference. He wrote: "You had a great band out here and I am glad that it was UCLA's musicians who were playing against you and not the SC Trojan Band, which hasn't had time to get started this year.... You were far better than any Big Ten band ever seen here."[34]

The following day the Aggie Band was the guest of the brand-new Disneyland Park, which had just opened that year. The musicians marched down Main Street and played a concert in the park, thrilling and impressing the thousands of tourists at Disneyland. After the concert the cadets enjoyed the park courtesy of Walt Disney himself before boarding the train for the trip back to College Station.[35]

Adams said he got a lot of correspondence about that trip but was most proud of the letter he received from the manager of the hotel where the band stayed in Los Angeles. "He said we were the only college group that had stayed in his hotel that hadn't taken anything when they left. Not even a wash cloth was missing," Adams said.[36]

The Colonel, it seems, taught his band members a lot more than how to march and play music. He was proud of everything he taught them. "My first speech to the new members of the band each year," he said, "includes a statement that they're going to learn something in the band that isn't taught anywhere else: the ability to perform under stress and strain, to carry out an assignment to perfection with their minds blanked out to everything else except what they're doing. I'd had many former bandsmen tell me the lessons of concentration they learned in the band were of great value in their professional lives."[37]

Adams's duties as band director included complete responsibility for the band members. This included not only directing the band and designing drills but also discipline and such routines as dormitory room inspection. One morning during such an inspection he found two seniors in bed sound asleep. They had been up very late studying and were so tired that they slept right through the inspection. The Colonel let them know that he had been there, though, and that their room did not pass inspection. When the seniors awoke, they found the Colonel's initials, "E. V. A.," written in the dust on their dresser.[38]

Many people know the story of the Aggie mascot, a dog named Reveille. The original Reveille was a mongrel brought to campus in 1931 by some cadets who had found her on the highway near Navasota, Texas. She spent a lot of time with the band after the bugler brought her back to the band dormitory one morning. The band members fed her, and she started marching with the band.

By the time Adams returned to direct the band in 1946, the original Reveille had passed away.

During Adams's early years as band director a new Reveille was donated to the college. This one was a collie that lived in a doghouse outside the band dormitory, Harrington Hall. Because the original Reveille liked to march with the band, it was thought that Reveille II should do the same. In the early 1950s she would be let loose from her leash at the beginning of the band's halftime drill. She would run straight down the field and bark and prance around with the band. At least that was the idea. Reveille II was a young dog and was perhaps excited by the cheering of the crowd; she began to stop and use the grass on Kyle Field as her personal restroom. When the cadets began to make wagers on which yard line she would utilize, Colonel Adams banished Reveille II from marching with the band. Sometime later her doghouse was burned down. After that she was assigned to one of the other cadet units for safekeeping. The successor to that unit is the present Company E-2, known as the Mascot Company.[39]

Over the years there has been some friendly rivalry between band members and other cadets. This has sometimes led to massive water fights between the band and the rest of the Corps. Who started these fights was not always clear, but perhaps some were started over the band members' policy of not letting anyone but band members walk on their private drill field adjacent to the band dormitory. At one time band members were required to keep buckets of water handy to throw on anyone caught walking on the drill field.

The band dormitory is at the far end of the cadet dormitory area. During the water fights the Cadet Corps usually advanced toward the band dormitory with buckets of water while band members tried to drive them back with similar buckets of water filled from the dormitory shower room and passed out through the windows. The band was always outnumbered but consistently made a valiant effort in those fights. Legend has it, however, that once in the late 1950s a band member returned from his small hometown with one of the community's volunteer fire department pumper trucks, which he hid behind the dormitory. When the fight started that night

and the aggressors approached the band dormitory, the band made a surprise counterattack with their secret weapon and won the fight.[40]

Perhaps some of the water fights had something to do with cadence. In 1982, Haynes W. Dugan of the Class of 1934 compiled the history of his class in *The History of the Great Class of 1934*. In that book he reports on a complaint that other members of the Corps of Cadets had made, on more than one occasion, that the band did not keep proper time by which the Corps could march without getting out of step. Most of the band members always thought it was a peculiar complaint because the band itself depended on a proper beat to always be in step. At one time, because of those complaints, Colonel Adams even changed the drum roll-off that preceded a march to a simple eight straight beats. In addition, he taped stopwatches to the top of the bass drums.

Dugan, however, provided Burt E. Nowotny's explanation to those who complained about the band's cadence. Nowotny was the band commander in 1931 and apparently intended his explanation to end the controversy.

It has been rumored that there has been some criticism of the time in which the band has been playing for the retreat formation. I would like to explain the difficulties under which the band labors in trying to play music to which the whole Cadet Corps might keep time.

In elementary physics we learn that sound travels at the rate of 1094 feet per second at 60 degrees Fahrenheit. We also learn the phenomena of reflection of sound (echo). The echo, being in itself sound, travels at the same rate.

It has been stated that a body of troops marching to the music of the band is required to change step at the drum solo. Sound produced by drums, being more resonant than the more regular music tones, creates a more noticeable echo.

The distance from the band position to Mitchell Hall is about 2 feet. At the instant the marching column passes that building, it receives the impression of the echo in contradistinction to the original sound from the drums to which they had been marching. Furthermore, there is another cross reflection from Gathright Hall which is very noticeable if one stands on the walk at a point between the entrance to the Assembly Hall and the residence of the president. There is a conglomeration of sound at this point but it is not, however, as abrupt as that caused by the impact of sound on Mitchell Hall.

We, the band, would gladly welcome any suggestion on a way to overcome this phenomenon.[41]

Nowotny's humorous response in 1931 did not end the complaints, which are still occasionally heard today. The band has continued to maintain its innocence of any attempt to change the cadence. Standard military cadence is 120 beats per minute, and the band continues to use that cadence when playing for Corps of Cadets parades and reviews. During halftime performances, however, the band has marched at 120 beats per minute and 116 beats per minute. Currently the organization has reduced that cadence to 104 beats per minute for halftime performances.[42]

In 1951 Adams decided it was time for the music of Aggieland to be recorded. Bill Turner, who was director of both the Singing Cadets and the Aggieland Orchestra, agreed to participate. The recordings were sponsored by the Office of Student Activities, and the Recording Publications Company of New Jersey sent representatives to campus to handle the recording work. The Aggie Band, the Singing Cadets, and the Aggieland Orchestra made the recording separately in Guion Hall, the campus auditorium, which was at the present site of Rudder Auditorium.

The album, titled *Songs of Texas A&M*, was introduced to the campus in a special program at Guion Hall on February 19, 1951. Onstage that night to talk about the music were authors J. V. "Pinky" Wilson, who wrote "The Aggie War Hymn"; Lil Munnerlyn, who wrote "The Twelfth Man"; and Colonel Richard J. Dunn, the retired band director who wrote "The Spirit of Aggieland."[43] This is believed to be the only time these three individuals were ever together.

In 1968 the band began a series of stereo recordings. Volume 1 was titled *The Fightin' Texas Aggie Band*. Under Adams's direction it became the top-selling college band recording in the nation. The "gold record" that marks that accomplish-

ment hangs in the E. V. Adams Band Hall and will be moved to the new John D. White '70–Robert L. Walker '58 Music Activities Center prior to its anticipated opening in the late summer of 2019.[44]

In 1970, Colonel Adams directed a second stereo album, volume 2, *Big! Brassy! Beautiful!* The series of recordings was continued over the years by his successors with volume 3, *Live from Kyle Field* (1973); volume 4, *Centennial Brass* (1976); volume 5, *Live from G. Rollie White* (1979); and volume 6, *Noble Men of Kyle* (1985). With volume 7, *Recall! Step Off on Hullabaloo* (1989), the format changed from records and tapes to compact discs. Volume 8, *Texas Aggie Band Centennial* (1993), continues this new format. Subsequent directors have continued to make CDs: the Aggie Band has released five new CDs since 1994, and the Aggieland Orchestra, a part of the Aggie Band, has recorded one CD. In addition, the Texas A&M Wind Symphony, under the direction of Dr. Timothy Rhea, current director of Bands and Music Activities, has released fifteen CDs, eight in a series called *Legacy of the March*, and seven in a set titled *Wind Band Masterworks*, in addition to CDs recorded at various concerts, clinics, and music educators' meetings nationwide.[45]

These recordings have been made possible through the sponsorship of an organization that also is part of Adams's legacy. Adams believed for many years that it was important to have an organization of former band members that could meet to relive their time in the Aggie Band and provide the emotional and financial support the band needed. The first reunion of former band members took place on November 6, 1965, in Duncan Dining Hall adjacent to the band dormitory on the Texas A&M campus. The assembled group voted to authorize Tom Murrah of the Class of 1938 to form a committee to organize an association of former band members. Murrah chose the members of his committee, and the organization was endorsed by the executive director of the Texas A&M Association of Former Students, Richard "Buck" Weirus of the Class of 1942.[46]

Ten days later the committee met to organize the association. The chair was Dr. Martin

McBride of the Class of 1936, who was assisted by John E. West of the Class of 1957. The first members included Colonel Adams '29, Wayne Dunlap '51, Walt Johnson '60, W. D. "Bill" Longley '47, Chartier Newton '55, Edwin Smith '61, and Cecil Steward '56. The basic concept of the organization was apparent to all. A constitution and bylaws were discussed, as were ways the organization could help Colonel Adams and the band with several problems. McBride and West were authorized to represent the others in seeking approval from Texas A&M's Association of Former Students to formalize the new organization. A name, the Texas Aggie Band Association, was selected.

In November 1966 a suggested slate of officers and bylaws was submitted by mail to all former band members who could be located by the organizing committee. By January 3, 1967, the ballots had been returned approving both the officers and the bylaws. The first officers were Murrah, president; W. Taylor Riedel '44, vice president; Joe Buser '59, secretary; and McBride, treasurer. The first dues were five dollars for a two-year membership, and the first meeting under the name Texas Aggie Band Association was set for October 7, 1967.

Since the establishment of the association, it has not only produced the record albums, but also established and maintained both a fund to pay tutors to help band members with their studies, and a loan fund for use by band members. The association continues its financial support for the band in various ways, but an important part of the group in recent years has been the appearance of former band members in a Reunion Band. The Texas Aggie Band Association has been a great service to the band and its members. It exists today because Colonel Adams made the effort with former band members to make it happen.[47]

In 1970, Adams realized another dream when the Aggie Band got a new rehearsal hall. For thirty-one years the band had been crammed into the fourth-floor rehearsal hall in the band dormitory, a room first built for about two hundred band members. It was enlarged in 1965 but still wasn't large enough. The room was, in fact, so small and its acoustics so bad that something had to be done. The new building provided plenty of room for three hundred band members and a large office for the director, as well as smaller rehearsal rooms for six to eight people, conference rooms, storage space, a library, and an instrument repair area.[48]

Colonel Adams had achieved his goals. He had created the finest and largest military marching band in the nation, building on what Colonel Dunn had accomplished before him. He had directed the recording of a best-selling record, helped establish the Texas Aggie Band Association, and convinced the university—yes, the Agricultural and Mechanical College of Texas became Texas A&M University while Adams was band director—to build a proper rehearsal hall next to the band dormitory.

In 1973, after twenty-seven years of being "The Colonel" to thousands of band members, E. V. Adams stepped down. Former band members and other friends gathered in Duncan Dining Hall for a farewell tribute. In recognition of Adams's emphasis on precise timing, that event was scheduled for 7:02 p.m. That night Adams looked at his stopwatch and, when it was time for him to speak, informed the crowd that the invocation had not been delivered until 7:09 p.m.

At the celebration dinner, H. C. "Dulie" Bell, a former band member in the Class of 1939 and a member of The Texas A&M University System Board of Regents, said, "The best public relations firm could never conceive an idea that would add as much to the good name of this great university as the Aggie Band." Emory Bellard, the football coach at the time, said at the tribute that he had "only one burning desire"—he "someday wanted to field a football team with the same precision and determination as the Fightin' Texas Aggie Band."[49]

When E. V. Adams retired, he was the dean of Southwest Conference band directors and had 209 straight halftime victories to his credit. In September of Adams's retirement year, the new band hall was named the E. V. Adams Band Hall and a plaque was unveiled. It read:

This building is dedicated to LT. COL. E. V. ADAMS Class of 1929.

For twenty-seven years (1946–73) he was the master bandmaster and mentor of more than 3,000 Aggie Bandsmen, offering to each man dignity, self-discipline and enduring pride . . . and they stepped off—for "The Colonel"—with a special marching magic that turned the heads and stirred the hearts of all who watched.

On September 22, 1982, Colonel E. V. Adams passed away. He was buried in his army dress uniform with the Stars and Stripes on his bier. The bugler who played "Taps" at the funeral was Aggie Band junior Jim Williams of the Class of 1984.

At the conclusion of that final bugle call, Cadet Williams removed the Aggie Band lyre from his collar and placed it in the casket. Williams had received that lyre from Edward V. Adams Jr., of the Aggie Band Class of 1961, when he was freshman.

The next evening, as the Aggie Band marched its halftime drill-ending block "T" down the field, the drum major stopped the "War Hymn" and halted what was now the three-hundred-piece Fightin' Texas Aggie Band at midfield. They stood quietly in tribute to "The Colonel," and then instead of running off the field as traditionally done, they walked slowly back to the stands in silence.[50]

Colonel Adams used miniature figures to plot the Aggie Band's halftime drills in the late 1940s and early 1950s, before he developed the special paper charts that divide the football field into thirty-two inch step intervals. Courtesy Mrs. E. V. Adams.

Colonel Adams directs the Aggie Band at a concert in Guion Hall in 1949. 1949 *Aggieland y*earbook, courtesy of Cushing Memorial Library & Archives, Texas A&M University.

Members of the 1950 Aggie Band stood silently in place for twenty minutes waiting for their shadows to fall perfectly in line for this photograph. Courtesy Mrs. E. V. Adams.

Midnight Yell Practices, like this one in 1951, were one time when cadets marched in other than their uniforms and displayed less military bearing than usually required by Colonel Adams. 1952 *Aggieland* yearbook, courtesy of Cushing Memorial Library & Archives, Texas A&M University.

Members from the Class of '52 Fish Band await the start of a parade. Courtesy of Cushing Memorial Library & Archives, Texas A&M University.

In 1953 Colonel Adams placed only seniors on the bugle rank, thus improving the overall appearance of the band. This photograph of the band parading in downtown Houston is the earliest evidence of that change. The senior bugle rank tradition has continued since that time. 1954 *Aggieland* yearbook, courtesy of Cushing Memorial Library & Archives, Texas A&M University.

April Fools Day in 1953 allowed freshmen to reverse roles with sophomores for a day. Here, "fish" of the Class of '56 inspect sophomore Larry Lightfoot '55. Courtesy Buddy Patterson '56.

Famous 1950s band leader Ray Anthony brought his group to Aggieland for a concert in 1953. Anthony and his vocalists visited backstage with Aggie Band seniors, who wore their band sweaters for the occasion. The sweaters are awarded to band members near the end of their junior year. Courtesy Carol E. Jordan '80.

Class of 1956 Fish Band leads the Freshman Battalion in a parade in downtown Dallas before the 1952 SMU game. Courtesy Buddy Patterson '56.

Five members of the Class of '56 Fish Band practice looking tough in preparation for their sophomore year. Courtesy Buddy Patterson '56.

This 1956 halftime drill marked the first time the Aggie football team won in Memorial Stadium in Austin. The Aggies beat the Longhorns 34–21 that day. Courtesy Olin Brown '60.

Texas A&M President Dr. David Morgan presents the General Moore Trophy, which recognizes the outstanding unit in the Corps of Cadets, to Cecil Steward '56 (*left*) commander of the 1955–56 White Band, and Buddy Patterson '56, White Band drum major. Courtesy Buddy Patterson '56.

Members of the Class of 1957, including bass drummer Karl "Gordo" Stephens '57, made up the last of the fish bands. Courtesy Karl Stephens '57.

Nighttime water fights were frequent occurrences in the 1950s. Here David Eller '59 (*center*), White Band commander and later chairman of The Texas A&M University System Board of Regents, and his classmates await the counterattack. Courtesy Olin Brown '60.

Bugle rank members stand at attention as the Corps of Cadets marches into Kyle Field for a 1961 football game. 1962 *Aggieland* yearbook, courtesy of Cushing Memorial Library & Archives, Texas A&M University.

Like other Aggie Band directors, Colonel Adams needed to be cognizant of what was happening on the football field at any given time. Here he prepares to give the downbeat as soon as the timeout is called. Courtesy Mrs. E. V. Adams.

The 1967–68 Combined Band Staff was under the direction of Henry Cisneros '68 (*front center*), who would go on to become mayor of San Antonio, a member of the Board of Regents of The Texas A&M University System, and U.S. Secretary of Housing and Urban Development under President Bill Clinton. 1968 *Aggieland* yearbook, courtesy of Cushing Memorial Library & Archives, Texas A&M University.

Former band members killed during the war in Vietnam included Air Force Captain Albert Tijerina '65, who served as Head Drum Major in 1964–65. Courtesy Sylvia Ann Tijerina.

In an effort to out-do all other classes, the Class of '70 band sophomores went all the way to the Trinity River bottom to find the largest log for the 1967 Bonfire. Although the tree was in about four feet of water, they managed to cut it down and bring it back to campus. It was the biggest log that year. Courtesy John Otto '70.

Juniors from the Class of '69 trying on their senior boots for the first time are (*from left*) Robert Wilkerson, Michael Koenig, Charles Eads, William Wilkinson, Lawrence Lippke, Morris Vogel, Michael Curd, Doug Scott, James J. Hall, and Arthur "Buzz" Erickson. Courtesy James J. Hall '69.

The number of band members grew consistently during Adams's tenure. When dates sat with the band, as they did in this 1969 photograph, close to 400 people filled the band's section at Kyle Field. Courtesy Mrs. E. V. Adams.

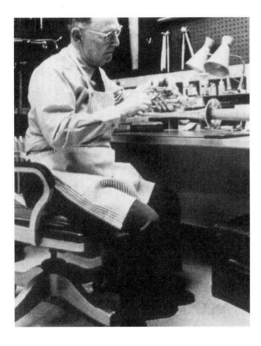

Colonel Adams enjoyed the challenge of repairing instruments throughout his career as bandmaster. This photo is circa 1970. Courtesy Mrs. E. V. Adams.

In 1970, Colonel Adams directed the first rehearsal in what was later to be named the E. V. Adams Band Hall. The new rehearsal hall was a longtime dream for the Colonel and band members. Courtesy Mrs. E. V. Adams.

Newly appointed drum majors Harry M. Fong, James F. Connally, and Ernest E. Johnson, all of the Class of '71, shortly after being named to their new posts at the end of their junior year. Courtesy of Cushing Memorial Library & Archives, Texas A&M University.

Final Review is an emotional time as Aggie seniors take their final salutes from their fellow cadets. In 1973 Colonel Adams joined the line of seniors to take his final salute as director of the Fightin' Texas Aggie Band. Courtesy Mrs. E. V. Adams.

4

The Big Bold Sound
Colonel Joe T. Haney, 1973–89

My job is not to build up the band. It's there, through the untiring and dedicated efforts of Colonel Adams. My job is to keep it at that exceptional level.

—JOE TOM HANEY

There is a legend that the Association of Former Students wanted an Aggie to take over the Texas Aggie Band when Colonel Adams retired. According to the story, they searched their files to find former students of Texas A&M who were band directors. They produced two names: E. V. Adams, director of the Texas Aggie Band, and Joe Tom Haney, director of the Mexia, Texas, High School Band.

Sometimes Aggies like to make up stories, but it is true that Haney enrolled at Texas A&M in 1944 as a member of the Class of 1948 and marched and played in the Aggie Band for Colonel Dunn. According to Haney, "One side of my family all bleeds maroon. They are completely Aggie, so I was completely brainwashed to come to A&M when I was a young lad. There was no place for me but A&M. I was in the Aggie Band. I wouldn't want to be in anything else. But we were in the war at the time, and when you were 18 you were gone."[1]

Haney spent the war years in the 282nd Army Ground Forces Band, and that convinced him that his career should be in music. Thus, after leaving the service, Haney decided to pursue a music degree, which he couldn't get at Texas A&M. Believing his best choice for music in the Southwest Conference was Southern Methodist University, he earned his music degree at SMU.

Even though Haney was forced to leave Texas A&M during World War II, he remained a dues-paying member of the Texas A&M Association of Former Students and is still proud of his playing days in the Fightin' Texas Aggie Band. Although the story holds that the alumni organization searched its files for an Aggie to direct the band, it is more likely that Haney was handpicked by Colonel Adams, just as Adams had been personally selected by Colonel Dunn. Haney met and became friends with Adams through their memberships in the Texas Bandmasters Association. There were other similarities: Haney had become a high school band director just as Adams had in his early career, and Haney had his high school musicians march in the military style Adams was perfecting with the Aggie Band. In 1957, Haney became director of the Mexia High School Band and began to build an award-winning program. When Haney and Adams learned that they both loved to hunt quail, they became even closer friends. Meeting each year at the Bandmasters conference, they would then go hunting together. During those annual visits, Adams learned of Haney's talent for arranging and composing music.

One day in early 1968, Adams called Haney and asked whether he would be interested in writing a new arrangement of "The Spirit of Aggieland." Haney replied that he would be honored to do so and set to work. He completed the arrangement and tried it out with the Mexia musicians. After a few minor adjustments Haney believed he had the sound Adams was looking for, so he sent the score to the Aggie Band's director. That was in late spring. When Haney had not heard from Adams by early fall, he concluded that Adams had not liked the arrangement. The younger bandmaster was disappointed, wishing that Adams had at least told him what was wrong and worked with him to "fix" it.

A short time later, however, Haney was playing golf on a Saturday afternoon and one of his companions, an Aggie, had a portable radio so he could listen to the Aggie football game while they played. When the game started, Haney was astonished to hear his arrangement of "The Spirit of Aggieland" being played by the Aggie Band.

The next week Adams called to say that the band was using the arrangement and asked about coming up to Mexia to hunt quail. During the hunting trip that was subsequently arranged, Adams asked Haney whether he knew a tune called "Kindly Step to the Rear." Haney did. After the two had walked a little farther, Adams asked whether Haney had heard the tune "Hey, Look Me Over." Haney responded that he knew that one, too. After walking another two hundred yards, the two hunters sat down on a rock to rest and Adams turned to Haney and said, "I want you to write me a song that's half way between 'Hey, Look Me Over' and 'Kindly Step to the Rear.'" Haney replied that he knew exactly what Adams was looking for. He went home, wrote a tune called "Gig 'Em," and

immediately sent it to Adams. This time Adams called Haney back right away and said he wanted to use the number on an album the band was recording. It was the band's second album in the stereo series, *Big! Brassy! Beautiful*!

Adams said he wanted to pay Haney for the work he had done. Haney refused payment. "I told him just doing it was enough for me," Haney recalled in a later interview, "but he insisted." The two musicians eventually reached an agreement that focused on their other common love, hunting. Haney asked for and Adams agreed to a puppy out of Freckles, Adams's favorite hunting dog. The puppy was delivered following Freckles's next litter as payment for writing the arrangement of "The Spirit of Aggieland" that is still used by the Aggie Band today and for the march "Gig 'Em" on the band's second stereo album.[2]

A mandatory retirement age of sixty-five existed at Texas A&M when Adams approached that age in 1972. Unlike Dunn, who was anxious to retire from his duties at Texas A&M, Adams was not particularly ready to put down his baton. If he had to, however, he could think of no one better for the band than Haney. To provide a transition period, Haney was brought in to be the associate director of the Texas Aggie Band during the summer of 1972. Adams had never hired anyone to be his assistant, and there had never been an associate director of the band. "With Mr. Haney many things can be accomplished that were not possible in the past with one person doing the work of five," Adams said in an article in the June 16, 1972, edition of the *Bryan–College Station Eagle*.

The Texas State Guard followed what was now Aggie Band tradition and commissioned Haney a major when he joined the band as associate director. Haney served one year in that position and became director upon Adams's retirement at the beginning of the fall semester of 1973. Haney's first act as director was to design a drill honoring Colonel Adams, which the band performed at the Wichita State football game on the same day the band hall was named for Adams.[3]

Colonel Adams's shadow was long over Haney during the first year. He worked in the E. V. Adams

Colonel Joe Tom Haney, Director, 1973–89.
Courtesy Texas Aggie Band.

Then-Major Haney, shown here out of uniform, served for a year as associate director of the band, working closely with Colonel Adams throughout the 1972–73 school year. Courtesy Mrs. E. V. Adams.

Band Hall with E. V. Adams's picture on the wall, and most of the musicians had played under Adams. He must have been told how wonderful Adams was many times during that first year. Apparently many people were concerned that the Aggie Band would change under a new director. After all, the university had changed dramatically during the last several years. The once all-male, all-military college was now a coeducational university—a major research institution. Membership in the Corps of Cadets was no longer mandatory. The school was a much larger and more diverse institution than it had been when Adams arrived in 1946.

When questioned about his plans for the band, Haney said, "Marching format, cadence, musical arrangements, beginning and ending drills with 'The War Hymn,' the signature block 'T' . . . all will be the same."[4] Haney emphasized that the band's intriguing, intricate maneuvers would be performed just as they always had been, and just

as Colonel Adams had promised Colonel Dunn, Haney promised to continue to play the national anthem in the same way Colonel Dunn had.

"My job is not to build up the band. It's there, through the untiring and dedicated efforts of Colonel Adams. My job is to keep it at that exceptional level. I will do my best to go along with the established procedures," Haney reported in September 1973 in Texas A&M's alumni magazine, the *Texas Aggie*. To help in that job, he hired Joe McMullen to take his place as associate band director. McMullen had been a successful band director at Clear Lake High School near Houston and he, too, received a commission in the Texas State Guard when he joined the Texas Aggie Band.[5]

During Haney's first semester a decision was made to admit women into the Reserve Officer

Training Corps program at Texas A&M University the following year. The question immediately arose about women in the Fightin' Texas Aggie Band.

The Aggie Band was—and still is—unique among college bands. No other college band at a major university lives together and eats together as a military unit. Aggie musicians wear uniforms every day—to class, to drill, to meetings, and to other functions on campus. The demands on the Texas Aggie Band far exceed those on other bands. The band performs at more football games than any other band. Through the 1993 football season the band had performed from coast to coast at 125 of the last 131 Aggie football games—including 42 straight from 1981 through the 1984 season. The fans demand the presence of the band. Once many years ago a woman returned forty football tickets when she learned the band would not be making the trip to the Aggie football game being played in her city.[6]

Even the football coaches acknowledge that the Aggie Band can help win football games. When asked how much advantage having the band at Louisiana State University was, Aggie coach Gene Stallings '57 replied in a September 23, 1970, article in the *Houston Post*, "I don't know, but we've gone over to Baton Rouge in the past without them and lost. This time we took them and won." The coach in 1993, R. C. Slocum, voiced the same opinion about the team's loss to Tulsa in 1991—the only trip the band missed that year.

In addition to the football games, the band then played for yell practices, Corps of Cadets reviews and Corps Trips, parades, Corps march-ins at football games, Aggie Muster ceremonies, basketball games, and other parades and concerts. It still plays for all those events except basketball games, which are now covered by a smaller pep band called the Hullabaloo Band, which, as part of the A&M Athletic Department, performs at basketball and volleyball games. In order for the Aggie Band to accomplish its intricate precision drills and meet the demands for participation in other events, it is important that the organization

make efficient use of its time. Living together and taking meals together helps create both efficiency and cohesion. In 1973, many people thought women could not be introduced because of the living conditions and the relationship that had to be established between band members.

On December 7, 1973, Shirley Pfister, writing in the *Houston Chronicle*, said, "While most all-male strongholds are under siege, boys in the band at Texas A&M University are as safe as Fort Knox." She quoted the university's president, Jack K. Williams, as saying, "The question (of admitting women to the band) has not even come up. We have no plans to change our all-male band policy in any way. This is a unique institution and we'd like to keep it that way."

Within six years, however, when a female cadet was denied the right to be part of a Corps of Cadets color guard, she filed a sex discrimination suit. The 1979 suit was filed against Texas A&M University and all of the all-male organizations that were part of its Corps of Cadets, including the band. The young woman who filed the suit did not play a band instrument and had never applied for membership in the band, but because the band was the best known of the Corps organizations named in her lawsuit, it was the band that was mentioned in headlines and stories about the suit.

Although there is no evidence that the lawsuit and the threatened admission of women to the band affected Haney's leadership, it must have been on his mind, because he had long stated he did not want anything to disrupt his ability to direct not only the music and the marching but the daily activities of the three hundred band members.

The membership of the Texas Aggie Band Association and the university administration were clearly against admitting women to the band in 1979. Both groups thought that such a change in Aggie tradition would destroy the band. In November 1979, in a letter to the president of the Texas Aggie Band Association, a former band member wrote, "We have finally arrived at that point in time where the Aggie Band Association will have to muster the forces to perform the task for which it was created—the preservation of the Fightin' Texas Aggie Band."[7] The former band member wanted the association to take whatever action was necessary to prevent women from joining the band.

The response of the Texas Aggie Band Association's president included these words:

> Yes, I would prefer that the Fightin' Texas Aggie Band remain all male. It has worked well that way for generations. It has built a reputation of which we are all proud, a reputation which I hope will continue for many more years, a reputation for precision military marching, a reputation for the big brass sound of patriotic music; and to those of us who have been there, a reputation for leadership training that has served us well in our chosen careers. I assume that this is what you have in mind when you say that you are interested in the preservation of the Fightin' Texas Aggie Band.
>
> I cannot speak for all former band members and I certainly cannot speak for the university but I can state that in my opinion the important issue in this matter is the continuing existence of the finest military marching band in the United States. . . .
>
> I believe that the position of the Texas Aggie Band Association in this matter should be one consistent with the objectives stated in our Association's constitution, "assistance for the Texas Aggie Band and its objectives in any fashion or method deemed appropriate." In my opinion it would not be appropriate for the Texas Aggie Band Association to take an active part in this issue. Any action on this association's part toward barring women from the band would not be in the best interest of preservation of the Fightin' Texas Aggie Band and not in the best interest of the university.[8]

In January 1985, a court order was issued forcing the band and other organizations within the Corps of Cadets to admit women. That fall, three women applied and were admitted to the band as freshmen in the Class of 1989. They were Jennifer Peeler, Carol Rockwell, and Andrea Abat. Because of the living arrangements of the band, the three women were housed in a women's dormitory and came to the band drill field and the band rehearsal hall for band practices and events.

They were part of the band, but they were not part of the band. Living elsewhere, they were unable to build the strong relationships that Aggie Band members had always enjoyed. They wanted to be part of the full Aggie Band experience.

Reporters were calling the women for interviews, and widespread attention was generally making it difficult for them to function as students, cadets, or band members. Haney recognized the problem and arranged a press conference in an effort to end the curiosity about the female band members. The women wanted so much to be part of the band that they would not agree to reporters' requests for photographs unless their "fish buddies" were in the pictures, too.

At the press conference, Tom Hale, the band commander, said, "Most members of the Aggie Band see no problem with girls being in the band and we expect no problems." Hale further stated that school, band, and Corps pressures were enough of a burden for the trio to shoulder without having to operate under a media microscope.[9] It was tough being a freshman in the Texas Aggie Band. It was tough being a sophomore, junior, or senior in the Texas Aggie Band. It was going to be even tougher for the three young women to be the first and to have to do it living in another dormitory.

According to Haney, 33 percent of the people who joined the Aggie Band did not make it through all four years. The odds were clearly against the women. Peeler and Rockwell dropped out during their first semester; Abat made it through her freshman year. She talked about her inspiration to persevere. "I will be wearing those boots," she said during her freshman year.[10] She was, of course, referring to the knee-high leather boots that Joseph Holick and his sons had been making for so many years—the boots that prove one has been good enough and proud enough and tough enough to become a senior in the Corps of Cadets at Texas A&M University.

"When we stepped off for the first halftime performance at Kyle Field my freshman year, I was very nervous," recalled Abat. "I felt like I had to be twice as sharp as the guys in order to fit in. But when we were introduced and the drum major blew the whistle we started into the routine and my concentration took over. Everything went well and when it was over, I felt so proud. It was a tremendous thrill to hear the crowd yelling for us—it is a truly unique and wonderful experience."[11] This truly unique and wonderful experience has been shared by thousands of other members of the Fightin' Texas Aggie Band—a shared experience to which they all can relate.

Haney realized that for the women to have any chance to succeed and have that wonderful experience to the same extent as the men, they were going to need the same opportunities to fully participate. Without any public announcement, Haney integrated the band dormitory. Abat was joined by other women in the fall of 1986 as they quietly moved into the previously all-male band dormitory. They were placed at the end of the first floor, and the restroom and shower at that end of the building were designated for women only.

Now when the band was ordered to "fall out," everyone in the band ran out of the dormitory together. Now when there was room inspection, everyone in the band stood at attention together. Now when they marched to meals, everyone marched together. Now when anybody in the band had a problem, they were all there together to solve it. It wasn't the way everyone wanted it, but at last now everyone had a chance to succeed and a chance to make it work.

In spite of these distractions, Haney was making progress. He emerged from Adams's shadow and began to add to the legend of "The Colonel," as he was promoted from major to lieutenant colonel in the Texas State Guard. Only one uniform change was made while Haney was director. The white Sam Browne belt worn by earlier band members had been abandoned in the late 1960s. Since that time the band uniform had been the same as that of all other cadets. In 1981, at the suggestion of

then commandant James R. Woodall '50, the band added a white belt with a brass buckle to its dress uniform, thereby returning to the practice of white accessories.[12]

Haney began to write new marches for the band—marches that were right for the big, bold sound that could be produced by the heavy brass instrumentation found in the Aggie Band. Haney's march "Noble Men of Kyle," written in 1973, became the group's signature piece. It was published by the Southern Music Company, became a best seller, and was used by six state championship high school bands in their winning performances. In continuing the stereo series of recordings, Haney included "Noble Men of Kyle" in the first recording he directed, *Live from Kyle Field.*

He would go on to record three more albums in the series, with the last one appropriately titled *Noble Men of Kyle.* The opportunity to record was available in part because the playing ability of the band was improving. Haney began to have sectional rehearsals to improve and concentrate on just one section of the band at a time. Haney also gives credit to the high schools for sending better musicians to the Aggie Band. "We would have 20 to 22 All-Stater's each year," Haney remembered during an interview in 1993. "It helped the overall playing quality of the whole band."[13]

In 1974, the improved playing ability prompted Haney to suggest to the drum majors that a section be added in each drill where the band would halt, face the stands, and play. He even prepared a new arrangement of Civil War marches that he called "The Blue-Grey Medley," designed to showcase how well the band could play. "They didn't want to do that because it hadn't been done before," Haney said, recalling the band's opposition to his plan. The director suggested the band members view it not as a change but as an addition to the drill because they played so well. He told them he wanted everyone to know just how well they played.[14]

Haney recalls the opposition to the idea: "Our drum major at that time was Brad Harrison '75 and he was one of my favorite old boys. I guarantee you he was real Old Army and he came in and said, 'Sir, I don't think we ought to do this.' I said to him, 'Brad, I'm going to tell you what. I've written this arrangement and we're going to go over to the side and turn to the people for about 30 or 40 seconds and if the people don't just go wild and really enjoy it I promise you we'll never do it again.'" Harrison replied that he'd do it because Haney wanted to, but he still didn't like it.

In the drill the band moved right to the sideline and played the last section of the medley, "The Battle Hymn of the Republic." In Haney's words, the band played the song "real slow and big and full with a great ending, and the people went wild." Haney remembers that Harrison came to see him the following Monday morning at 8: a.m. and admitted he had been wrong, encouraging Haney to keep the innovation. Based on the reception the band received and the acceptance of the drum majors, Haney wrote other arrangements in a grandioso style that could be used in the same manner and continued this addition to the drills.[15]

Haney maintained the basic concept that Adams had developed but added new variations that thrilled the crowds. New wedge entrances, double chevron drills, and oblique movements were performed, all using the basic *Army Drill Manual* but with formations that had never been seen before. It was Haney's band now, and praises calling it the best band in the country were starting to roll in.

In 1975 the band traveled to Arkansas for the game between the Aggies and the University of Arkansas Razorbacks in Little Rock's War Memorial Stadium. The Aggie Band was seated in the end zone while the Arkansas band had much better seats at about the fifty-yard line, a location where they could be seen on television as they played in the stands. As the game progressed, the ABC roving camera operator continued to come to Haney and ask that the band play at almost every time out. Finally, just after the start of the fourth quarter, the cameraman asked one more time for the Aggie Band to play. Haney replied that to be fair he really ought to ask the Razor-

back Band to play as much as the Aggie Band. The cameraman spoke briefly into his headset microphone and returned to Haney, saying, "The director says he doesn't want to hear the Arkansas band, he wants to hear the Aggie Band."[16]

Others favored the band as well, many with compliments such as these collected by band member John West of the Class of 1957:

"My band kids were simply amazed at the Texas A&M Band's precision; especially the countermarches. There is no better military band than A&M."—Houston Band Director

"What's better than superlative? The Fightin' Texas Aggie Band, that's what."—Texas A&M staff member

"You are a credit to the tradition."—Former band member, Midland

"The finest marching band in the nation."—Jacksonville, Florida

"The Texas A&M marching band show is the most precise performance that I have seen anywhere. Most precision drill teams are unable to march with such precision but when you add the extra factor of playing a musical instrument you get a performance that is breath taking!"—Corporate vice president.[17]

But then disaster struck. What other college band could make headlines by making a mistake? On October 24, 1981, the Fightin' Texas Aggie Band made a mistake during its precision drill in Rice Stadium in Houston. Each of the Aggie Band's halftime drills had to be so exact in order for the maneuvers to work that even the smallest mistake, causing a member to be only inches out of place in the constantly moving pattern, could cause a domino effect. Each band member also had to perform his or her function exactly as designed or other band members could not perform theirs. It was a team effort.

On that day the crowd in the stands was stunned as the drum major suddenly stopped the drill before the block "T" was formed. To the trained eyes of former band members it was apparent that, seconds before, something had gone wrong. Part of the crisp marching style was no longer crisp. Band members who normally passed inches from each other now collided. The disaster that the Aggie Band had always avoided had finally happened. There was no way to complete the drill.

Rumors immediately spread. One of the first was that the Aggie Band had done it deliberately to mock the Rice band known as the MOB (Marching Owl Band), which was noted for undisciplined and antagonistic stunts. "We're not interested in that kind of stuff," Haney said in addressing the rumor. He added that each member of the Aggie Band was supposed to be concentrating on putting on a flawless performance. He also said that several of the band members had reported that their concentration was disturbed "for a brief second," which caused four drill leaders to turn too soon.[18]

This gave rise to the second rumor, one that still persists decades later. The rumor was that members of the Rice band blew whistles to confuse the Texas A&M band. Aggie Band members responded to both whistles and baton commands from their drum majors. In response to questions about this rumor, Major Joe T. McMullen, the associate band director, said that there was no truth to it.[19] To this day, however, all Aggie Band drills performed in Houston are done with baton commands only, movements are made on predetermined yard lines, and no whistle commands are used at all.

At one game a few years ago hundreds of whistles could be heard in seating areas of the Astrodome during an Aggie Band performance at a University of Houston football game. Stores near the University of Houston campus reported that they had sold out of whistles that week. Fortunately the Aggie Band policy of no whistle commands in Houston had gone into effect immediately following the Rice game in 1981, and the band gave a perfect performance.

The mistake at the 1981 Rice game was such an event that newspaper articles continued throughout the week, and then, on the following Saturday at Kyle Field against Southern Methodist University, the band performed one of the most difficult drills ever designed and did it flawlessly. Each drill for the rest of the season was more difficult than the last. Each called for individual movement and intense concentration.

After the University of Arkansas game that year, the editor of the *Bryan–College Station Eagle* wrote in the November 22, 1981, edition: "We all thought we knew how good the Aggie Band was—until the Arkansas game a week ago. That was the most incredible halftime performance I have ever witnessed. . . . A&M probably is the only school anywhere that throws in a free football game with its band performance. One of these days I fully expect the band to be invited to a bowl game—and to be told it can bring along its football team if it wants to." The Aggie Band survived its worst nightmare and ended the season with its collective head held high and praises ringing in its ears.

Haney continued to compose and arrange music during his time as director. He wrote the words and music to "Centennial March" to commemorate the centennial of the university in 1976. The Fightin' Texas Aggie Band and the Singing Cadets made history by appearing together for the first time on Kyle Field at the Texas Tech football game that year to perform the song. He wrote new arrangements for "Stars and Stripes Forever" and many other familiar marches. He also continued to compose original music for the Aggie Band, including "Brasso Brillante," "Brazos Brigade," and "March Furioso."

"You have to create a stadium sound," he said later. "We're the only band in the Southwest that plays all of the time. You can't just march down the field playing just any march. You have to have music that sounds big and full. That's why I wrote all those marches—to give the band marches that could take advantage of the band's instrumentation and produce that Aggie Band sound."[20] In all, Haney wrote fifteen marches for the Fightin' Texas Aggie Band. Some of the new music was used on the recordings produced by the Texas Aggie Band Association, bringing additional income to support the band's operation.

Under Haney the band began to travel more. Thanks to the successful football program at Texas A&M, Haney took the band to eight bowl games—more than any other director. In 1982, 1983, and 1984 the band was at every game the team played. During his last seven years as director the band missed only two of the seventy-nine football games played. In 1988 in a trip reminiscent of the 1955 trip to California for the early season game with UCLA, Haney took the band to New York City for the Kickoff Classic game with Nebraska. The game was actually played in the Meadowlands Stadium in New Jersey, and like the trip to California, it required an early return to campus for band practice. This time there was a difference; the band made the trip by air. But as on the California trip, the band drew praise from everyone who saw it perform.

Although it was thought impossible, the band's reputation grew even greater during Haney's tenure as director. The band's membership increased from year to year, and Haney was able to march as many as 303 on several occasions. He said that was the ideal number because it gave the musicians the room they needed on the field to perform some of the much-anticipated Aggie Band maneuvers. Colonel Jay Brewer '81, the current senior associate director of the Aggie Band, reports that since Haney's tenure the band has marched as many as 400 people. He says the band's "best current block" is 360—twelve files by thirty ranks—but that the count changes frequently, especially for away games where only sophomores, juniors, and seniors travel.[21]

As the university's enrollment increased, Haney expanded the instrumental music program to give opportunities to more students. In 1972 as associate director he had formed a Concert Band. He followed that by reestablishing the Aggieland Orchestra, which had been a popular part of Texas A&M in the years right before and after World War II. The orchestra had formerly been led by the director of the Singing Cadets, and although some members of the Aggie Band were among its members it was not then a part of the band.

The Aggieland Orchestra was really a dance band that played Glenn Miller–type music, the so-called Big Band sound of the 1930s and 1940s. The orchestra had been disbanded in the early 1960s, and all the music had been given away to the Bryan High School music program. Haney obtained new music and started the orchestra again, this time with members from the Aggie Band. Haney himself was the vocalist for the orchestra, and the group proved to be so popular that it was booked for dances almost every weekend the Aggie Band wasn't playing. Because of its popularity, the Aggieland Orchestra recorded an album in 1985.

Haney also created the Texas A&M Symphonic Band to meet the needs of students who were not in the Corps of Cadets but still wanted to play band music. There were a lot of All-State musicians on campus who did not want to participate in a military-type organization, so this gave them an opportunity to continue their music. In addition, Haney reorganized the Drum and Bugle Corps, which played for the Corps of Cadets when they marched to meals. It had existed for some time, but Haney's reorganization made it a more meaningful experience for those who participated.

"When I came to Texas A&M there was one instrumental music group—the Aggie Band," Haney said. "When I got through there were five—the Aggie Band, the Concert Band, the Symphonic Band, the Aggieland Orchestra, and the Drum and Bugle Corps."[22]

During the 1970s fewer and fewer high school bands were marching in the military style used by the Aggie Band. Many bands had changed to what is ironically called Corps Style. This is essentially a style in which the band moves onto the field and stands and plays show tunes and popular music. In these bands the members play music, but they don't do much marching. In military style the band marches and plays at the same time.

To encourage more high school bands to use the military style—and thus produce potential members for the Aggie Band—Haney contacted the National Association of Military Marching Bands about the Aggie Band's hosting a marching competition each year on the Texas A&M campus. The first such contest was held on a weekend without a football game in the fall of 1987. The competition was conducted on Kyle Field to attract outstanding high school military-style marching bands to campus each year. At the end of each contest the Aggie Band gave a demonstration drill that always brought the high school musicians to their feet with loud, appreciative cheers. The contest continued at Kyle Field, run largely by band members, until the field was converted back to grass in 1996.[23]

It was also during Haney's tenure that the Texas Aggie Band Association began to form a Reunion Band of former band members. The first Reunion Band appearance was at a spring football game where football coach Jackie Sherrill had invited "old" football players to come back and play. It seemed appropriate for old band members to come back and play, too. The Reunion Band met every other year on a fall football weekend for a number of years and sometimes marched onto Kyle Field with the Corps of Cadets. The largest Reunion Band marched on September 25, 1994, to mark the band's centennial. The details of that halftime performance are included in chapter 5.

In 1982 Major Joe McMullen, the associate band director, passed away and was replaced by Bill Dean, who had directed the Odessa, Texas, High School Band before coming to Texas A&M. Dean directed the Symphonic Band and assisted Haney in some of his other duties. He was the first director of the Reunion Band and was the first associate director who did not wear a military uniform. In 1986 Dean was honored by the Texas Bandmasters Association by being named Bandmaster of the Year.

As the duties and responsibilities increased for the band director, it became apparent that an assistant band director would be needed in addition to the associate director. The band had been using student assistants to help with many of the logistics involved in supporting a large organization.

These assistants were students who had completed their four years in the band but were still in school. One of these assistants was Jay O. Brewer of the Class of 1981. When Brewer finished his student assistant year Colonel Haney decided he was too good to let go, so the position of staff assistant was created and Brewer became a full-time employee. It was Brewer who became the first assistant director of the Texas Aggie Band in 1986. Haney said he needed someone like Brewer because he was doing everything himself. "I hired Jay as a student to do all the legwork and when he graduated I kept him on because he already knew his way around."[24]

"I was no more qualified than anyone else who had ever marched in the Aggie Band," Brewer related in an interview in 1993, "but I was lucky enough to get to stay." Brewer quickly learned instrument repair because the band was involved in so many performances that instruments could not be sent out when repair was needed. "I was sometimes repairing instruments until two or three o'clock in the morning," he said, "but it was needed and I find it very satisfying to know that I'm responsible for seeing that all of the instruments function properly."[25]

In 1988 Haney decided it was time to retire after directing the Fightin' Texas Aggie Band for seventeen years. Those were years of expanding programs and bigger bands performing bold new halftime drills, of new music with a massive sound written especially for the Aggie Band, of women successfully integrated into the band, and of an expanded staff to meet the needs of the multiple music organizations.

In reflecting on his tenure as director of the Aggie Band, Haney said his biggest thrill came when the band was preparing for the 1987 Cotton Bowl against Ohio State University. The Ohio State Band had a proud heritage and a reputation as one of the best of the Big 10 bands. They called themselves "The Best Damn Band in the Land."

"I always told our band I could take them anywhere in the United States and they could stand against any band, anywhere," Haney recalled.

"Ohio State has an all brass band. Most of the members are music majors and they are really good. I thought, 'You've been telling the band they can go against the best, and Ohio State says they're the best.' Let's see how we do."

Haney beams as he remembers that New Year's Day: "Our band outdid themselves. They were fantastic. When the Aggie Band finished, the band director at Ohio State came over to me and said, 'They are as good as I've heard they were. They're outstanding and I've never seen anything like it.' That was my highlight because we have just a bunch of old country kids—no music majors at all—and they were as good as a band full of music majors."[26]

Haney was still speaking highly of his experiences with the band in 1993. "The Aggie Band is everybody's band," he said. "You have to really think about what you're doing. If you try to change something you have to think about what's involved. The Aggie Band belongs to the world. It's one of a kind. There's not another one like it."[27]

As Haney prepared for his final year, so too did Andrea Abat. The only woman of the original three who enrolled in 1985 fulfilled the promise she made when she arrived: "I will be wearing those boots." She put on her senior boots to march at the Kickoff Classic game at the Meadowlands Stadium in New Jersey. In recalling her first year, she said, "I set out to earn my senior boots and I wanted to be able to wear my senior ring for all of the halftime performances at Kyle Field this fall."[28] She attained both goals and during her senior year she hung a sign on her dormitory room door that proudly proclaimed "Noble Woman of Kyle."[29] Abat's success as a pioneering woman in the Aggie Band affected her family, too. Her father, Paul Abat, is a graduate of the University of Texas. His daughter said in an article in the Au-gust 27, 1988, edition of the *Bryan–College Station Eagle*, "He's a converted Aggie fan now, but it took him a full semester."[30]

On November 16, 1991, the band drill field adjacent to the band dormitory was named the Joe T. Haney Drill Field. During his time with the Aggie Band, Haney was promoted to the rank of full colonel by the Texas State Guard, making him the only director of the Fightin' Texas Aggie Band to achieve that rank at that time. The dedication of the drill field was a fitting tribute to the man who became "The Colonel" to the men and women who marched in the Aggie Band from 1973 to 1989.

The marker for the Haney Drill Field was donated by the Class of 1992, which was the last class to enter the band under his direction. It reads:

JOE T. HANEY
DRILL FIELD

This drill field is named in tribute and honor of Colonel Joe T. Haney, Director of the Fightin' Texas Aggie Band, 1973–1989. Over his 17-year tenure, he inspired thousands of Aggie bandsmen to devote themselves to hard work, perfection of precision drills, and in every step encouraged nothing less than superior performance.

Colonel Joe T. Haney—who wrote "The Noble Men of Kyle" and was deserving of being called one—died on March 9, 2016, at the age of eighty-eight. He suffered from Alzheimer's disease during the last several years of his life. Up until his Alzheimer's diagnosis, he had remained active in Bryan–College Station, judging bands, playing golf, and enjoying life with his wife, Mary, who still resides in the area, and occasionally directing the Fightin' Texas Aggie Band during a football game at Kyle Field. An Aggie Band bugler played "Taps" at his funeral.

Major Joe McMullen (*right*) was associate director under Colonel Haney from 1973 until his death in 1982. Courtesy Texas Aggie Band.

Aggie Band members and their dates march to a Midnight Yell Practice in 1973. Aggies march to the stadium at midnight to practice yelling for their team the following day. 1974 *Aggieland* yearbook, courtesy of Cushing Memorial Library & Archives, Texas A&M University.

On a rainy game day like this one in 1974, it's nice to have a band date with an umbrella. The Aggie Band may be the only college band that allows dates to sit with band members at football games. 1975 *Aggieland* yearbook, courtesy of Cushing Memorial Library & Archives, Texas A&M University.

The 1974–75 bugle rank prepares to step off in Kyle Field. 1975 *Aggieland* yearbook, courtesy of Cushing Memorial Library & Archives, Texas A&M University.

Band members were limited in the ways they could keep warm, or cool, when temperatures during the 1975 football season ranged from sweltering to freezing and almost everything in between. Blankets were a favorite of both the musicians and their dates when the temperatures dropped. 1976 *Aggieland* yearbook, courtesy of Cushing Memorial Library & Archives, Texas A&M University.

The 1976–77 Infantry Band staff included (*left*) Drum Major William Cummings '77, Wilbert J. Sennette, Jr. '77, Brad Garrett '78, Commander Charles P. Briggs IV '77, Rolando H. Santos '78, Martin E. Bryant '77, and Richard A. Stunts '77. 1977 *Aggieland* yearbook, courtesy of Cushing Memorial Library & Archives, Texas A&M University.

In a rare joint appearance, Texas A&M's Singing Cadets joined the Aggie Band in celebrating the university's centennial in 1976. Photo by John West '57.

Colonel Haney designed spectacular new drills for the Aggie Band, including this version of the spider drill in 1976. Courtesy of Cushing Memorial Library & Archives, Texas A&M University.

Bruce Hamilton '78, 1977–78 drum major, prepared to salute while passing the reviewing stand during Final Review 1978. 1978 *Aggieland* yearbook, courtesy of Cushing Memorial Library & Archives, Texas A&M University.

The Aggie bass horns take a rest outside Kyle Field before a 1979 football game. 1980 *Aggieland* yearbook, courtesy of Cushing Memorial Library & Archives, Texas A&M University.

Ruth Hunt, shown here with band freshman Chris Breaux '84 in 1980, has served as the "fish lady" to more than a generation of band freshmen and to other freshmen cadets. Although retired, she comes to campus each day to her adopted table in the Memorial Student Center to listen and to encourage young people who are adjusting to life in the Corps. 1981 *Aggieland* yearbook, courtesy of Cushing Memorial Library & Archives, Texas A&M University.

Elizabeth Hughes, age 2, shows she knows how to direct Mark Beach '81 in his push-up exercises. Young Elizabeth went with her Aggie family to meet the band when the buses carrying the musicians stopped for lunch in Abilene en route to the Texas Tech game in Lubbock in October, 1979. Elizabeth's brothers, James '82 and Robert '83, were both in the band at the time. Other Aggie kin include her father, J. Harold Hughes '52; her sister, Kathryn Hughes Holmes '86; and her brother-in-law, Marty Holmes '87. One of her brothers became band commander; the other served as liaison between the band and the Corps staff; and her brother-in-law became head yell leader. Courtesy J. Harold Hughes '52.

An Aggie Band saxophone player concentrates on his music during a 1980 football game. 1981 *Aggieland* yearbook, courtesy of Cushing Memorial Library & Archives, Texas A&M University.

The 1980–81 Fightin' Texas Aggie Band enters Kyle Field through the north end zone tunnel led by Drum Majors Randy Nelson '81, David LePori '81, and David Rogers '81. 1981 *Aggieland* yearbook, courtesy of Cushing Memorial Library & Archives, Texas A&M University.

Freshman Jerome Kelly '84 stands on the sidelines of the band practice field in 1980 with the drum major's clipboard and bullhorn, waiting to be called to duty while the band practices for a 1980 halftime performance. 1981 *Aggieland* yearbook, courtesy of Cushing Memorial Library & Archives, Texas A&M University.

Colonel Haney consults with Drum Majors Jason Clark '82, head in hands, Rodger Kret, '82, and Rodney Kret '82 after the band failed to complete its halftime drill at Rice Stadium on October 24, 1981. Rumors ran rampant over what had caused the disaster, and to this day all drills done in Houston are performed without the aid of whistle commands. Photo by Kathy Young, Bryan–College Station *Eagle*.

Head Drum Major Randy Nelson '81 stands ready on the Kyle Field wall during a night game in 1980. 1981 *Aggieland* yearbook, courtesy of Cushing Memorial Library & Archives, Texas A&M University.

It is the duty of Aggie Band sophomores to provide the outhouse for the top of the annual Aggie Bonfire. Here the Class of '84 outhouse, decorated with a donated Austin City Limits sign, is hoisted to the top of the 1981 stack. 1982 *Aggieland* yearbook, courtesy of Cushing Memorial Library & Archives, Texas A&M University.

"Drown Outs," or "Quadding," involving both band members and other cadets, were a common occurrence on the Quad in the 1970s and 1980s. 1981 *Aggieland* yearbook, courtesy of Cushing Memorial Library & Archives, Texas A&M University.

Members of the Aggie Band traditionally run from the field at the conclusion of the halftime drills. *1981 Aggieland*.

Physical training, including outfit runs through the campus like this one in 1981, have been a part of the band experience for many years. 1982 *Aggieland* yearbook, courtesy of Cushing Memorial Library & Archives, Texas A&M University.

In order to perfect its intricate drills, the Aggie Band must practice rain or shine. Drummer Charles Williams '84 demonstrates that dedication on a rainy day in 1983. 1984 *Aggieland* yearbook, courtesy of Cushing Memorial Library & Archives, Texas A&M University.

Colonel Haney re-established the Drum and Bugle Corps as a separate organization within the Aggie Band. The unit included volunteer freshman and sophomore brass and percussion players from the band who played for marching to "chow" and for certain special occasions. 1985 *Aggieland* yearbook, courtesy of Cushing Memorial Library & Archives, Texas A&M University.

These 1984 bass horn players show that turning with the massive instruments in a confined space can be tricky. 1985 *Aggieland* yearbook, courtesy of Cushing Memorial Library & Archives, Texas A&M University.

Freshmen members from the Class of '89 included (*from left*) Jeffrey Starr, Michael Kelly, Jennifer Peeler, Ronald Felden, Carol Rockwell, and Andrea Abat. Abat, Rockwell, and Peeler were the first women in the band, joining in September of 1985. Shown here after a press conference, they refused to be singled out for a photograph unless some of their other "fish buddies" were included. It is tradition in the Aggie Band that you look out for your fish buddies. 1986 *Aggieland* yearbook, courtesy of Cushing Memorial Library & Archives, Texas A&M University.

The music of the Fightin' Texas Aggie Band under Colonel Haney was dominated by a big brass sound created by a strong contingent of bass horn players. While the Haney-era bands generally marched twenty-four to thirty bass horns, a world-record forty of the massive horns marched with the organization during the 1993 football season. Courtesy Texas Aggie Band.

When marching in diagonal files in the squad drill, the 1985–86 Aggie Band was spread over more than forty yards of the TCU stadium. 1986 *Aggieland* yearbook, courtesy of Cushing Memorial Library & Archives, Texas A&M University.

January 1, 1986, marked the Aggie Band's first appearance in a Cotton Bowl game since 1968, but it would be the first of three straight New Year's Days in Dallas. The Aggies won the football game against Auburn 36–16. Courtesy Robert C. Barker '71/Barker Photography.

Drummer Jeff Pehl '89 leads his file down the sideline during a 1988 halftime drill. 1989 *Aggieland* yearbook, courtesy of Cushing Memorial Library & Archives, Texas A&M University.

Kevin Roberts '89 was the Aggie Band's first black drum major. 1989 *Aggieland* yearbook, courtesy of Cushing Memorial Library & Archives, Texas A&M University.

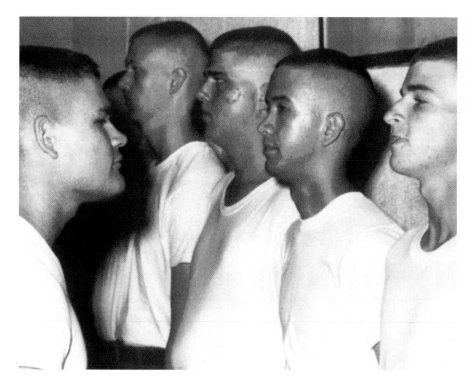

New fish are treated to a hall inspection by sophomore Rod Hadder '91 in 1988. Photo by Texas A&M University Photographic Services.

The Aggieland Orchestra was re-established during Colonel Haney's tenure as director. The current group is directed by Colonel Jay O. Brewer '81, fourth from right on the bottom row. Courtesy Texas Aggie Band.

The Fightin' Texas Aggie Band and former band members in the Reunion Band joined forces on Kyle Field to honor Colonel Haney following his retirement in 1989. The combined group played the band's signature march, "Noble Men of Kyle," which Haney had written in 1973, and the current musicians spelled his name on the field. Courtesy Texas Aggie Band.

Drum Major Mike Sammis '90 leads the band during a 1989 halftime performance. 1990 *Aggieland* yearbook, courtesy of Cushing Memorial Library & Archives, Texas A&M University.

The 1988 football season got off to an early start in the Kickoff Classic at the Meadowlands in New Jersey. Band members returned to campus early to prepare their drill, which ended with the traditional block "T." The football team was outscored by Nebraska, 23–14, but the freshman band members earned their lyres before classes had even started. Photo by George Hamilton '61/Barker Photography.

The Fightin' Texas Aggie Band spells out "Gig 'em Aggies," at halftime at Kyle Field. Photo by SNS Photographics.

Bass drum players Jason Blevins '94, *front*, and Kacey Gabriel '94, *rear*, "eat" their bass drums as part of the maneuver required to turn the cumbersome instruments in the tight formation of a countermarch. Photo by Glen Johnson/Johnson Photography.

The highlight of each football season is the development and execution of the various complicated versions of the cross-through. The band performed a wide double cross-through at the University of Texas' Memorial Stadium in Austin in 1990. Courtesy Robert C. Barker '71/Barker Photography.

Bugle rank members lead each halftime drill and must be exact in every movement in order for the complicated drills to be completed with perfection. 1990 *Aggieland* yearbook, courtesy of Cushing Memorial Library & Archives, Texas A&M University.

The Fightin' Texas Aggie Band marches in the shadow of the Capitol during President George H. W. Bush's inaugural parade in Washington, D.C., in 1989. Photo by Robert C. Barker '71/Barker Photography.

The band spells out "Aggies" during the halftime of the TCU game in 1986. The football team won the game, 74–10, and, as always, the Fightin' Texas Aggie Band won the halftime. Courtesy of Robert C. Barker '71/Barker Photography.

As part of one of the two annual Corps Trips, the Aggie Band paraded through downtown Dallas in November, 1992, prior to the SMU football game. Courtesy Robert C. Barker '71/Barker Photography.

Seniors Ken Stover, Bruce Cummings, Tom Rheinlander, Greg Dew, and Dillard Stone, all from the Class of '80, having completed their last parade, bid good-bye at the 1980 Final Review. 1980 *Aggieland* yearbook, courtesy of Cushing Memorial Library & Archives, Texas A&M University.

Band Commander Jeremy Schubert '93 surrounded by other members of the 1992–92 Fightin' Texas Aggie Band during a performance at Kyle Field. Photo by Glen Johnson/Johnson Photography.

Dorothy Hopkins, administrative assistant to the director of the Texas Aggie Band, joins Colonel Haney to celebrate the naming of the band's practice field in his honor in 1991. The special ceremony was planned by the band's Class of 1992, which was the last class to enter Texas A&M while Haney was director. Courtesy Texas Aggie Band.

5

The Legend Continues
Lieutenant Colonel Ray E. Toler, 1989–2001

It's magic. —RAY E. TOLER

The date was September 18, 1992; the scene was the airport in Columbia, Missouri. The Fightin' Texas Aggie Band, clad in battle dress uniforms (also known as fatigues), had just landed in two 727 jet aircraft in anticipation of supporting the Aggie football team at the next day's athletic contest. The days of sending the band by train had ended many years before, but what had not changed was the band's reputation, which had spread even to Columbia. Media representatives were there to meet the planes. During an on-camera interview with a Missouri journalist, the band's director was asked how it was that the Aggie Band was able to perform such amazingly impossible maneuvers. Lieutenant Colonel Ray E. Toler's reply was simple: "It's magic."[1]

Colonel Toler had indeed continued the magic of the Texas Aggie Band since becoming its director on September 1, 1989. His appointment also continued the practice of the retiring director personally picking his successor.

When Toler was growing up in Marlin, Texas, he worked in a store owned by Joe Tom Haney's uncle. During the summers when Haney returned to his hometown on vacation from his high school

band duties in Mexia, he taught trombone to young Ray Toler. Toler must have learned well, because he later earned a music scholarship to Texas Christian University in Fort Worth. According to Toler, most of the young men in Marlin went to college at Texas A&M; although he, too, aspired to Aggieland, he couldn't earn a music degree there and instead selected TCU. He graduated from the Fort Worth university in 1964 with a degree in music education and became a high school band director in Weatherford, Texas.

Before being called to active duty in the armed services, Toler auditioned for the Air Force Band Program and was accepted. While playing the trombone in the Air Force Band of the West, he applied for a position as an Air Force Band officer and entered Officer Candidate School. He received his commission as a second lieutenant in February 1968 and was immediately named director of an air force band—only the second person ever to become a director right out of Officer Candidate School. He directed several other air force bands, both in the United States and overseas. Included in his air force career were some unusual assignments like arranging music written by the king of

Thailand for the monarch's twenty-fifth anniversary of his ascension to the throne, and recording the music of West Africa. His 1984 recording by the Band of the Air Force Reserve, titled *Comin' at Ya*, was nominated for a Grammy Award.[2]

Toler eventually became chief of bands and music for the US Air Force, with responsibility for that service's overall music program. He was fulfilling those duties when Aggie Band director Joe Tom Haney called to see whether he would be interested in becoming the director of the Fightin' Texas Aggie Band upon Haney's retirement. Haney had followed Toler's career since Marlin and had kept in touch with him during his various air force assignments. Haney recommended Toler to the university administration, and it was agreed that Toler was, indeed, the right person for the job.[3]

Following the precedent set by Haney, Toler first became associate band director, assuming that position in September 1988, for a transition year before Haney's pending retirement. Haney had served seventeen years with the Aggie Band; Toler had spent twenty-two and a half years with the air force. In September 1989, Toler became only the fourth full-time director of the Aggie Band. "I had been working with professional musicians in the air force," Toler commented later. "I had to remind myself that I was now working with students. I had to become a teacher again, but I quickly learned that the quality of the students was just amazing. We have such high academic standards here that the students we get are in the top 10 percent of their high school class."

Toler had to endure the same questions as Haney had before him. Because the style of the Aggie Band was so distinctive and because people expected so much of the Aggie Band, they did not want to see anything happen that would "change" the style and high quality they had come to expect. "The first thing everyone asked me when I got to Texas A&M was, 'You're not going to change anything about the band, are you?'" Toler said. "I told them the Aggie Band would remain the unique, number one, precision marching military band that it is. We do the thing that we do

Lieutenant Colonel Ray E. Toler, Director, 1989–2002. Courtesy Texas Aggie Band.

best, better than anyone else in the world; a man would be a fool to change that."

Toler was also wise enough to know that the band director's position at Texas A&M required more than just directing music. The director was responsible for many aspects of the cadets' daily lives. Toler spent at least twenty hours each week as a mentor to students in the Aggie Band and to those in the university's Symphonic Band, who were primarily noncadets and thus not members of the Fightin' Texas Aggie Band.

When Toler became director in 1989, he set goals and objectives for the band under his direction. First, he was determined to maintain the marching preeminence of the organization; second, he wanted to continue the progress Haney had started in improving the playing of the music. In order to do that he promoted Jay Brewer from assistant band director to associate band director and brought in Jim McDaniel as assistant director.

Brewer, a member of Texas A&M's Class of 1981, had served Colonel Haney as student assistant during the 1981–82 academic year. Recognizing Brewer's abilities, Haney promoted him to staff assistant in 1982 and then to assistant director in 1986. With his promotion to associate director in 1989, Brewer began to take a more prominent role in the administration of the band. He continued to repair instruments as he had done under Haney, but because of his experience with the band—a total of twelve years at the time, including his four years as a student—Brewer became the one to see that the important traditions of the Aggie Band were continued under Toler's direction.[4]

Brewer was also made responsible for the care of the Haney Band Drill Field and the band dormitory. In actuality, the "band dorm" had become two residence halls (a new term for dorm)—Harrington Hall, or Dorm 11, and Whiteley Hall, or Dorm 9—as the number of band members was now more than the capacity of one hall. Brewer also assisted Toler as mentor and counselor, bringing the perspective of a former band member to his discussions with the cadets. The band's extensive music library was also Brewer's responsibility, and he served as director of both the Aggieland Orchestra and the Texas Aggie Band Association's Reunion Band. In addition, he shared with Toler the responsibility for directing the smaller version of the Aggie Band that then played at basketball games.

Both Toler and Brewer were assisted by McDaniel, who earned bachelor's and master's degrees from Texas Christian University and came to Texas A&M as assistant band director in 1990 from Martin High School in Arlington, Texas, where his bands were among the most successful in the state. McDaniel, as assistant director, led the University Jazz Band, a new organization of students who were not members of the Aggie Band. After Toler came to Texas A&M, the jazz band became affiliated with Texas A&M's instrumental music program, a part of the Department of Philosophy and Humanities in the College of Liberal Arts. McDaniel also assisted Toler in directing the Symphonic Band, which was open to all students at the university and usually included a small number of Aggie Band members among its musicians. McDaniel was the second member of the band's staff not to wear a military uniform; Bill Dean, associate director under Haney, had been the first. McDaniel left the band in 1993 to return to the public schools and was replaced by Tim Rhea.

Rhea graduated with honors from the University of Arkansas with a degree in music education and earned a master's of music in conducting at Texas Tech University. He was a teacher and band director in the La Porte, Texas, Independent School District before coming to Texas A&M. Rhea, a composer as well as a conductor, wrote "The Texas A&M Centennial March" as one of three specially commissioned pieces of music to commemorate one hundred years of the Aggie Band. He followed the earlier tradition of Aggie bandmasters by accepting a commission as a lieutenant in the Texas State Guard.[5]

Another valued member of Toler's staff was Dorothy Hopkins. Hopkins had come to Texas A&M as secretary to Haney in 1982 and was promoted by Toler to staff assistant and then administrative staff assistant. In that role, she handled all the office and administrative duties for the band. She was responsible for making all the travel arrangements for the band's many road trips. The band now traveled by air on long trips, using two chartered 727 jet aircraft. Shorter trips continued to be by bus—eight modern, air-conditioned vehicles for each trip. When the trips were very short—like the ninety-mile journeys to Houston, Waco, or Austin—band members usually made their own travel arrangements and assembled at a designated location at a specific time. For these short trips, Hopkins engaged a moving van to carry the ten thousand pounds of instruments to the staging area. On the longer trips, the instruments traveled in the baggage compartments of the planes or buses.

A few years ago, on trips to Arkansas and Lubbock, the band would take a ten-hour bus ride, play for four hours at a football game, get back on the buses, and travel another ten hours back to College Station. Fortunately, those twenty-four-hour bus trips are over, and the band now has the luxury of spending the night in a hotel at or near the site of the game or the event at which it is appearing. In many cases, the band uses the same hotel rooms that the football team used the previous night, thus allowing the university to cover the "two-night minimum" that many hotels impose on football weekends. Just as Adams reported in 1955, the band is always a welcome guest at these hotels. Hopkins says the group "is always invited back."[6] An excited hotel staff in Columbia, Missouri, posed for souvenir pictures with band members; a Dallas hotel where the band stayed for the 1993 Cotton Bowl displayed the words "Thanks Aggie Band!" on their outdoor sign for all to see. Hopkins cited the long bus trip to El Paso for the John Hancock Bowl in 1989 as the toughest of the group's road trips, and the pleasant visit to San Diego, California, for the 1990 Holiday Bowl as one of the best.

In addition to her regular duties, Hopkins, who has grown children of her own, was the unofficial "Band Mom" and liaison with many Aggie Band parents, especially those living out of state. "Being a long way from your son or daughter when that son or daughter is having a tough time is difficult for parents," she says. "It's not easy being in the Aggie Band. I try to help both the parents and the band members understand what is going on and why." When asked to describe her duties, Hopkins says, "If it's not marching or playing music, I do it."[7] By handling the details, she gave Colonel Toler the time to provide the leadership needed to maintain the quality of the Fightin' Texas Aggie Band.

And that's exactly what Toler was able to do. He achieved the goals he set of maintaining the marching preeminence of the Aggie Band and continuing to improve its musicianship. The marching preeminence that began under Adams has continued, with both Toler and Brewer designing new halftime drills. In addition, it has become a tradition in recent years for each of the three drum majors to design a drill each year. "These are some of our best drills," reports Brewer. "The drum majors really come up with some new challenges for the band."[8]

With the marching at such a high level, the band is always in demand for performances away from campus, but the high academic standards of the university make it impossible for the band to accept all these requests. Band members have come to Texas A&M first and foremost to earn their degrees. Both the organization's directors and its support organization, the Texas Aggie Band Association, are well aware of that fact, and the association assists the students by providing money for tutors if necessary. Despite its members' academic schedules, the group has appeared in numerous parades and events, including presidential and gubernatorial inaugurations. The band has also appeared at special civic and community programs and National Football League games, all the while continuing its tradition of appearing at more of its own team's football games than any other college band, including ten bowl games during Toler's twelve years as director.

The enhanced musicianship that Haney brought to the Aggie Band continued under Toler, as did the recordings. Volume 7, *Recall! Step Off on Hullabaloo*, was released in 1989, and a new recording, volume 8, *Texas Aggie Band Celebration*, was released in 1993 to commemorate the one-hundredth anniversary of the band. It includes the march written by Colonel Haney in honor of the centennial. Titled "Maroon Tattoo," the march features the big, bold sound for which Haney's marches are known. When the centennial recording was made, the recording engineer noted the improvement in the band. "We are discarding takes this time that would have made the recording four years ago. We have so many more really good ones this time around."

Toler reports that at meetings of the College Band Directors National Association many highly respected directors compliment the Aggie Band. "Everyone from the Big 8 has heard wonderful things about the band because of its performance at the University of Missouri in 1992," he said before the Big 8 became the Big 12 and Texas A&M joined the conference in 1994. "They tell me we set a standard there that had not been seen forever, practically." The director takes pride in the healthy respect for the band that remains based on other performances, including its 1986 Cotton Bowl drill. "Several members of the staff at Ohio State always mention how their band is still talking about the Aggie Band. We get those same kind of comments all over the country."

Under Toler the Aggie Band was back at full strength. The number of women in the band continued to increase, with their full participation in all aspects of the band including the regimented lifestyle and the 5:30 a.m. military-supervised physical training three days a week, in addition to the drills and rehearsals. In talking to prospective students about the Aggie Band, Toler was always very straightforward. He was known for telling the students and their parents that being in the band wasn't easy, that it required living a disciplined lifestyle. "It's not for everyone," he told them, "but for those who are willing to accept the challenge of living that regimented lifestyle—in the Corps of Cadets twenty-four hours a day, marching to early chow as a complete band, doing physical training as a military unit, taking the evening meal as a military unit, living in the dormitory together, and studying together at night—there's no greater reward."

Toler also stressed what a student can get from the band: the leadership training, learning to be a follower and then a leader. "One of these years you're going to have to get up early in the morning on a daily basis regardless, so you might as well learn it early as we do here at Texas A&M. A band member gets up early, goes all day, and finally gets to bed at 11 p.m. or midnight, having put in a full day's work in academics, the Corps of Cadets, and the band," he often told prospective members.

Although auditions were required in the early days of the Aggie Band, none have been required since the days of Colonel Dunn through Toler's tenure. The Aggie Band accepted anyone who was qualified to enroll at Texas A&M University, had experience marching and playing in a high school band, and was ready to accept the challenge of participation in the Corps of Cadets. There were no band scholarships, but incoming musicians were eligible to compete for other financial assistance offered through the university and the Corps of Cadets.

Only about eight hours a week were spent perfecting the drills because of the other demands on the cadets' time. According to Toler, this was less time than other bands spent on perfecting the one drill they would repeat and repeat with only minor variations each week all season. The Fightin' Texas Aggie Band presented a new drill each week, a feat that Toler says could be accomplished only because of the leadership provided by the cadet officers and the discipline inherent in the band's structure. The Corps of Cadets, and the Aggie Band, taught that discipline.

"We are only on the drill field for an hour each day, and during that time there is no fooling around. Everyone concentrates for the full hour," says Toler. "We have a commitment to excellence. That's why we are able to do what we do. We did 12 different drills during the 1992 football season. When I tell my counterparts that they shudder." The videotapes of the band's various drills that Toler took to the annual meetings of the College Band Directors National Association were among the most popular items in the information area. Toler says the other directors just couldn't believe the Aggie Band did different drills each week with different memorized music. He told his colleagues that this was routine for his musicians. "I didn't originate that, of course. That's always the way it's been. Wherever we go, we get a standing ovation because people appreciate quality."

That quality continues to be recognized throughout the country. Even before former president George Bush decided to build his presidential library at Texas A&M University, he determined that he liked the Aggie Band and invited the group to march in his inaugural parade. The band's big patriotic sound thrilled the crowds that lined the streets that day in January 1989. Since that time, George Bush has paid tribute to the Aggie Band each time he has visited the campus.

When asked about women in the band, Toler pointed out that although there were only two women in the organization when he arrived in 1988 as associate director, during the centennial year, 1994, there were more than thirty. "We are now at the point where more young women are joining each year," he said then. Toler added that the transition of the band from an all-male organization to one that included both men and women was very easy. One additional change in the women's housing was made after he became director. Haney had successfully moved the women into the band dorm to help them feel they were part of the organization, but as the number of women increased some still felt isolated from their fellow band members because all the women were still housed at the end of the first floor. The women came to Toler and said they really wanted to be part of their individual units within the band. They felt they were missing too much by being segregated to one area of the dormitory.

Under Toler's direction the band remained organized in two bands, the way it had been for the previous fifty years. Under Dunn the two were designated the Field Artillery Band and the Infantry Band, reflecting the branches of the army in which the cadets trained. When the cadets' military options expanded to include other branches of the armed services, Adams changed the names of the units to the Maroon Band and the White Band. Bowing to band tradition, Haney reinstated the Field Artillery and Infantry designations in 1976. The two bands had been divided into two company-sized units, A Battery and B Battery in the Field Artillery Band, and A Company and B Company in the Infantry Band until 1982–83, when Corps administrators attempted to add additional units within the band, an idea that lasted only two years. In 2013–14, however, a C Battery and a C Company were added to create more reasonably sized units than were allowed with just the four groups.[9]

Although the women were living in the band dormitory during Toler's early leadership, they were not living with the units to which they were assigned. Toler sought permission from the Corps commandant, Major General Thomas G. Darling '54, to make the requested change on an experimental basis. Darling agreed, and the change was successful. Women are now housed on every floor in the band dormitories, and they are beginning to take on responsible leadership positions as full participants in all band duties and activities. "Women are an asset to the Aggie Band," Toler said. "They have proven themselves. We lost fewer women than men during the 1992–93 school year."

When asked about his decision to retire from the air force and come to Texas A&M, Toler said, "I wouldn't change places with anybody. I bleed maroon now." Toler gives credit to his staff for making his transition from the air force to the Aggie Band easy. "Dorothy Hopkins, my administrative staff assistant, was invaluable. She had been here 12 years when I arrived. She's the 'Band Mom.' Jim McDaniel was a fine musician; it was a big help to have him here to help with the Symphonic Band and the Jazz Ensemble. I also expected big things with Timothy Rhea. His arranging and composing will be big assets for the band."

Other than the cadet leadership in the band, Toler reserved his highest praise for his associate director, Major Jay Brewer '81. "Jay has grown up with the band," Toler said with a smile. "He was a band member, a student assistant, an administrative assistant, the assistant band director, and now the associate director. He made the transition between directors go smoothly. He is a friend and a confidant."

Brewer's direct experience with the band began in 1977 when he joined it as a freshman, but his first contact with the organization came long before that time. His father was a member of the Class of 1943, so Brewer knew about Texas A&M from the time he was a small boy. As a junior high school trombone player, he was best friends with a boy who was the brother of one of the Aggie Band's drum majors. Brewer says one of the highlights of that time was coming to campus to visit his friend's brother and staying in the band dormitory.

One year, Brewer's parents came to campus for the Texas A&M–University of Texas football game and told the band director of their son's interest in the Aggie Band. Colonel Adams, who was director at the time, sent the Brewers back to their Channelview home with some gifts for their son—a copy of the band's first stereo album, *The Fightin' Texas Aggie Band*, and the trombone music for "The Aggie War Hymn." The young man played the album and the music over and over again and dreamed of one day being in the Fightin' Texas Aggie Band. In a later interview, Brewer said twelve young men from Channelview came to Texas A&M in the fall of 1977. Three, including Brewer, joined the band; the other two dropped out the first week. Only four of the twelve graduated. After his time in the band was over, Brewer was pleased to be given the opportunity to stay. "Sometimes I have to pinch myself," he said, "and wonder 'Is this a dream or is this really Jay Brewer's life?'"[10] Brewer pays tribute to Haney for giving him a chance and to Major Joe McMullen, Haney's associate director, whom he calls his mentor, his teacher, and his friend.

The members of the Texas Aggie Band Association consider Brewer such an asset to Colonel Toler and to the Aggie Band and its traditions that they voted to financially support his progress toward a master's degree at the VanderCook School of Music in Chicago, where Colonel Adams studied. Brewer spent his summers in Chicago until he was awarded his master's in 1993. Although Brewer did not play and march for Adams, he has affectionate and fond memories of the man who sent him his first Aggie Band music. Adams died in 1982, but his picture hangs on the wall behind Brewer's desk. "It's so I'll always be aware that he's looking over my shoulder," Brewer explains.

When Brewer first came to Texas A&M in 1977, Adams had already retired, and the first time they ever met was in the fall of 1981. Brewer was the band's new graduate assistant and was in the band hall to ready it for an open house for the Texas Aggie Band Association. The young assistant came out of his office and saw Adams, in a maroon blazer and gray pants, opening the door. Adams saw Brewer in his Texas State Guard lieutenant's uniform and said, "Who the hell are you?" to which Brewer replied, "Well, who the hell are you?" Adams, whose formal portrait was on the wall immediately adjacent to where he was standing, said, "I like that. I just wanted to find out what kind of man you are."

In telling the story of that first meeting, Brewer turned around and took an army officer's hat off a shelf in his office and said, "A short time later, I saw Colonel Adams again and he said he had something for me. He gave me this hat—his hat—and said, 'Someday, Lord willing and the creek don't rise, maybe you can put that on and wear it.'" Brewer was finally qualified to wear the hat after he was promoted to major and has worn it selectively ever since, but only on specific occasions—at Texas Aggie Band Association reunions and when the band does the midfield crisscross maneuver that Adams designed.

Colonel Adams's hat is just one of the band's traditions. Not many people know about the hat because it is Brewer's personal story, but Brewer also keeps up with other traditions important to the collective band and individual band members. When asked about those traditions, Brewer cites the band's long-standing commitment to excellence. "The really important traditions of this band are found on the outside of this building [the E. V. Adams Band Hall]," Brewer often says, quoting the plaque that dedicated the band hall to Colonel Adams: "dignity, self-discipline, and enduring pride." Brewer says those three phrases "are the real tradition of the Aggie Band. . . . We create mature, responsible leaders who have self-confidence and who, because of what they have to do in the Aggie Band, pay attention to minute details. That serves them well in whatever profession they choose."

When pressed, however, he admits to other traditions, some serious and some not so serious. Just being in the Aggie Band is a tradition for some families. Band rosters—and stories—tell of fathers and sons sharing the experience across generations, and there are several examples of brothers being in the band at the same time or in consecutive years as mandated by their ages. There were twin brothers—Rodger and Rodney Kret—who served as the side drum majors in 1982–83. Senior boots have been passed down along family lines, as has family participation in either the Field Artillery or the Infantry Bands. A notable example of multigenerational participation is found in the Adams family. E. V. Adams of the Class of 1929 was, of course, the band director for whom the band hall is named. His son E. V. Adams Jr., of the Class of 1961, marched and played for his father for four years, and his grandson E. V. "Rusty" Adams III, of the Class of 1996, has become the third generation in the Fightin' Texas Aggie Band.

In another long-standing tradition, freshmen in the band are called fish, as are other freshmen in the Corps of Cadets, and when the fish arrive they are given very short haircuts. The women must have a hairstyle that does not touch their uniform collar. The fish are issued their uniforms but are not allowed to pin on their band lyres, the brass military collar insignia for the organization, until completion of their last home drill performance of the season on Kyle Field, in conjunction with other fish in the Corps donning their own brass. At one time, band fish earned their lyres by performing in a perfect Aggie Band halftime drill, which usually occurred near the start of the season. The new method encourages consistency across the entire Cadet Corps. Until that time, all fish wear a brass AMU pin on their collars.

In addition to other activities associated with football games, there is an important tradition associated with the last drill of each football season at Kyle Field. At that time the band's announcer—Colonel Jay Brewer, associate band director and a member of the Class of 1981—reads a special dedication honoring the organization's seniors as they begin their final performance on Kyle Field.

The traditional dedication reads:

> Ladies and gentlemen, tonight's halftime drill is dedicated to the senior cadets of the Fightin' Texas Aggie Band who march tonight in their final performance on Kyle Field. These seniors have given freely of their time and talents, demonstrating an admirable leadership to those bandsmen who follow in their footsteps. Tonight, they join the rank and file of an endless legion of Aggie Bandsmen whose dignified footsteps and echoing brass have filled this stadium to the brim through decades past. May each senior leave feeling confident that they have contributed largely to the development of that concentrated will and desire to excel that is the hallmark of all Aggie Bandsmen. We ask that you join in wishing them all a true cadence and steady tempo as they step out into the bright tomorrows that follow this grand finale on Kyle Field.

The Aggie Band is part of many campus traditions. One of the best known was the Aggie Bonfire, a massive log stack that was constructed each year just before the football game with the University of Texas, referred to as "t.u." by Aggies everywhere. The bonfire was burned each year to symbolize the Aggies' "burning desire" to beat t.u. on the gridiron. That tradition came to a crashing end at approximately 2:42 a.m. on November 18, 1999, when the massive stack, still under construction, collapsed, killing twelve people—eleven current students and one former student—and injuring an additional twenty-seven. That accident and its aftermath led to the withdrawal of Texas A&M University sanctions for the annual project. Although a bonfire is still constructed annually off campus by interested students and former students, building or participation in the burning of that fire is not an event officially sponsored or funded by Texas A&M.[11]

Aggie Band members from before 1999 remember a bonfire tradition that included the band. For many years it was the responsibility of the band's sophomores to "acquire" the outhouse—or t.u. tea house—that sat on top of the stack. Since outhouses eventually became scarce, the band sophomores would build an outhouse, deliver it to the bonfire site to be hoisted to the top of the stack of logs, and finally watch it go up in flames with the rest of the bonfire.

Another traditional band sophomore duty was making the torches the yell leaders and drum majors carried before home football games as they led the students from the Corps housing area to Kyle Field in a torchlight parade to practice yelling for the coming game. Tradition holds that the band sophomores tried to make the torches as heavy as possible as their way of "getting back" at the seniors.[12]

Each class in the band and the Corps of Cadets has certain differences in uniforms that may not be noticeable to the untrained eye. Fish wear no braid on their caps, sophomores wear black braid, juniors wear white braid, and seniors wear a gold and black striped braid. Fish and sophomores wear black belts, whereas juniors and seniors wear white belts, and of course seniors wear boots. Many years ago when there was a separate fish band, the fish had to wear a piece of coat hanger in their caps to make them absolutely straight on top. Band fish were referred to as "skate heads" because of the bladelike appearance of their caps. Supposedly it was punishment for the theft of the bear cub mascot of Baylor University by a previous band fish class. The tradition ended when the fish band was merged back into the Aggie Band in 1954.[13]

One of the Aggie Band's most important traditions is the process of selecting the drum majors. There are three drum majors—a head drum major and two side drum majors—and all are seniors. This process, too, has changed over the years. Each spring, interested juniors submit their names for the drum major positions. To be eligible, they must turn in their official transcript proving they have a specified grade point ratio (the same is true for juniors applying for positions on the bugle rank). There are preliminary tryouts to see whether the candidates have mastered the basics of conducting and the required drill terms. Based on the way the candidates march and handle the baton, the number of finalists is reduced.

The second phase of the selection process takes two days. On the first day each candidate, again one at a time, conducts the band in the rehearsal hall in either "The Spirit of Aggieland" or "The Star-Spangled Banner," and a march selected by the directors. On the second day the band moves to the drill field, where the candidates explain and then lead the band through a drill.

When all candidates have had their turn, the band is dismissed and the work of the selection committee—the three drum majors and the three directors—begins. Each candidate is honestly discussed and everyone has a vote. The combined band commander is then given an opportunity to express his or her opinions to the directors, and decisions are made. Later that day or the next, a meeting is held on the Joe T. Haney Drill Field with as many of the band members as are available. Each drum major then announces his or her successor and presents that person with a new baton.[14] "It's an exciting time for the cadets," Colonel Brewer says. "Some, of course, are disappointed, but they can move on to other opportunities, like the bugle rank or unit leadership positions." The reason for the change in the selection process—and for most changes in the Aggie Band and Texas A&M University—has to do with the increased size and complexity of Texas A&M's academic programs, a Corps of Cadets–wide emphasis on grades, and the increased size of the Aggie Band, which now numbers more than 420 musicians. The number of band members provides new challenges in both scheduling and performing.[15]

Band members from previous decades may remember a different selection process, in which the band hall was locked, with only the selection committee—which was much larger and included representatives of each class—inside. No one entered or left until the selection process was completed. The band director served as mediator in the open discussion that took place. All members of the committee, regardless of class, were encouraged to speak freely and all votes counted the same. When the selection was made, one of the fish on the committee was then dispatched to the band dormitories, no matter what the hour, to inform the other fish that the selection had been made. The fish class blew whistles as the signal for all band members to return to the band hall. Only band members were admitted. When all had returned to the band hall, the announcement was made. It, too, was a very emotional time for every member of the band as the new drum majors thanked the other candidates for their participation in the process and the retiring drum majors passed to their successors the treasures that each drum major had passed to the next drum major for untold years. Long ago the new head drum major received an old pair of red socks that legend holds were "acquired" from a Southern Methodist University drum major even though he did not wish to part with them. Rumor had it that the socks could not be washed because they had never been washed before, and they had to be worn under the drum major's boots at the SMU game. The Field Artillery Band drum major allegedly received a special set of spurs, and the Infantry Band drum major was given a special belt buckle. An old tradition was that the Infantry Band drum major was the ugliest person in the band. At the end of their year as drum majors, each kept the baton used during the year. Colonel Brewer does not know whether there is still a pass-down tradition among the drum majors, "although I have not heard about these particular pass-downs in many years."

Next to the drum majors, the most important position for precision marching is that of bugle rank member. The twelve senior bugle rank members are chosen for their leadership and marching ability by a committee made up of those who will be juniors and seniors the following year. Traditionally, bugle rank members keep their bugle banners after their year of service.

A relatively new tradition preserves the look and some of the maneuvers of the Aggie Band for all to see. Visitors to the Sam Houston Sanders Corps of Cadets Center on the university campus can view a miniaturized band on a made-to-scale football field in a display case. The figures in the case were constructed by the late Bob Lang of the

Class of 1949. Lang started manufacturing the figures in 1985 and perfected his technique over the next several years. The figures on display were made in 1992 from a combination of metals and painted to accurately reflect the band's current uniforms. Through the course of the year, the figures are moved into different maneuvers on the miniature football field, including countermarches and crisscrosses. Instrumentation is exactly the same as it is in the actual band, and additional figures with various instruments were made so the display can be changed if the band's instrumentation changes. In addition to modeling the current band, Lang has also created replicas of the band from earlier eras.[16]

One of the most emotional traditions at Texas A&M is the monthly Silver Taps ceremony, and certain members of the Aggie Band play an important part in that solemn ritual. When an Aggie dies while still enrolled in school, students gather in front of the domed Academic Building in the center of the campus at 10:30 p.m., the campus lights are dimmed, and three rifle volleys are fired in salute. Then from the dome—spreading across the campus through the night air—comes the sound of "Silver Taps," a harmonized version of "Taps" played by the band's Silver Taps team. Silver Taps team members are known only to themselves and are selected each year by the previous group's members.[17]

Being in the Fightin' Texas Aggie Band is a special privilege that no band member ever forgets. Your life is never the same after you have been a member of the finest military marching band in the nation. The friends you make in the Aggie Band are your friends forever, and that is true not only for your classmates but for all who served in the band with you; as band members get older, it becomes true for anyone who ever served. That is why the Texas Aggie Band Association was founded—because of the members' love for one another, for the Fightin' Texas Aggie Band, and for their shared experience that has remained virtually unchanged for generations. Most of today's living former band members lived in the same dormitories, ate in the same dining hall, marched on the same practice field, and learned about dedication as they all stepped off on Hullabaloo. And that is why former band members return for reunions, to celebrate the band's history and to welcome the new fish to their fellowship, and why those former members form a Reunion Band, coming from all over the world to participate.

The experience of being in the Aggie Band has served its members well. There is no school of music at Texas A&M; band members major in everything from aerospace engineering to zoology. Aggie Band members have therefore become leaders in many professions and can be found as bank presidents, doctors, lawyers, dentists, psychologists, architects, engineers, teachers, professors, university administrators, ministers, merchants, farmers, ranchers, pilots, Peace Corps workers, judges, mayors, Cabinet members, military officers, all kinds of business leaders, and many more occupations, including, of course, band directors.

Edwin H. Cooper '53, a former band member who later became dean of admissions at Texas A&M, once said: "In 1953 I packed my trombone away for the last time as an Aggie Band member. The slide was worn thin from the sand and grit of the practice field, parade grounds, football fields, and streets of Dallas, Fort Worth, Houston, and Norman, Oklahoma. I thought I had contributed something to the band and to Texas A&M. But now I find the reverse has been true. The band has contributed to me. With each passing year I grow more aware of the fact that membership in the Aggie Band is not service—it is an investment in your own future, an investment which grows magnificently with time."[18]

For 125 years members of the Fightin' Texas Aggie Band—with dignity, self-discipline, and enduring pride—have stepped off for "The Colonel" with a special marching magic that turns the heads and stirs the hearts of all who watch. In doing so they bring honor to their school, to themselves, and to all of those they touch.

While Toler was director the band celebrated its centennial in 1994 with a series of special events held around Texas and on campus. There was special music composed, concerts performed statewide, and a fund-raising effort called the Eternal Aggie Band that focused on raising $1 million to ensure that the band would be able to "march on forever." In addition, a weekend-long Centennial Reunion brought hundreds of former band members back to campus and resulted in a halftime performance on September 24, 1994, that featured both that year's Aggie Band and a Reunion Band, together numbering more than eight hundred musicians, including the band's oldest living member at that time.[19]

Near the end of the Aggie Band's drill—but before the formation of the block "T"—the Reunion Band marched onto the field to form the largest Fightin' Texas Aggie Band ever assembled on Kyle

An ambulance rushes to the center of Kyle Field to carry Jack Jernigan '56 to the hospital. Courtesy of Cushing Memorial Library & Archives, Texas A&M University.

Field. The two groups formed a giant block "T," did one countermarch, and stopped for the presentation of a $1 million check to the university to establish the Eternal Aggie Band Endowment by Texas Aggie Band Association president Donald B. Powell '56. As the bands halted the formation and Powell crossed to the fifty-yard line for the presentation, Kyle Field went suddenly silent—someone had collapsed among the former musicians. The fans in the stands realized what had happened before those on the field did. A trainer from the opposing team—Southern Mississippi—rushed to the fallen man, as did several doctors who were among the former band members. The emergency medical technicians who are always on hand on game days responded, as did the various physicians from both football teams. No one knew the identity of the fallen Aggie, just that he hadn't gotten up and things didn't look good. Soon a name was passed among the onlookers. The victim was apparently Jack Jernigan of the Class of 1956. The musicians quietly left the field as the fans and football players, who now lined the sidelines, watched helplessly. Powell said after the event that "there were probably more prayers uttered at Kyle Field that day that weren't about football than ever before."[20]

Jack Jernigan died twice that day on Kyle Field—his heart stopped beating and he was revived, but he left Kyle Field alive in an ambulance and was rushed to St. Joseph's Hospital in Bryan (now CHI St. Joseph). By the time Jernigan's family arrived at the hospital, Aggies had already assembled there to offer their support. Some had been at the game, and some had heard about what had happened on the radio. That support was offered steadily throughout Jernigan's stay at the hospital. Margaret Rudder, the widow of former Texas A&M president James Earl Rudder '32, offered

Jack's wife, Marilyn, a place to stay at her home near the hospital. A local car dealer provided a vehicle for the family's use. Countless Aggies brought blankets and pillows for the cardiac care waiting room, along with food and snacks, greeting cards, get-well gifts, and emotional support for the family. Thanks to the exceptional care offered at St. Joseph's—and especially to Dr. J. James Rohack—Jernigan recovered and was eventually able to hold a press conference at the hospital at which he profoundly thanked all the new members of his "extended Aggie Family" for their prayers and support throughout his ordeal.[21] Jernigan, who eventually moved to College Station, died in January 2015 of heart failure caused by complications of pneumonia. The eighty-year-old had lived twenty years after his death on Kyle Field.[22]

Toler continued as the band's director until the end of the 2001 football season. He worked tirelessly to improve the musicianship of the group, which was getting larger every year. Eventually he, too, like the directors before him, sought a less regimented lifestyle. After twelve years as director of the Aggie Band and a growing instrumental music program, he and his wife, Catherine, decided to retire to a lakeside home on Lake Livingston and enjoy increased time with their children and grandchildren. He continued his longtime avocation as a music adjudicator at various state and national competitions and occasionally attended an Aggie football game at Kyle Field as a guest of the band. Catherine died of cancer in 2003, and Colonel Toler eventually remarried a friend he and Catherine had known in college at TCU. Like the directors before him, Colonel Toler had put his selected successor in place years before, when he hired Timothy Rhea as an assistant director of the band in 1993.

Colonel Toler's first rehearsal as Aggie Band director came during Freshman Orientation Week in 1989, when he directed the new fish band. Photo by Texas A&M University Photographic Services.

Directors have traditionally watched the band practice from the northeast corner room on the fourth floor of Dorm 11, as Toler does here in 1989. Photo by Texas A&M University Photographic Services.

Like the directors before him, Colonel Toler is a dedicated football fan who was quick to show his approval for a good play during the 1989 football season. Courtesy Texas Aggie Band.

Led by the drum majors and bugle rank, the new fish perfect their marching skills during Freshman Orientation Week in 1989. Photo by Texas A&M University Photographic Services.

The 1989–90 bugle rank stands at attention prior to the start of a drill on Kyle Field. 1990 *Aggieland* yearbook, courtesy of Cushing Memorial Library & Archives, Texas A&M University.

Sometimes a few push-ups are helpful in perfecting a drill. These Class of 1993 fish learn perfection under the supervision of two sophomore drummers during a practice session in the fall of 1989. 1989 *Aggieland* yearbook, courtesy of Cushing Memorial Library & Archives, Texas A&M University.

Aggie Band bass drummers Rod Hadder '91, *left*, and David Wallace '91 keep time during a 1989 Midnight Yell Practice. 1990 *Aggieland* yearbook, courtesy of Cushing Memorial Library & Archives, Texas A&M University.

Piccolo player Teresa Jones '91 concentrates on her music during a 1989 football game. 1990 *Aggieland* yearbook, courtesy of Cushing Memorial Library & Archives, Texas A&M University.

Trey Gamble '83 of the Texas Aggie Band Association presents a new bugle to bugle rank member Rod Hadder '91 during a pregame ceremony in 1990. The Band Association, a group made up of former members and friends of the band, donated the twelve new bugles to the band. Photo by Texas A&M Photographic Services.

Members of the Texas Aggie Band Association's Reunion Band "hump it" to give the Fightin' Texas Aggie Band yell prior to taking their seats before the Southwestern Louisiana game in 1990. The Aggies won the game, 63–14. Photo by Texas A&M University Photographic Services.

Drum Majors (*from left*) Christopher Alexander '91, Russell Griffin '91, and Richard Wariner '91 pose in front of the scoreboard at the Sea World Holiday Bowl in San Diego on December 29, 1990. The Aggie football team defeated Brigham Young University 65–14, virtually shutting down BYU's Heisman Trophy winner Ty Detmer. Courtesy Robert C. Barker '71/Barker Photography.

Senior band buddies from the Class of '91 pose by a jet fighter during the band's trip to the 1990 Sea World Holiday Bowl in San Diego. Courtesy Robert C. Barker '71/Barker Photography.

In 1991 the tradition of the "fish band" was recreated when Colonel Toler replaced the Drum and Bugle Corps with an all-freshman unit to play for selected events. The difference in this and the original fish bands immediately after World War II was that the group was under the field direction of the Aggie Band drum majors as opposed to a freshman drum major. 1992 *Aggieland* yearbook, courtesy of Cushing Memorial Library & Archives, Texas A&M University.

The 1991–92 Fightin' Texas Aggie Band forms Texas A&M's ATM logo on Kyle Field in 1991. Courtesy Robert C. Barker '71/Barker Photography.

Tom Pradel '94, 1991–92 corps bugler, blows "Taps" to signal the end of another day on the Quad. A sophomore member of the Aggie Band is appointed as the Corps bugler each year to provide bugle calls for the cadets. 1992 *Aggieland* yearbook, courtesy of Cushing Memorial Library & Archives, Texas A&M University.

The Aggie Band's 1992 "invasion" of Columbia, Missouri, was covered by a central Missouri television news team as the band marched from their two chartered airliners to the awaiting buses. The band was in Missouri for the game with the University of Missouri. The Aggies won the game, 26–13. Photo by Robert C. Barker '71/Barker Photography.

Band members struggle with members of Company C-2 of the Corps of Cadets during the annual Flight of the Great Pumpkin. During the Halloween ritual, the band freshmen must guard their dorm as Company C-2 attempts to help one of its members dressed in a large carved pumpkin head to run through the dorm. 1990 *Aggieland* yearbook, courtesy of Cushing Memorial Library & Archives, Texas A&M University.

The Aggie Band also supports its school's basketball team. At one time, the whole band attended each and every home game, but when the group grew to more than 300 the Maroon and White bands began to alternate games. Currently, a specially selected basketball band of 50 pieces plays for basketball games. Photo by Glen Johnson/Johnson Photography.

The 1992 bass horn section shows off the band's newly purchased instruments in front of the Clayton W. Williams Jr. Alumni Center, home of the Association of Former Students. Courtesy Texas Aggie Band.

The Aggie Band spent January 1, 1992, at the Mobil Cotton Bowl in Dallas. Courtesy Robert C. Barker '71/ Barker Photography.

Associate Band Director Major Jay O. Brewer '81 observes baritone horn players Robyn Lunsford '94, *left*, and Craig Bryant '93 during a sectional rehearsal in 1992. Courtesy Texas Aggie Band.

Texas Aggie Band Association staff members Pamela Netzinger Burleigh '92, *left*, and Jean S. Stanley review registration for a TABA reunion. Photo by Texas A&M Photographic Services.

The 1992 Texas Aggie Band Association Reunion Band, led by (*from left*) Drum Majors Richard Alexander '65, Chris Alexander '91, and Scott Yerigan '85, marches into Kyle Field on September 12, 1992, prior to the Tulsa game. Courtesy Robert C. Barker '71/Barker Photography.

Ed Perry '43, Ben Schleider '43, and Joe Gordon '43, the three drum majors featured in the 1942 Hollywood movie *We've Never Been Licked*, returned to campus for their fiftieth class reunion in 1993. Photo by Robert C. Barker '71/Barker Photography.

6

The Expanding Music Program
Dr. Timothy B. Rhea, 2002

I knew that I wanted to be a musician from an early age—probably elementary school. The path never changed for me.

—TIMOTHY RHEA

In anticipation of the celebration of the Aggie Band's centennial in 1994, then director Colonel Ray Toler began to seek composers to create special music to mark the occasion. Three marches were ultimately commissioned: one composed by the band's past director, Joe Tom Haney's "Maroon Tattoo"; one written by TCU music professor Curtis Wilson called "March Reveille"; and one, "A&M Centennial Celebration," penned by a young band director and composer named Timothy Rhea. That was the beginning of Rhea's association with the Aggie Band, which is now entering its twenty-fifth year.

Rhea had known about the Aggie Band since high school in De Kalb, Texas. "I grew up in a high school band that marched 6 to 5 precision military style, so the Aggie Band was often referenced by my high school band director. But I did not see the Aggie Band perform until my senior year of high school, when I attended a college recruiting trip at the University of Arkansas in Fayetteville. The football game ranks as one of the coldest experiences of my life. I left as soon as the two bands had performed at halftime."[1]

Despite that experience, Rhea attended college at the University of Arkansas, majoring in music education. He says those four years are the only ones he's ever spent outside Texas, but he does acknowledge that the University of Arkansas totally funded his undergraduate education through band, music, and academic scholarships that enabled him to have three years of private study with director of bands Eldon Janzen, "which provided my foundation in how to teach and rehearse musical groups." He says he chose Arkansas for a simple reason. "To pursue the career path I wanted, collegiate degrees in music were required. As it was not possible to obtain a music degree at Texas A&M it was never a consideration." Following his 1989 graduation, he returned to Texas to pursue a master's degree in instrumental conducting at Texas Tech University in Lubbock. He calls his time at Tech "two great years—I was a graduate assistant who really

Dr. Timothy Rhea, director of the Fightin' Texas Aggie Band since 2002. Courtesy Texas A&M University Department of Music Activities.

served as an assistant director, did most of the arrangements for the marching band, and conducted two complete concerts with the university's top symphonic band." Rhea says the late James Sudduth, then director of bands, "gave me musical opportunities that I had never experienced. I miss him very much."

Following receipt of his master's degree, Rhea accepted a position in the music program at the La Porte School District near Houston. Through participation in the Texas Music Educators Association, Rhea had met Colonel Toler while working on his master's degree at Texas Tech. At that time he was also doing many marching band arrangements for groups all over Texas. During his year in La Porte, Colonel Toler commissioned Rhea to write a march to celebrate the centennial of the Aggie Band. At the next Texas Music Educators gathering, the two met face to face, and Toler encouraged Rhea to come to the Texas A&M campus for a visit and to discuss an open position as an assistant director of the Aggie

Band. "Teaching at the college level had always been my major career goal," Rhea recalls. "To be offered the position at A&M when I had been teaching for less than a year—at the age of 24—seemed almost impossible. I had never expected it to happen so fast. The decision was not a difficult one for me." Rhea joined the Aggie Band staff in 1993, just in time to celebrate the centennial, with the march he composed as one of the commissioned works performed that year.

Working alongside Colonel Toler and then Lieutenant Colonel Brewer, Rhea learned the Aggie Band from the ground up. Knowing of his new hire's skill as a conductor, Toler shifted major responsibilities for the Texas A&M Symphonic Band his way. Rhea became director of that group, which was later renamed the Texas A&M Wind Symphony, in 1995. He has conducted the Wind Symphony at conventions of the Texas Music Educators Association, College Band Directors National Association, and American Bandmasters Association. On several occasions he toured with the symphony throughout Texas, including performances at the Meyerson Symphony Center in Dallas and the Wortham Center in Houston, as well as in San Antonio and Austin. He began conducting the Wind Symphony in Europe in 1999, subsequently returning in 2001, 2004, and 2007. Under his direction the group has performed concerts in England, Ireland, Austria, Germany, and the Czech Republic.[2]

Building on the legacy established by his predecessors, Rhea has worked hard to develop what is now referred to as the Bands Program at Texas A&M. In addition to serving as director of the Aggie Band, he also holds the title of director of bands and is the administrative head of the instrumental music department and contributing composer and arranger for all Texas A&M Band Department ensembles, which includes "the nationally famous Fightin' Texas Aggie Band," four concert bands (the Wind Symphony, Symphonic Winds, Symphonic Band, and Concert Band), two jazz bands, the Aggieland Dance Orchestra, and two university orchestras (the Philharmonic Orchestra and the Chamber Orchestra). The

At Hallsville High School en route to the Louisiana Tech game, Rhea observes a marching practice from ground level. Courtesy Texas A&M Corps of Cadets.

combined instrumental program serves around one thousand students each semester, making it one of the largest such programs in the country. "Our groups participate in a wide variety of performances which include athletic events, formal concerts, informal concerts, parades, gatherings and ceremonies," Rhea explains. "Our performance venues span 100,000 seat stadiums, famous concert halls, national and state music conventions, European cathedrals, small recital spaces, presidential inaugural parades, and many others. Our students come from every department and major at Texas A&M and have found that there is time to be a part of the various ensembles while maintaining their busy academic schedules at A&M." Rhea adds that membership in each of the groups requires prior experience and an audition, which can be arranged by contacting the Band Department.[3]

In addition to his responsibilities on campus, Rhea also earned his doctorate in instrumental conducting with a minor in composition from the University of Houston. He worked full time with the A&M bands while pursuing his doctorate full time. "I was young and not married at the time," he recalls. "It was pretty much all I did for three years—work, and go to school, and drive back and forth between College Station and Houston." He adds that even now, "my biggest issue has always been one of time. Because my job here includes many responsibilities in addition to the Aggie Band, and because I maintain a very active professional profile as a conductor and music educator, my schedule is very demanding —and time-consuming." In his role as a professional music educator, Dr. Rhea is justifiably proud of his service first as president-elect and then as president of the American Bandmasters Association, which he considers the most prestigious organization in his profession. According to its website, the ABA was founded in 1929, with John Philip Sousa as its honorary life president. The organization recognizes "outstanding achievement on the part of Concert Band conductors and composers. The current membership (by invitation only) comprises approximately 300 band conductors and composers in the US and Canada and 80 Associate Members (music businesses and corporations that provide significant services to bands and the publication of band music)."[4]

Although an acknowledged composer and arranger of band music, Rhea stresses that he owes his invitation to become part of the association largely to the young men and women of the bands under his direction. He says it was the ever-improving performance level of the Wind Symphony that brought him to the attention of the group and eventually gave him the opportunity to serve as its president. "This invitation-only organization is based on the quality of your performances and what you have accomplished on a national level during your career," he explains. "I was one of the youngest persons elected to mem-

bership and am one of the youngest to serve as president. This type of recognition from those most accomplished in your profession helps to reaffirm that you are, hopefully, doing the correct things in your career." During his early years in the organization, College Station hosted the convention of the ABA, and the Fightin' Texas Aggie Band was the first-ever marching band to perform at an ABA convention. "I believe that experience, along with the performances that were given that week by the Wind Symphony and the Aggie Band, had a great deal to do with my ascending to the presidency of the ABA," Rhea states. He is quick to add, however, that his greatest accomplishment "is the success of my students and the relationships that I have enjoyed with many of them after they leave the university. I hear from at least one of them practically every day."

Although the achievements of the "other" bands are a source of pride for Rhea, he is quick to acknowledge that the Aggie Band is still the centerpiece of the university's music program. "As with

Taking the field in Baton Rouge for the 2013 LSU game. Courtesy Texas A&M Corps of Cadets.

any university, the marching band—in our case, the Aggie Band—is always the most visible group that you have. They have a built-in audience every week during the fall, and function as a major face of the university. In my opinion, they are one of the most positive public relations tools available to Texas A&M. The Aggie Band is unique in that we are the only major university marching band in the nation that has retained the 6 to 5 military precision style of marching, along with the performance of traditional march music. When combined with those factors of influence through the Corps of Cadets, it makes for a unique and appreciated organization. The success of the Aggie Band has certainly played a role in allowing for the growth and expansion of instrumental offerings throughout the years. In order for everything to continue to move forward, it is most important that the Aggie Band retain the traditions it has held for the past 125 years."

The current director is quick to acknowledge that maintaining the Aggie Band—or any of the other groups within the Band Department—is a group effort that begins with him and the student musicians but would be impossible without his staff, which includes Colonel Jay Brewer, senior associate director of the Aggie Band; First Lieutenant Russell Tipton, associate director of bands; Travis Almany, director of orchestras and associate director of bands; Chris Hollar, director of jazz ensembles and the Hullabaloo Band; and Susan Haven, administrative assistant and business contact. "To be successful, you must surround yourself with others that are great at what they do, provide them with your expectations, then let them do their thing," Rhea says, citing his management philosophy. "I am blessed to work with colleagues who are some of the most outstanding people and musicians around. They are completely dedicated to Texas A&M University and the musical and personal success of our students. Rhea's wife, Jennifer, says the group is much more like a family than a staff, and that pleases her husband, who is quick to praise her as well. "Jennifer came into my world and Texas A&M after I had already been here for

several years," he says. "She quickly embraced everything—especially since she is a major college sports fan—and continues to love it. There is no one more supportive of what I do. Much like my parents, Nina and Boyce Rhea, she has probably attended more marching performances and concert events than most people do during a lifetime." He also credits Jennifer, who is a public school administrator in College Station but not a musician, with "picking up everything very quickly." He says his parents have also probably witnessed more marching and concerts than most parents ever will. "But they provided both me and my brother a wonderful life while growing up that included all the skills we needed to be successful in life. They have always been supportive of me in all my endeavors," he adds. Of all his related endeavors, he says he now considers himself primarily a conductor, a position that both he and Leonard Bernstein confirm is also a teacher. "Over the years I have been a composer, an arranger, a director, a conductor, a teacher, and an administrator, but I now consider myself primarily a conductor. I have continued to learn from others throughout my career. I still do some arranging and composing, which I really enjoy, but on a much more limited basis than several years ago, and I truly love conducting and the teaching that goes with it."

Rhea said he would be remiss if he didn't give special mention to one individual and one organization that have played and continue to have important roles within the Aggie Band. Colonel Jay Brewer of the Class of 1981 has been part of the band since he signed on as a fish in the fall of 1977. He is its longest continuous employee, having known Colonel Adams and worked with Colonel Haney, Colonel Toler, and Dr. Rhea. Both Toler and Rhea acknowledge the role Brewer played in helping them get acquainted with the nuances of working with the Aggie Band, including passing on his knowledge of the traditions that have been an important part of the band's history. Colonel Adams gave him his parents' sheet music to help him musically while he was still in junior high school and later passed on a hat that is one of Brewer's prized possessions. Colonel Haney hired him as a student worker and ultimately offered him an assistant director position, enabling him to join the staff full time following graduation. He knew the band from the inside out and willingly shared his knowledge with the newcomers who came to the band as either students or staff. The last chapter of this book shares some of his thoughts on his years with the Aggie Band and what those years have meant to him. Brewer has also been an almost continuous liaison with what both he and Rhea call an organization that is "vital" to the Aggie Band, the Texas Aggie Band Association (TABA), the official alumni and support organization of the band.

"There is no group that is more supportive of the Aggie Band than the TABA," Rhea states emphatically. "For me, it has been a pleasure to get to know those who marched with the band before my time here. They are always a great sounding board for advice and support. It's great for me to watch students that played in the band during my tenure become involved in this organization. The TABA does a great deal to honor our current band members with recognition dinners and gatherings and provides the funding for items that band members wish to keep after their time marching, like drum major batons and bugle banners. Their major contribution, however, is to provide funds for academic tutoring that enables cadets to maintain the grade point averages necessary to participate in and hold leadership roles in the band."

Although band traditions and rituals have changed over the past 125 years, the experience has remained essentially the same—the thrill of marching for the first time on Kyle Field; the pride of performing a difficult drill perfectly; completing your fish year; the emotion of representing yourself, your state, and your school in a presidential inaugural parade; and the delight in "getting back" at a bothersome upperclass cadet are all experiences former Aggie Band members have shared. The willingness of TABA members to share those experiences is important, especially to cadets who are having those same experiences today.

While tending to the musical, academic, and emotional needs of music students is an important part of the work of the band's staff members, lately Rhea has been very involved in his administrative work as head of music activities at Texas A&M. He has been focused on planning for and anticipating the fall 2019 opening of the new John D. White '70–Robert L. Walker '58 Music Activities Center on the corner of George Bush Drive and Coke Street on the main campus. The new building will bring together all the university's musical activities—instrumental and choral—for the first time in Texas A&M's history. It will include four large rehearsal halls with state-of-the-art acoustics, a hundred-yard artificial turf practice field for the Aggie Band that will eliminate uneven or unsafe rehearsal conditions, soundproof practice rooms with extended student access, libraries for both instrumental and choral music, and ample locker space for instrument storage. The 70,000-square-foot center will also provide opportunities to tell students, former students, and visitors about the proud traditions of musical organizations at Texas A&M. The new facility will house the Aggie Band, Wind Symphony, Symphonic Winds, Symphonic Band, Concert Band, two jazz ensembles, Aggieland Orchestra, Singing Cadets, Century Singers, Women's Chorus, Chamber Orchestra, Philharmonic Orchestra, and other student music ensembles. Texas A&M committed to providing half of the $40 million necessary to construct the Music Activities Center. A $10 million naming gift from the Corpus Christi–based Ed Rachal Foundation established the name for the new facility in honor of John D. White '70 and Dr. Robert L. Walker '58. Other leadership gifts for the new building came from Anne and David Dunlap '83, Elizabeth and Paul "Haskell" Motheral '52, and Patricia and Weldon Kruger '53. White and Walker are both former members of the Rachal Foundation board who were instrumental in establishing the board's relationship with Texas A&M. The Board of Regents of The Texas A&M University System approved the naming of the building in April 2016.[5] White, a former member of the TAMUS Board of Regents, is a Houston attorney whose practice is focused on commercial litigation, particularly in the energy sector. He has been active in a variety of Texas A&M alumni groups from the Association of Former Students to the Corps Development Council, as well as the American, Texas, and Houston Bar Associations, and was a director of the Greater Houston Partnership, the Texas Lyceum association, and the Houston Livestock Show and Rodeo International Committee.[6] Dr. Walker retired from Texas A&M in 2014 after serving nine different A&M presidents in a variety of fund-raising positions, including vice president for development and senior executive for development in the Office of the President. During his decades-long career, he was a well-known face on campus, being seen most often in the company of potential donors to the university. He is credited for attracting millions of dollars in gifts to his alma mater.[7]

The Music Activities Center will provide a new focus for music at Texas A&M, but it won't change the challenges members of the Fightin' Texas Aggie Band face, Rhea says. "Being in the Aggie Band is a challenge—mentally and from a time standpoint. As our society continues to turn toward instant gratification and immediate satisfaction, it is so easy for students to quit things these days. Unfortunately, the pendulum seems to be swinging from group success to individual

The John D. White '70–Robert L. Walker '58 Music Activities Center broke ground on September 8, 2017. Shown here under construction in Spring 2019, it accommodates more than 1,300 band, orchestra, and choral musicians at Texas A&M.

success. Students these days seem to want to be involved in everything, but they face major issues regarding their time management. They stress out quickly." Many members of the Texas Aggie Band Association say after the fact that the most important thing they learned in the Aggie Band was time management. They learned to begin a project and stick with it until it was completed successfully. For the past and current members of the Aggie Band, it's a different project—a different and more complex drill—each week during football season.

Rhea believes it is "very important" that the Aggie Band always remains a "6 to 5" precision military marching band, taking six steps for every five yards, utilizing appropriate music, and functioning as a major unit within the university's Corps of Cadets. "Any change from that would alter the band in a major way," and its legacy would be gone. "It also must always embrace the highest standards, both musically and when marching."

So he continues to work toward that end as director of the Aggie Band. He also spends considerable time educating others regarding "the why, what, and how as related to music education and the Aggie Bands program. Because there is no formal school of music here, making people aware of what we do and how we do it continues to be a vital part of my job." In addition to that task, he believes his major contributions to the Aggie Band in his twenty-five years with the program are threefold—"first, enhanced expectation of quality music performance, with consistent levels of playing and marching; second, contributions of numerous arrangements and compositions that we perform; and third, expansion of drill ideas, including individual assignments for each musician and drills charted exactly to the musical phrases." His contributions to the Music Activities Department are also threefold—first, the establishment of the department and the expansion of musical offerings for all Texas A&M students; second, the construction of the Music Activities Center; and third, "continuing to elevate our performance expectations for all groups, a large part of which has been through the hiring and retention of outstanding directors for our staff."

For Timothy Rhea, the challenges will be identical in the years ahead—maintaining the legacy of the Fightin' Texas Aggie Band and increasing the visibility and musicality of the other elements of the Music Activities Department for which is he responsible.

The band marching in the Battle of Flowers Parade in San Antonio, April 2014. Courtesy Texas A&M Corps of Cadets.

A morning practice on Haney Drill Field in 1995. Courtesy of Cushing Memorial Library & Archives, Texas A&M University.

The Fightin' Texas Aggie Band performed at the Astrodome during the band's Centennial year. 1990 *Aggieland* yearbook, courtesy of Cushing Memorial Library & Archives, Texas A&M University.

Drum Major John Fugitt '98 waits with the band before halftime of the Iowa State game. Courtesy Texas A&M Yearbook Collection, Cushing Memorial Library and Archives.

The trumpet section stands at attention before a halftime in 1997. Courtesy Texas A&M Yearbook Collection, Cushing Memorial Library and Archives.

Drummer Bryan Weidenbach '98 and his section mates race off the field after another successful halftime show. Courtesy of Cushing Memorial Library & Archives, Texas A&M University.

The bugle rank is ready to march onto the field in South Bend, Indiana, for the 2000 season opener against Notre Dame. Courtesy of Cushing Memorial Library & Archives, Texas A&M University.

There was snow on the field and in the stands at the Independence Bowl Game in Shreveport, Louisiana on December 31, 2000. Nevertheless, Drum Major Jesse Clayborn '01 gives the order to take the field for halftime. Courtesy of Cushing Memorial Library & Archives, Texas A&M University.

In lines as straight as arrows, the Fightin' Texas Aggie Band marches in a parade in 1996. Courtesy of Cushing Memorial Library & Archives, Texas A&M University.

Drum Major Urbane Martinez '16, who went on to be commissioned as an officer in the U.S. Marine Corps, exemplifies the spit and polish that have made the band famous. Courtesy of Texas A&M Corps of Cadets.

Honoring Colonel Toler's impending retirement as the 1986 band had done for Colonel Haney, the band spells out their director's name during a 2001 drill. 2002 *Aggieland* yearbook, courtesy of Cushing Memorial Library & Archives, Texas A&M University.

Commemorating his 25 years of service to Texas A&M University in 2018, Dr. Rhea leads the Texas A&M Wind Symphony in its Anniversary Concert. Courtesy Texas A&M University Department of Music Activities.

A view of the precise turns necessary to execute the close-order drills that have made the Fightin' Texas Aggie Band famous. 1997 *Aggieland* yearbook, courtesy of Cushing Memorial Library & Archives, Texas A&M University.

Sitting in the east stands of Kyle Field, band members typically get plenty of sun on game days. 1998 *Aggieland* yearbook, courtesy of Cushing Memorial Library & Archives, Texas A&M University.

The Fightin' Texas Aggie Band marched in the Governor's Inaugural Parade in Austin in 2015. Courtesy Texas A&M Corps of Cadets.

7

"On the Road Again . . ."

The life I love is making music with my friends,
and I can't wait to get on the road again.

—Willie Nelson

Two things make the Fightin' Texas Aggie Band unique among college bands. The first is the amount of time it has spent on the road; the second is the amount of time it has spent on the air. The Aggie Band has probably been on the road more than any other college marching band, and it is the only band to have a regularly scheduled television show that has aired on stations throughout Texas since 1995. During the 125 years of its existence, the Aggie Band has been available to far-off audiences through not only travel and television, but also a wide variety of recordings.[1]

Although the size of the organization and the cost of transporting more than four hundred people by train, bus, or plane has become cost prohibitive, the mileage and audience counts—assembled by unofficial Aggie Band statistics keeper Dr. Bruce Bockhorn '74—speak for themselves. According to Bockhorn's figures, the Aggie Band has joined the Texas A&M football team on the road for fifty football games since 1994, in addition to performing a new drill at every home football game in Kyle Field and marching in nineteen bowl games.[2] Unlike most college bands, the

Aggie Band performs a different drill at each performance. Although the same elements and formations—countermarches, block band formations, wedges, chevrons, divisions into sections, and variations on the crisscross—are often seen from drill to drill, they are combined in a different order each week and the complexity increases from drill to drill, meaning those marching are responsible for independent movement apart from those around them. The band is also moving almost continuously through most drills. The lone consistent factor in each drill is that each performance ends with some version of the block "T." And variations exist even within the "T," which is sometimes formed horizontally and other times vertically, with the stem of the letter extending down the length of the field or across the width. The letters "A" and "M" are sometimes added, and on rare occasions the group returns to a past tradition and spells something out on the field. The band has traveled more than fifty thousand miles since 1994, performing before audiences of more than 17.6 million fans in that same period. In recent years, many of those trips have been by bus

Drum Major Beau Voelkel '99 leads the band during the march-in for the 1998 Texas Tech game. Courtesy Texas A&M Yearbook Collection, Cushing Memorial Library and Archives.

(to locations like Lubbock, Stillwater, Fayetteville, Baton Rouge, and El Paso), although some were made in private vehicles (to closer venues like Waco, Austin, and Houston), and still others utilized chartered aircraft (to Denver, Los Angeles, San Diego, New York City, and Notre Dame in Indiana).

Although those figures reflect only recent trips, the Aggie Band has also traveled by special train at least twice. For the October 1930 football game against the University of Nebraska, the college's administration chartered a train to take Colonel Dunn and the band to Lincoln, where it paraded through the downtown and gave an "outstanding performance at the game." According to the 1931 yearbook, the group "gained considerable commendations from the Northern press and from the University of Nebraska." Another major train trip took place in 1955 when Colonel Adams was director. At that time, a chartered train took 250 bandsmen to California for the opening of that year's football season against the University of California at Los Angeles in the Los Angeles Coliseum. Travel for that many people was expensive even then. Raising the money for the trip turned out to be no problem. When former students learned of the need, they contributed $25,000 in a matter of days to make the trip possible. More on this trip, which included a chance for the band

to visit the brand-new Disneyland, is included in chapter 3.

In the Aggie Band's early years and through most of the twentieth century, the challenges of taking the band to football games were simpler. But as the Aggie football team joined new and more widespread conferences—and the size of the band grew—travel became more difficult and more expensive. The Southwest Conference, which A&M was part of for eighty-two years, was originally made up of schools in Texas that were fairly easy to reach for both bands and football fans.[3] The SWC school farthest from College Station was the University of Arkansas, which played most of its home games in Fayetteville but occasionally traveled to Little Rock. Both were bus trips, although lengthy ones. Texas Tech in Lubbock was also a considerable distance, but doable. Aggie teams became affiliated with the new Big 12 Conference (an expansion of the old Big 8) in 1994.[4] Although the new conference included longtime rivals Texas, Baylor, and Texas Tech, it added Oklahoma and Oklahoma State to the so-called South Division, with Kansas, Kansas State, Colorado, Nebraska, Missouri, and Iowa State as the North Division. Football teams played each team in their division every year, as well as two or three teams from the other division. Conference championship games were also played, mostly in states in the North Division. Thus the football world of the Texas Aggie Band expanded. During its first two years in the Big 12, both the band and the football team were committed to making sure the Aggie Band marched in every Big 12 stadium.[5] Visiting bands had not been the norm in the Big 8 as they had been in the SWC. Some locations claimed they couldn't make room for band members without decreasing the seats available to their own alumni and visiting fans, which were also limited. The distance to the Big 12 stadiums made plane travel necessary. Once the original visits had been made, the Aggie Band was forced to restrict its trips to Big 12 away games and eventually traveled as a smaller band that did not include its freshman members.

A similar situation occurred when Texas A&M left the Big 12 to join the Southeast Conference, an even more geographically diverse group of schools. New athletic opponents included the Universities of Alabama, Arkansas, Florida, Georgia, Kentucky, Mississippi, Missouri-Columbia, South Carolina, and Tennessee, as well as Auburn University, Louisiana State University, Mississippi State University, and Vanderbilt University.[6] As in the Big 12, visiting bands were not a tradition in the SEC, and the increasing cost of chartered planes, jet fuel, accommodations, and meals for the cadets, as well as the academic demands involved in pursuing a degree at Texas A&M and the need to miss classes while traveling, all contributed to the decision to further limit out-of-town trips. Band members still attend one or two away games each football season, often depending on the site and other factors, and always accompany the football team to bowl games.

In anticipation of the band's 1994 centennial celebration, two former band members—Donald B. Powell '56 and Robert C. Barker '71—embarked on a project to spread the story of the Aggie Band to a larger audience. Powell wrote, and Barker, who owned Barker Productions in Bryan before his retirement, produced a documentary-length video called *Recall! The Story of the Fightin' Texas Aggie Band*. Although it contained much of the historical information included in the 1994 edition of this book, the information was told from the viewpoint of a grandfather (played by former band member Gene W. Clark '43) telling his young grandson (played by Matthew Oberhelman '09) about the history of the Aggie Band. The video was shot in the Sam Houston Sanders Corps of Cadets Center on campus and included many of the photographs from this book, film clips from various old and newer band drills at a variety of locations, and the voice talent of many of those

The Fightin' Texas Aggie Band traveled to Jacksonville, Florida, for the Gator Bowl game against North Carolina State in December 2018. Courtesy Texas A&M Corps of Cadets.

listed in this book's acknowledgments. Several thousand copies were sold, Barker says.[7]

Collectively, Powell, Barker, and Bockhorn were also involved in another endeavor that makes the Aggie Band unique—*The Texas Aggie Band Show*. The Aggie Band is the only college band to have its own weekly television show that airs commercially and includes the band's complete halftime drill during the football season and other historically significant performances on programs not shown during the traditional marching season. Bockhorn has been the lone host of the show since 2004 and was cohost with Powell, the show's originator, in 2002 and 2003. Powell and Barker, who had been filming the band since the early 1980s for use by its directors and drum majors, had noticed that television networks broadcasting college football games gave little time to marching band performances because of their need to provide scores from around the National Collegiate Athletic Association and, yes, the advertisements that allowed the broadcasts to air. As owner of Barker Productions and the administrative secretary of the Texas Aggie Band Association, Barker also sold tapes of the drills performed during each specific football season's halftime performances for the TABA. As former Aggie bandsmen, both Barker and Powell knew the work that went into the drills and agreed that it was a shame that fans no longer saw the halftime performances. After campaigning for coverage with local and national broadcasters, Powell realized that perhaps one of the reasons TV didn't cover marching bands was that it simply didn't know how. Another problem was that by this time, many college bands didn't actually march. They were what Powell was fond of calling "Stand and Play Bands," meaning they took their place on the field and generally played a medley of show tunes and pop music, with a patriotic tune thrown in from time to time around major national holidays. Because the Aggie Band was different—marching for almost its entire halftime drills and rarely playing show tunes—Powell sought to help directors

and camera operators know that this band was different by sharing with them what was coming and enabling them to anticipate interesting video opportunities. He began to work with Colonel Toler to be able to "chart" the drills so television personnel knew what to expect when.

Barker soon joined the effort, which achieved limited success. Since Barker had long been the official photographer at Corps of Cadets march-ins and the videographer of record for the band's halftime performances, the two eventually went to a local television station, KYLE-TV, seeking airtime for the limited-edition program.[8] That marked the birth of the half-hour shows featuring the complete Aggie Band halftime, highlights of any visiting band, and studio-shot features about life in the Aggie Band and the Corps of Cadets. Less than a year after the show's premiere, when KYLE-TV faced ownership changes and a different programming focus, Barker and Powell found a new opportunity with KAMU-TV, Texas A&M's public television affiliate. In addition to airing the program several times each week, KAMU uploaded the show to a PBS satellite, which made it available to any other PBS station that wished to pick it up for use in its market. Members of the Texas Aggie Band Association and Aggie Band parents called PBS stations in their communities, asking them to air the show. By the late 1990s, the show was broadcast several times a week on KAMU and on PBS stations in other communities state-wide, including Dallas–Fort Worth, San Antonio, Lubbock, Longview, Tyler, and even Austin for a short time. The program did not, however, air in the Houston area. Rumor had it that the operator of the Houston PBS station—the University of Houston—wouldn't air the program because of a long-standing rivalry between A&M and UH, which Aggies had long referred to as "Cougar High." Both KUHT and KAMU are on the cable system in the Bryan–College Station area and often show the same programs at the same time, noted then director of educational broadcasting Dr. Rodney Zent '75, who added that KAMU serves the smallest PBS market in the state, while

KUHT is the oldest and largest market in the country. "Maybe they just didn't want to compete with us," Zent was known to joke.[9]

During its early years, Powell and his wife, Mary Jo, did all the research and prepared the scripts for the show, sharing the manuscripts with Barker so that he would know what shots were needed at the football games and what features would need to be filmed in advance in his studio. When each week's game was over, Barker would go back to his editing suite at Barker Productions and edit the show, turning it in at KAMU on campus only a few days after the filming of the featured halftime drill. Powell was always quick to point out that the credit belonged mostly to Barker. "I was just the face in front of the camera, but the band and Bob always did most of the work," he said shortly before turning the show over to Bockhorn.[10] Yet in 1995, the format of the show was altered dramatically when the Aggie Band flew on a chartered plane to Denver, Colorado, to march at a football game between the Aggies and the Colorado Buffaloes in Boulder. Barker, both Powells, and *Texas Aggie Band Show* cameras went on that trip and did that week's show entirely "on the road." The show never returned to the studio again, and since then its format has included segments filmed on various football fields; in the E. V. Adams Band Hall, the band dormitories, and the Corps of Cadets housing area known as the Quad; in classrooms and study areas; and around the community at special TABA events like the fish barbecue, the junior sweater-presentation dinner, and the senior banquet. Powell and Barker did a total of 77 shows together before bringing Bockhorn on board for an additional 12 shows in both 2002 and 2003. Barker filmed and produced a total of 210 shows before retiring in 2013 and selling the bulk of his equipment to RDM Pros of Bryan, which took over producing the show.[11]

Bockhorn continues to write and host the show and has been seen in 242 individual episodes as of the conclusion of the 2017–18 academic year. Shortly after Barker's retirement, Bockhorn negotiated a new agreement to air the program on KAGS-TV and KCEN-TV, two commercial stations owned by Tegna, Inc., a publicly traded broadcast, digital media, and marketing services company headquartered in McLean, Virginia. Under the new agreement, the show is syndicated to nine other Tegna-owned TV stations across the state, in communities including Abilene, Beaumont, College Station, Dallas, Houston, San Angelo, San Antonio, Tyler, and Waco. In addition, it is provided to www.TexAgs.com, which has an audience of almost five hundred thousand Aggie sports fans interested in all things Texas A&M. The show also continues to run on the Corps of Cadets Association (CCA) website, www.corpsofcadets.org. In the spring of 2015, the show took another leap forward by covering an entire academic year, fall to spring, from the point of view of the Texas Aggie Band and the Corps of Cadets. That continued in both 2016 and 2017. The commercially aired show is presented under the sponsorship of BJ's Restaurant and Brewhouse, whose CEO is former Aggie Band member Gerald W. "Jerry" Deitchle '73, and the Texas A&M Corps of Cadets Association. Additional underwriting opportunities are available through RDM Pros at either 979–260–1925 or www.rdmpros.com.[12] In the years since Bockhorn and his wife, Carobeth, assumed responsibility for the content of the program they have worked to see that individual band members get a lot more "face time." Cadets introduce each segment of the show, conduct interviews, and share both their responsibilities and opinions about the challenges of life in the Aggie Band.

In addition to the traveling and the television show, the Aggie Band—and indeed the Texas A&M Bands Program—has issued first recordings, then tapes, and now compact discs that are available across the nation and worldwide, increasing the number of appreciative listeners. The dates and titles of those recordings are listed in chapter 3.

The dedication and devotion shown by people like Powell, Bockhorn, and Barker is not unique to these three. They are among thousands of former Aggie Band members—doctors, dentists, lawyers, bankers, members of the military (including Brigadier General Joe E. Ramirez Jr. '79, the current commander of A&M's Corps of Cadets), college administrators, teachers, ministers, accountants, musicians, and virtually every profession imaginable—who have experienced the Aggie Band firsthand and want others to have that same experience.

A group of former band members have also received special recognition by the university and the Corps by being chosen for induction into the Texas A&M Corps of Cadets Association's Corps Hall of Honor. The Hall of Honor was established in 1993 to recognize those who contribute or have contributed to the Corps "in a matter that is above and beyond the call." Those inducted into the Hall of Honor have "lived a life that exemplifies the Texas Aggie Spirit. . . . By possessing the values upon which the Corps was founded: honor, loyalty, service, pride, patriotism, faith, leadership and honesty." The eleven former band members who have received this honor are General Otto P. Weyland '23, Colonel E. V. Adams '29, Lieutenant General Ormand R. Simpson '36, Joseph "Searcy" Bracewell Jr. '38, George Linskie '38, Colonel Willie Frank Bohlmann '50, Donald B. Powell '56, Arno W. Krebs Jr. '64, Ronald L. Skaggs '65, Rick J. W. Graham '66, and David D. Dunlap '83.

Like the Hall of Honor inductees, all former Aggie Band members share similar memories of working hard to achieve the same goal and learning to manage their time to ensure that happens for others. They were tough enough and good enough and proud enough to be called members of the Fightin' Texas Aggie Band.

Them basses! Each spring the band plays for the Corps of Cadets' pass in review at Parents' Weekend (now Family weekend), as in this photograph from 2011. Courtesy Texas A&M Corps of Cadets.

Lots of indoor musical preparation is required before the band takes their work onto the drill field, as shown in this photograph from 1996. Courtesy Texas A&M Yearbook Collection, Cushing Memorial Library and Archives.

In 2002, band member John Dunbar '04 served as bugler for the Corps of Cadets. Courtesy Texas A&M Yearbook Collection, Cushing Memorial Library and Archives.

The drummers play for the Fish Review in 1996. Courtesy Texas A&M Yearbook Collection, Cushing Memorial Library and Archives.

Band seniors lead the Elephant Walk in 2005. Courtesy Texas A&M Yearbook Collection, Cushing Memorial Library and Archives.

The Fightin' Texas Aggie Band performs during Parents' Weekend, 2006. 2006 *Aggieland* yearbook, courtesy of Cushing Memorial Library & Archives, Texas A&M University.

Drum major Andy Nelson '02 on the field during halftime of the Iowa State game. 2002 *Aggieland* yearbook, courtesy of Cushing Memorial Library & Archives, Texas A&M University.

The Fightin' Texas Aggie Band drummers appear on the Kyle Field video display board during the march-in for the game with Northwestern (Louisiana) State in 2018. Courtesy Texas A&M University Bands and Orchestras.

8

The Definitive Aggie Bandsman
Colonel Jay O. Brewer '81, 1977–

I'm not any different than anyone else who's ever marched in the Aggie Band.
—COLONEL JAY O. BREWER '81

Former members of the Fightin' Texas Aggie Band share many common qualities. They have been more than just Texas Aggies—they've been members of the band and the Corps of Cadets, each of which requires a commitment of time and dedication far beyond that of many other Aggies; they've been students in the traditional sense, attending classes and laboratories, taking exams, writing papers, giving oral reports, and participating in group projects; they've shared the pride of a job well done, whether marching on Kyle Field, representing their school in a parade, or doing well in the classroom; and they've watched the vast majority of students around them on the Texas A&M campus and elsewhere choose a different—and easier—path, free from the regimentation they endure as members of both the Corps and the band. And since 1977, they've also watched Jay Brewer—a stellar example of what being a devoted part of the Aggie Band is all about.

Brewer began his time in the Aggie band as a fish in 1977, where he was watched largely by the sophomores in the Class of 1980 in their traditional role in both the band and the Corps. They made him toe the line by standing inspections, cleaning his "hole" (the Corps term for one's dorm room), and teaching him that before you could lead, you first needed to know how to follow. He eventually became a student worker for Colonel Haney, who made it possible for him to remain with the band as a staff assistant following his graduation with a degree in mechanized agriculture. He has been part of the band staff ever since and has been the longest continuous employee in the band's history. He now serves as senior associate director of the Aggie Band and achieved the rank of colonel in the Texas State Guard, thus joining the tradition of a colonel being at—or near—the helm of the band. In his various roles he has come in contact with virtually every student who has played in the band since 1977, as well as countless university administrators, a large number of dignitaries, band personnel at other colleges and universities, high school musicians and band directors, potential Aggie Band members, and countless former

Colonel Jay O. Brewer '81, associate director of the Fightin' Texas Aggie Band since 1977. Courtesy Texas A&M University Department of Music Activities.

band members who want to share stories about their time in the band or the Texas A&M of days gone by.[1]

Pieces of Brewer's story appear throughout the earlier chapters of this book, reflecting his work with various band directors. In addition, he is the face, heart, and voice of the Aggie Band. He is a frequent speaker at A&M clubs, Texas A&M University Mothers' Clubs, Aggie Musters, and a variety of community organizations. Following the example set by one of his mentors, Dr. Donald B. Powell '56 (the coauthor of the 1994 version of this book), he accepts the first invitation he received to address an Aggie Muster—perhaps the most important Aggie ceremony in that it recognizes those Aggies who have passed on during the last year.[2] During this ceremony, another Aggie answers "here" when the deceased's name is called, indicating that even those Aggies

who have gone ahead of us are still with us and remembered. Although Brewer won't admit it, this author believes he arranged for the entire Aggie Band to answer "here" when her husband's name was called at the campus Aggie Muster in 2012, thus honoring his friend and mentor who had long been part of the Aggie Band.

Brewer is also the voice of the Aggie Band at Kyle Field and other locations. He is the one who delivers the now-famous words at the beginning of each halftime drill at Kyle Field—"And now, forming on the north end of Kyle Field, the nationally famous Fightin' Texas Aggie Band!" The last four words are drawn out for effect and the crowds say them with Brewer. He says he's never actually heard those words live—he delivers them from a soundproof booth in the press box—but his friends and family constantly tell him that the words have impact, and that it wouldn't be an Aggie halftime without them. While not everyone outside the band and the Corps of Cadets knows his face, there are literally millions of people who have heard his voice announcing the band's performances. Brewer says it almost doesn't matter where he is or what he's doing, strangers always ask whether he's "the nationally famous Fightin' Texas Aggie Band" once they hear his voice. He is proud to admit that he is and hopes he might continue to make those announcements after he's retired from being the senior associate director of the Aggie Band, something that may well happen in the next few years.[3]

For anyone who has ever met Brewer, there is no question that he is also the heart of the band. One can see it in his dealings with past, present, and future band members; in his attention to the traditions that have made the band what it is today; in how he talks with others about the Aggie Band; and in the way he holds himself when directing the band, whether or not he is wearing Colonel Adams's hat. There is no doubt that he carries the Aggie Band in his heart.

According to Brewer, anticipating the band's quasquicentennial (*Merriam-Webster*'s word describing a 125th anniversary) and the opening of the new John D. White '70–Robert L. Walker '58 Music Activities Center has given him time to reflect on what the Aggie Band has become, where it is now, and where it might be headed as it marches toward its sesquicentennial (or 150th) year. "We are in a time in our history where we have never been before," he notes, "where Aggies interested in music have the opportunity to perform in a wide variety of ways and venues. We've made things more like the 'real world' by creating other music organizations outside the Corps of Cadets," he adds, quickly acknowledging Joe Tom Haney for realizing that this need existed and working to establish the first symphonic band during his tenure as director.

He also credits Ray Toler and Tim Rhea for both further increasing the opportunities and vastly improving the musicality of all the groups and for their commitment to keeping the Aggie Band a military marching band. He's well acquainted with the words of Colonel Dunn, who said that in its early years, the Aggie Band "accepted anyone who knew which end of the instrument to blow in," but he notes that musicians must now audition for places in all musical activities, including both instrumental and vocal music groups. He says the biggest change he's observed in his time with the band has been "the evolution of the American college student. Today's students are different than those of the last century. They have grown up in a far different and more affluent world, with new technology impacting their lives almost every day. They have more choices now than ever before. They don't need to be in the Corps, they don't need to be in the band, they don't need to deal with the discipline and regimentation that exist in both those organizations. But young men and women continue to choose the Aggie Band because they want to or need to be involved in something that's way bigger than themselves."[4] Brewer is perhaps the definitive Aggie Band member in that he recognizes that fact and feels blessed both to have been in the band and to now be able to help the young men and women he works with become proud members

of the finest military marching band in the nation. "One of my claims to fame is that I'm really not any different than anyone else who has ever marched in the Aggie Band. I wasn't the band commander, I wasn't a drum major, I wasn't on the bugle rank. I just came along at the perfect time to be available for this job. I am eternally grateful to Joe Tom Haney for giving me the opportunity to remain a part of this band and to the subsequent directors who have encouraged me to remain in increasingly important positions within the organization. I lead a charmed life because of what I do for a living. The Aggie Band is absolutely about tradition and memories. The friends you make here are friends you'll have for the rest of your life. As many others have noted, they will be with you when you're married and when you're buried, and it's all because of the memories you've shared over time. The friendships endure. That becomes clearer to me each and every time I talk with a former band member and it's something I try to pass on to the new band members I see every day."

Like other band directors over time, Brewer acknowledges the support he receives from his wife, Judy. "She's also a teacher, so she understands," he says. The couple have two grown children, James and Natalie. "I've always been passionate about young people, and to have a chance to impact their lives each and every day is extremely fulfilling." Indeed, it is difficult to find a former Aggie Band member in the past four decades who can't recall some interaction with Brewer. Although some were not particularly pleasant at the time, they all were memorable. In addition to interacting with students, Brewer says he often becomes well acquainted with their parents. As instant communication has become a way of life, parents aren't hesitant to reach out to the adults who share responsibility with them for their offspring. Although most students who come to Texas A&M are already legal adults at eighteen, moms and dads still want to know what is happening with them and why. College students in the past used to have to rely on written letters,

The Fightin' Texas Aggie Band executes the famous "Block T" at halftime of the 2018 Clemson game. Courtesy Texas A&M University Department of Music Activities.

and it took a relatively long time for the letters to reach a student's hometown and for a reply to come back to College Station, but now text messages and FaceTime allow real-time communication concerning real or imagined wrongs by other students or members of the band or Corps staff. Brewer said such conversations are simply part of his job, and in that role he is the face of the Aggie Band to parents.

He is always quick to add that across the decades, students find that "their time in the band helped mold them into the successful adults they've become. They learn that being a part of a bunch of people committed toward a single goal is a valuable lesson than will serve them through-

out their lives. They also see through examples, and come to know over time, that the friendships endure and expand."

Brewer's words provide an apt closing for this volume marking the Fightin' Texas Aggie Band's 125th year. "The Aggie Band is more than just a single person or a single director. It's more than Joseph Holick or the early bandmasters, Colonel Dunn, Colonel Adams, Colonel Haney, Colonel Toler, Dr. Rhea, or even, yes, Colonel Brewer. It's a series of like minds combined in a single effort, working toward a single end—unmatched precision marching and music on the field. I and all Aggie Band members believe the band will march on forever, as it should."

March-in for the game with the University of Louisiana–Monroe, 2018. Courtesy Texas A&M University Department of Music Activities.

The trombones and basses belt out a military march on a typical fall "Aggieland Saturday." Courtesy Texas A&M Corps of Cadets.

The brass and drum sections play a pregame concert beside the fountain in Rudder Plaza in 2014. Courtesy Texas A&M Corps of Cadets.

Alabama Game Day march-in, 2016. Courtesy Texas A&M Corps of Cadets.

Marching in for the game with Ole Miss, 2016. Courtesy Texas A&M Corps of Cadets.

The band marches down Military Walk during Final Review 2014. Courtesy Texas A&M Corps of Cadets.

As expected, the Fightin' Texas Aggie Band won the halftime at the 2018 Auburn game, though the football team was barely outscored. Courtesy Texas A&M Corps of Cadets.

Good-bye. The Aggie Band marches off, in a parade in downtown Houston, before the Rice game, 1983. Photo by Jim Elmore, courtesy John H. Lindsey '44.

Appendix A

Band Leadership

Bandmasters and Directors

1894	Joseph F. Holick
1895	Arthur Jenkins
1895–97	George W. Gross
1897–1902	F. H. Miller
	(Joseph F. Holick–1902)
1903–1904	George W. Terrell
	(Joseph F. Holick–1904)
1904–17	Bradford Pier Day
	(Joseph F. Holick–1917)
1918–19	Alois Slovacek
1920	Howell Nolte*
1920–24	George Farleigh
1924–46	Richard J. Dunn
1946–73	E. V. Adams
1973–89	Joe T. Haney
1989–2001	Ray E. Toler
2001–	Timothy B. Rhea

*Member of the Class of 1918 and mentioned as director in the September 30, 1920, issue of the *Battalion*. No further record exists; may have filled in until Farleigh arrived.

Band Staff Members

Associate Directors

1972–73	Major Joe T. Haney '48
1973–82	Major Joe K. McMullen
1982–88	Mr. Bill J. Dean
1988–89	Lieutenant Colonel Ray E. Toler
1989–	Major Jay O. Brewer '81

2001–2004, 2007–2016	Dr. Paul Sikes
2004–	Major Travis Almany
2004–	Mr. Chris Hollar
2016–	Lieutenant Russell Tipton

Assistant Directors

1986–89	Captain Jay O. Brewer '81
1990–93	Mr. Jim McDaniel
1993–2001	Lieutenant Timothy B. Rhea

Graduate Assistants/Student Assistants (Listed by Class Year)

Marion D. McNair, Jr. '70
Cliff Chamberlain '71
John R. Williams '75
Gwynne Geddie '75
Billy Joe Jay '75
Jim Ramsey '77
Bill Byers '80
Jay O. Brewer '81
Curtis Wales '89
Michael Percifield '91

Staff Assistants

1982–86	Jay O. Brewer '81
1989–2004	Dorothy Hopkins
2004–2015	Jean Stanley
2015–	Susan Haven

Texas Aggie Band Association Presidents

1966–69	Thomas A. Murrah '38, San Antonio (two consecutive terms)
1970–71	Homer Hunter '25, Dallas
1972–73	Joseph J. Buser '59, Bryan
1974–75	Lawrence W. Christian '62, Tulsa
1976–77	Kenneth B. Livingston '56, College Station
1978–79	Donald B. Powell '56, College Station
1980–81	Charles S. Kinard '57, Bryan
1982–83	Charles E. Still '61, Bryan
1984–85	Billy G. Lay '53, College Station
1986–87	George A. Humble '48, Groesbeck
1988–89	John C. Otto '70, Bryan
1990–91	David P. Marion '65, Giddings
1992–93	James K. Hennigan '54, College Station
1994–95	Donald B. Powell '56, College Station

1996–97	Lawrence A. "Larry" Lippke '69, College Station
1998–99	Sigurd S. "Sig" Kendall '71, College Station
2000–01	Robert L. "Lee" Clayton III '72, Denison
2001–03	William R. "Bill" Howell '69, College Station
2004–05	James J. "Jim" Hall '69, Katy
2006–07	Robert A. "Bob" Flocke '68, Wimberly
2008–09	Bruce F. Bockhorn '74, Carmine
2010–11	Richard B. "Bruce" Stone '73, Humble
2012–13	Don W. Bailey '78, College Station
2014–15	Christopher M. "Chris" Sullivan '98, Bryan
2016–17	Michael A. Hudson '97, Bryan
2018–19	Harvey R. Schulz '69, College Station

Drum Majors and Commanding Officers

YEAR	DRUM MAJOR	COMMANDING OFFICER
1894	H. A. "California" Morse	F. D. Perkins
1895	J. Dahlich	A. Amthor
1896	E. H. Sternenberg	A. W. Ball
1897	H. Cotton	E. H. Sternenberg
1898	R. S. Farr	H. H. Tracy
1899	R. W. Cousins	W. F. Dyer
1900	H. Japhet	T. H. Clements
1901		
1902	J. Harrison	G. W. Risien
1903	F. Bauer	J. C. Burns
1904	F. H. Simonds	J. C. Burns
1905	W. B. Guinn	B. D. Marburger
1906	Guy T. Haltom	R. E. Schiller
1907	W. E. Sampson	E. L. Marek
1908	W. E. Sampson	H. F. Foy, Jr.
1909	H. C. Miller	C. P. Brannin
1910	H. C. Miller	Byron Gist
1911	S. W. Clark	B. M. Brown
1912	H. M. Brundrette	B. J. Manfield
1913	J. R. Hill	L. V. Leinhard
1914	H. M. Brundrette	S. H. Slay
1915	H. E. Runge	O. W. Greene
1916	J. R. Barnes	T. K. Morris
1917	G. C. Morris	G. B. Hanson
1918	J. H. Stacey	F. A. Cooper
1919	H. M. Bohn	F. V. Murrah
1920	W. W. Cox	H. N. Glezen
1921	H. E. De Lee	J. A. Walker

YEAR		DRUM MAJOR	COMMANDING OFFICER
1922		C. Reed Compton	G. L. Boykin
1923		C. Reed Compton	O. P. Weyland
1924		Wilson N. Reedy	S. C. Bartlett
1925		Wilson N. Reedy	A. W. Huff
1926		Earl F. Patterson	L. F. Lightner
1927		J. L. Pink	E. A. Dietel
1928		R. S. Dockum	F. M. Mabry
1929		R. S. Dockum	W. C. Morris
1930		R. S. Dockum	W. H. Dickinson
1931		T. B. Bagley	B. E. Nowotny
1932		T. B. Bagley	R. J. Sechrist
1933		Tom Speed	F. L. Bryan
1934		Thomas Terrell	T. N. Gearreald
1935		Alvin Canuteson	F. W. H. Wehner, Jr.
1936		H. G. Barton	D. J. Lewis
1937		M. B. Cramer	F. G. Prutzman
1938	Combined	J. S. Bracewell	T. A. Murrah
	Artillery	J. C. Clary	J. C. Clary
	Infantry	Paul C. Davis	Paul C. Davis
1939	Combined	G. A. Brock	B. T. Wehner
	Artillery	S. J. Marek	S. J. Marek
	Infantry	George Fulton	George Fulton
1940	Combined	W. R. Ledbetter	T. A. Balmer
	Artillery	John W. Bailey	H. L. F. Doerr
	Infantry	John M. Sharp	L .J. Wehrle
1941	Combined	J. P. Ledbetter	E. L. Wehner
	Artillery	J. W. Cargile	R. J. Chappell, Jr.
	Infantry	T. R. Harrison	L. J. Nelson
1942	Combined	A. M. Hinds	R. R. Russell
	Artillery	Claude C. Stewart	C. J. Toland
	Infantry	Jack M. Balagia	W. M. McReynolds
1943	Combined	B. H. Schleider	William Bucy
	Artillery	Joe F. Gordon	A. H. Munson
	Infantry	Ed Perry	O. L. Culberson

The War Years
June 1943–September 1946

	Freshman Band	W. E. Stackhouse, Freshman Drum Major	
1944	Combined	Eugene Fields	(None)
	Artillery	Don Hackney	Sid V. Smith
	Infantry	Kenneth Varvel	J. K. Stalcup

YEAR		DRUM MAJOR	COMMANDING OFFICER
June –September 1944		(None)	James T. Jarrett
September 1944–January 1945		G. C. "Pete" Stanley	John A. Veien
			W. A. Ray/1st Co.
			J. Clayton/2nd Co.
		Paul A. Allen succeeded Stanley in November 1944.	
January–June 1945		Paul A. Allen	Ernest Slaughter
			W. T. Brown
June 1945–September 1945		Paul A. Allen	C. E. "Fount" Ray
September 1945–June 1946			
	Artillery	W. T. Brown	W. T. Brown
	Infantry	I. E. Elkins	I. E. Elkins

I. E. Elkins served as Head Drum Major and Combined Band Commander when the Band performed together. Paul A. Allen then served as the third drum major.

YEAR		DRUM MAJOR	COMMANDING OFFICER
1947	Combined	Philip B. Kosub	Philip B. Kosub
	Artillery	J. B. Cooper	William S. Dixon
	Infantry	Paul A. Allen	Paul A. Allen, Larry Mangold
1948	Combined	R. B. Stanford	D. R. Howell
	Maroon	A. D. "Artie" Byall	William E. LaRoche
	White	Troy Prater	Richard H. Nichols
1949	Combined	T. A. Carlton	George R. Edwards
	Maroon	Carl B. Whyte	W. H. Smith
	White	R. Bruce Hurley	L. C. Kinard
1950	Combined	M. A. Moore	W. F. Thompson
	Maroon	W. E. Hollar	W. E. Hollar
	White	A. D. Waldie	C. R. Lundelius
1951	Combined	T. C. Alderson	Richard L. Goodwin
	Maroon	R. H. Buchanan	J. E. Rutherford
	White	Wayne Dunlap	C. H. Neeley
1952	Combined	James W. Rogers	Voris R. Burch
	Maroon	R. L. Robinson	Lowell A. Holmes
	White	Grover C. Ellisor	Grover C. Ellisor
1953	Combined	D. E. Krueger	D. E. Greaney
	Maroon	G. W. Berner	D. D. Howell
	White	J. I. Jordan	J. H. Thomas
1954	Combined	Hugh H. Philippus	R. N. Porter
	Maroon	W. B. Brogdon	D. C. Quast
	White	W. E. Narville	G. S. Fulghum

YEAR		DRUM MAJOR	COMMANDING OFFICER
1955	Combined	John F. Dornbusch	Paul E. Gentry
	Maroon	Earl Pike	Earl Pike
	White	D. P. Ashcroft	E. F. Willms
1956	Combined	Tommy Short	V. A. Moseley
	Maroon	Dwight Brown, Jr.	A. L. Cordes
	White	Buddy D. Patterson	W. C. Steward
1957	Combined	Gary W. December	C. H. Holley
	Maroon	Jay G. Cloud	M. B. Benton
	White	J. M. Cornwall	C. W. Rasco
1958	Combined	R. W. George	A. H. Grantham
	Maroon	R. E. Roycroft	W. R. Stallworth
	White		Olin W. Brown
1959	Combined	R. C. Schubert	W. J. Skaggs
	Maroon	J. F. Stoll	J. L. Guinn
	White	R. F. Hunter	David G. Eller
1960	Combined	David H. Arnold	Ralph E. Petersen
	Maroon	James F. Bailey	Billy B. Eitel
	White	Olin W. Brown	Robert B. McJohnson
1961	Combined	David L. Voelter	Walter R. Willms
	Maroon	Fred C. Buckner	Donald F. Boren
	White	Robert S. Harris	Aubrey C. Elkins, Jr.
1962	Combined	Manley McGill	Jimmie L. Coombes
	Maroon	John A. Betts	Sidney F. Stephenson
	White	Dennis W. Sander	Lawrence Christian
1963	Combined	Ronald P. Moon	William Barnhart
	Maroon	Cesar R. Guerra	Frank W. Grimes
	White	Conway R. Shaw III	Paul E. Bergstrom
1964	Combined	Wayne M. Noster	James M. Morgan
	Maroon	Robert Ridley	James R. Hottenroth
	White	David L. Creech	Robert L. Burgoon
1965	Combined	Albert Tijerina	Thomas R. Seely
	Maroon	Dennis B. Barr	Gilbert Kretzschmar
	White	Richard M. Alexander	Larry A. Phillips
1966	Combined	Ellis C. Gill	Cecil O. Windsor, Jr.
	Maroon	Ronald D. Winn	Roy L. May
	White	Charles T. McGinnis III	Rick Graham
1967	Combined	William M. Hensley	Jim R. Davidson
	Maroon	Freemen J. Jarrell	Andrew A. Tijerina
	White	Donald C. Burleson	David A. Kocian
1968	Combined	Richard C. Westbrook	Henry G. Cisneros
	Maroon	Marc A. Sheiness	Larry C. Hearn
	White	James W. Criswell	Dennis R. Parrish
1969	Combined	Michael B. Benton	William R. Howell
	Maroon	Lawrence A. Lippke	Melvin S. Beck
	White	James J. Hall	Jonathan M. Beall

YEAR		DRUM MAJOR	COMMANDING OFFICER
1970	Combined	John C. Otto, Jr.	Edwin Lamm III
	Maroon	Richard D. Garrett	Richard G. Sanchez
	White	Daniel Gower, Jr.	Roland F. Bonewitz
1971	Combined	James F. Connally	Sigurd S. Kendall
	Maroon	Harry M. Fong	Mitchell J. Timmons
	White	Ernest E. Johnson	Ralph K. Jenke
1972	Combined	Steven T. Sullivan	Michael A. Langston
	Maroon	John R. Dye	Adrian A. Arriega/Fall
			Stephen F. Brock/Spring
	White	Richard A. Smith	C. L. Hubbard III
1973	Combined	Alan H. Gurevich	Paul Herrington
	Maroon	Richard W. Minix	Gilbert Rodriguez
	White	Richard B. Stone	Russell A. Braden
1974	Combined	Steven C. Moore	Mike Phillips
	Maroon	Choya Walling	Leon R. Bennett, Jr.
	White	Bruce F. Bockhorn	Pat L. Phillips
1975	Combined	F. Brad Harrison	Jon R. Bullock
	Maroon	W. H. Richards	John A. Kincaid
	White	Burton T. Owens	Marcus G. Dudley
1976	Combined	Mic Comley	Jim C. Ledlow
	Maroon	Lacy C. Gilliam	Thomas W. Henry
	White	Clifford L. Simmang	Robert N. Townsend
1977	Combined	William P. Schwennsen	Robert E. Spiller
	Artillery	Nathan J. Ramsey, Jr.	Terry H. Tooley
	A Battery		Kyle Braswell
	B Battery		Chris J. Roach
	Infantry	William Bryan Cummings	Charles P. Briggs IV
	A Company		Robert P. Gottlich
	B Compay		Otto Hanneman
1978	Combined	Joseph Bruch Hamilton	Joseph Alan Spann
	Artillery	Lynn Balinas	Rodney J. Boehm
	A Battery		Lawrence D. Boyd
	B Battery		Michael J. Close
	Infantry	James A. Earl IV	Grady Garrett
	A Company		Danna Ray Foy
	B Company		David Dodson
1979	Combined	Larry Haag	William McKerall
	Artillery	Michael McCartney	Steve Smith
	A Battery		Ronald Greenwade
	B Battery		Dennis Halleron
	Infantry	Connie Williford	J. Dean Nelson
	A Company		Robert Fields
	B Company		Joe Ramirez

YEAR		DRUM MAJOR	COMMANDING OFFICER
1980	Combined	James Dees	Greg Dew
	Artillery	Phil Gougler	Thomas Rheinlander
	A Battery		Rob Ferguson
	B Battery		Mike Harp
	Infantry	Bill Byers	Tim Gaither
	A Company		Bruce Fain
	B Company		Jeff Presnal
1981	Combined	Randy Nelson	Cullen Shiffrin
	Artillery	David LePori	Charles Fields
	A Battery		Wes Osburn
	B Battery		Wes Klett
	Infantry	David Rogers	Eddie Conger
	A Company		Wayne Shortle
	B Company		Curtis Donaldson
1982	Combined	Jason L. Clark	James H. Hughes, Jr.
	Artillery	Rodney Kret	Tom Wilkes
	A Battery		Patrick Doyle
	B Battery		Kenneth LePori
	Infantry	Rodger Kret	Duane Schwarz
	A Company		Jeffrey Badders
	B Company		Dennis McQueen
1983	Combined	Bill Pilcher	Shane Doering
	Artillery	John Grigsby	Stuart Wood
	A Battery		Larry Marek
	B Battery		Dave Womack
	C Battery		Kevin Harris
	Infantry	Ross Rutherford	Dane Whitaker
	A Company		Tom Bone
	B Company		Glen Hackemack
	C Company		Ken Roberson
1984	Combined	Adrian Burke	Dayton Robertson
	Artillery	Kenny Barton	Kevin Smith
	A Battery		Kim Fuschak
	B Battery		Steve Shea
	C Battery		Tom Kallina
	Infantry	Nick Evanoff	Kevin Vaille
	A Company		Brian Culhane
	B Company		Robin Ryan
	C Company		Robert Green
1985	Combined	Mark Allen	John Ripley
	Artillery	Glen Emshoff	Gregory Stephens
	A Battery		James Morris
	B Battery		David Sandridge
	Infantry	Richard Scott Yerigan	John F. Davis, Jr.
	A Company		Max Caramanian
	B Company		Bill Giessing

YEAR		DRUM MAJOR	COMMANDING OFFICER
1986	Combined	Craig Sims	Tom Hale
	Artillery	Paul Marvin	Russell Hevenor
	A Battery		Michael Mittag
	B Battery		Sean Peters
	Infantry	Keith Lyons	Louis Meneghetti
	A Company		Ronald Terrell
	B Company		Rodney Terrell
1987	Combined	Dale Crockett	Eric Smith
	Artillery	Byron Spencer	Cody Hurdt
	A Battery		Kevin Laughbaum
	B Battery		Gordon Greaney
	Infantry	Mike Bond	Chris Smith
	A Company		William Cade
	B Company		John Hyatt
1988	Combined	Les Cardenas	Keith McKnight
	Artillery	Dennis Garth	Richard Pfeil
	A Battery		Michael John
	B Battery		Steve Hall
	Infantry	Andreas Garza	William Hostetler
	A Company		Todd Greenberg
	C Company		Perry Barth
1989	Combined	Chad Corbett	Allan Hess
	Artillery	William Nabors	James Owens
	A Battery		Derrek Hryhorchuk
	B Battery		Tim Graham
	Infantry	Kevin Roberts	Mark Fulton
	A Company		Jeff Pehl
	B Company		Eric Jackson
1990	Combined	Mike Sammis	Alan Blackmon
	Artillery	Steve Hare	Matt Long
	A Battery		Russell Downey
	B Battery		Brian Weir
	Infantry	Troy Yoakum	Mike Watson
	A Company		Brent Millican
	B Company		Zac Crouch
1991	Combined	Russell D. Griffin	Russell S. Lewis
	Artillery	Christopher Alexander	Craig N. Davis
	A Battery		Steven Baine
	B Battery		Joe Seago
	Infantry	Richard J. Wariner	Jody Schubert
	A Company		Rod Hadder
	B Company		Gary Hendershot
1992	Combined	Joe B. Gamertsfelder	Mark Lane
	Artillery	L. Steve Beller	Christian Williams
	A Battery		Darren Boarnett
	B Battery		Michael Keller

YEAR		DRUM MAJOR	COMMANDING OFFICER
1992 (*cont.*)	Infantry	Nicholas A. Luggerio	Scott de Villeneuve
	A Company		Lane Miller
	B Company		Rudy Vacek
1993	Combined	Matt Daniel	Jeremy Schubert
	Artillery	Daylen Borders	
	A Battery		Greg Sawyer
	B Battery		Brian Box
	Infantry	Michael Suerth	
	A Company		Russ Gregg/Fall
			Kirk Richards/Spring
	B Company		Mike Scott
1994	Combined	Jason Blevins	Jason Hearnsberger
	Artillery	Troy Davidson	
	A Battery		David Sprinkle
	B Battery		Lance Clark
	Infantry	Michael Davison	
	A Company		Kacey Gabriel
	B Company		Jason Patterson
1995	Combined	Jake Battenfield,	John Cyrier
		Wade Johns	
	Artillery	Jason Williams	Todd Neander,
			Paul Reininger
	Infantry	Wade Johns,	Juan Nava,
		Eric Oliphant	Jaime Santana
1996	Combined	Jonathan Luikens	Will Koeck
	Artillery	Tom Pool	John Davidson,
			Sheldon Blackwell
	Infantry	Hung Lee	Guy Gregg,
			David Childers
1997	Combined	Shane Tanner	Mike Hays
	Artillery	Michael Voinis	Ted Vierling,
			Frank Hinds
	Infantry	Louis Migliaccio	Chris Morgan,
			Joel Neuenschwander
1998	Combined	John Fugitt	Clay Kennedy
	Artillery	John Pluff	David Veach,
			Ryan Barton
	Infantry	Christopher Sullivan	Daniel Moran,
			Cory Burk
1999	Combined	Samuel Udovich	Beau Voelkel
	Artillery	Jonathan Scott	Matthew Bauerschlag,
			John Christie
	Infantry	Brian Marks	Jason Eggenburger,
			Jace Neuenschwander

YEAR		DRUM MAJOR	COMMANDING OFFICER
2000	Combined	Mark Gandin	Jarrett Sonnen
	Artillery	Jason Bradford	Jose Guzman, Patrick Spies
	Infantry	Mike Maginness	Sean Penrod, Christopher Migl
2001	Combined	Jesse Clayburn	Ernest Hunter
	Artillery	Michael Waun	Adam Jenkins, Eric Gomez
	Infantry	Jason Griffin	Onni Hynninen, Ryan Zeitler
2002	Combined	Dean Dominy	Chip Wenmohs
	Artillery	Daniel Daly	Justin Hall, Jeremy Hall
	Infantry	Andy Nelson	Jason Fritzler, David Feith
2003	Combined	Alex Jones	Daniel Moran
	Artillery	Matthew Morrison	Ryan Hufford, Matthew Henley
	Infantry	Asa Selzer	Stephen Guillot, Scott Beimer
2004	Combined	Jonathan Dunbar	Ryan Knape
	Artillery	Adam Hurst	Travis Brown, Robert McClelland
	Infantry	James Sajewski	Michael Piazza, Kyle LaRocque
2005	Combined	Timothy Newman	David Moran
	Artillery	Travis Raine	Brian Faughn, Terry Gage
	Infantry	Marcos Azua	Michael Barbier, Casey Hays
2006	Combined	Brandt Owens	Jonathan Houston
	Artillery	Gary Davis	Brian Kendall, Abby Belitzer
	Infantry	Emmanual Guillory	Rider Barnes, Jeremy Bell
2007	Combined	Paxton Miller	Nathan Snow
	Artillery	Justin Partlow	William Byrne, Joseph Dannenbaum
	Infantry	Justin Loomis, Pete Moonjian	Reid Zevenbergen, John Pulvino
2008	Combined	Michael Valdez	Robert Will
	Artillery	Nathan Fluker	Luke Netardus, Ryan Chance
	Infantry	Jake Poulsen	Nathan Fluker, Austin Cox

YEAR		DRUM MAJOR	COMMANDING OFFICER
2009	Combined	Elliot Stump	Pedro Vega
	Artillery	Samantha Clements	David Pitcher,
			Randal Hartsfield
	Infantry	Adam Broussard	Joel Varner,
			Danny Hernandez
2010	Combined	Cody Works	Kason Knight
	Artillery	William O'Gorman	Jovan Martinez,
			Riley Roach
	Infantry	Benjamin Rush	Jason Schladt,
			Trevor O'Flaherty
2011	Combined	Austin Welty	Josh Fritz
	Artillery	Chad Kloesel	Ruben Watson,
			Tony Cincotta
	Infantry	Bryan Rathke	Michael Foderetti,
			Bryan Rathke
2012	Combined	Mark Jessup	Dalton Fuss
	Artillery	Luke Ellis	Jacob Springer,
			Maxwell Anthony
	Infantry	Michael Blanchard	Larry Sullivan,
			Michael Young
2013	Combined	Michael Froebel	J. P. Barton
	Artillery	Andrew Mann	Brian Smith,
			Michael Froebel
	Infantry	Heather Ortega	Garrett Williams,
			Eric Espinoza
2014	Combined	Steven Hering	Trevin Hazel
	Artillery	Cody Ward	Allison Fuss,
			Scott Hartsfield,
			Stephen Hankins
	Infantry	Urbane Martinez	Patrick Casey,
			Kevin Moss,
			Joshua Hewett
2015	Combined	Tim McMillan	Parker White
	Artillery	Garrett Leach	Sara Carriker,
			John Price,
			Thomas Branyon,
			Chris Martin
	Infantry	Shaun Bruner	Justin Tash,
			Jordan Garcia,
			Ian Tenbrink,
			Spencer McDonald
2016	Combined	Timothy Cummins	Kevin Wilfong
	Artillery	Matthew McClure	Ryan Tschirhart,
			Luke Jacobson,
			Rex Ritchie,
			Allen Tschirhart

YEAR		DRUM MAJOR	COMMANDING OFFICER
2016 (*cont.*)	Infantry	Hayden Perry	Chris Wood, Andrew Hounsel, Mitchel Stipek, Jeffrey Knapp
2017	Combined Artillery	John Little Ross Bodeker	Matthew Rollins Benjamin Butler, DeForest Gordy, Ben Earnshaw, Glen Colby, Sheldon Snyder
	Infantry	Cole Bordner	Rachel Branyon, Mark Williamson, Cody Caraway, Samantha Blackmar
2018	Combined Artillery	James Shifflett Wyatt Thomas	Chris Morris Hannah Stacey, Wyatt Thomas, Kenny Adams, Conner Marek
	Infantry	Reid Webster	Scott Lauritsen, Tyler Flatt, Chris Weisberg, Reid Webster
2019	Combined Artillery	Claudio Trevino Chris Watson	Caleb Brown Cody Bliss, Harrison McClain, Matthew Molden, Ross McMahan
	Infantry	Josiah Caver	Douglas Mendelsohn, Jayson Cavazos, Josiah Caver, Matthew Papandrea

Appendix B

Rosters of Aggie Band Members

During the past 125 years more than 10,000 young men and women have marched as proud members of the Fightin' Texas Aggie Band. This roster lists only the year in which their names first appeared as members of the band, but they continue to step off in spirit each time they hear the command, "Recall! Step off on Hullabaloo." The roster was compiled from records of the Texas A&M University Archives, the Sam Houston Sanders Corps of Cadets Center, the Association of Former Students, the Texas Aggie Band Association, and various yearbooks. Some records, especially those from the early years and the years surrounding World War II, were inconsistent or nonexistent. Corrections and additions—which are welcomed and encouraged—should be submitted in writing to the Texas Aggie Band Association at taba@corpsofcadets.org.

Band Membership Years 1894–1993

Aaberg, W. J., 1949
Abat, Andrea A., 1985
Abbott, O. W., 1933
Abdullah, Henry, 1982
Abell, David, 1988
Abernathy, R., 1981
Ablers, Robert, 1985
Abney, Roy, 1984
Abrahamson, E. C., 1946
Abrego, Hector, 1993
Ackerson, Brian, 1992
Ackerson, Kevin, 1991
Acosta, Gerson, 1993
Adair, J. M., 1944
Adam, D. A., 1921
Adamcik, Merrill T., 1954
Adams, C. H., 1960
Adams, C. S., 1926

Adams, D. C., 1957
Adams, D. R., 1957
Adams, David E., 1961
Adams, Dell, 1972
Adams, E. V., 1925
Adams, E. V. Jr., 1957
Adams, E. V., III, 1992
Adams, Greg T., 1984
Adams, J. A., 1962
Adams, J. C., 1958
Adams, Joe M., 1972
Adams, John, 1980
Adams, John M., 1971
Adams, Kenneth, 1969
Adams, Michael W., 1969
Adams, Milton L., 1971
Adams, P. O., 1930
Adams, R. K., 1945
Adams, Rufe E., 1905
Adams, S. L., 1933
Adams, T. A., 1955

Adams, W. T., 1942
Adkins, Barry, 1979
Adkins, David, 1983
Adkisson, G. B., 1963
Adkisson, J. F., 1935
Adkisson, J. W., 1938
Adkisson, Mike Allen, 1947
Adkisson, W. T., 1951
Adlam, F. H., 1950
Adoue, J. B., 1957
Ahrens, Kenton S., 1955
Akin, J. F., 1953
Alanis, Edward, 1980
Albers, Robert, 1983
Albert, W. E., 1960
Albrecht, Frank J., 1947
Albright, M., 1968
Albright, Paul, 1983
Alcorn, David, 1981
Alcorn, Patrick, 1980
Alderdice, J. R., 1950

Alderman, D. R., 1962
Alderman, John H., 1956
Alderson, Thomas C. Jr., 1947
Aldrich, O. C., 1936
Aldrich, W. M., 1964
Aldridge, B., 1981
Alexander, A., 1968
Alexander, Bobby, 1978
Alexander, Christopher, 1987
Alexander, D. L., 1950
Alexander, D. S., 1953
Alexander, David, 1980
Alexander, G. L., 1951
Alexander, G. M., 1937
Alexander, Jon, 1980
Alexander, Jonathan, 1989
Alexander, R. B., 1940
Alexander, R. F., 1952
Alexander, Richard M., 1961
Alexander, W. R., 1916
Allan, Paul, 1979
Allan, Thomas, 1975
Allard, I. L., 1908
Allen, B., 1965
Allen, Dwight R. 1952
Allen, H. B., 1905
Allen, J., 1967
Allen, J. D., 1958
Allen, J. H., 1936
Allen, Jeffrey, 1989
Allen, M., 1967
Allen, Mark, 1981
Allen, Paul, 1980
Allen, Paul A., 1944
Allen, Richard G., 1985
Allen, T. E., 1924
Allen, Tom, 1978
Allen, W. E., 1950
Allison, E. C., 1914
Allman, B. L., 1941
Allman, S. H., 1941
Allphin, J., 1959
Allred, W. L., 1951
Almond, Derek, 1984
Alsmeyer, Charles R., 1947
Alsmeyer, Richard H., 1947

Alsobrook, Sam E., 1970
Alston, R. E., 1940
Altgelt, Franz H., 1928
Altman, Benny, 1934
Altus, James, 1978
Alvarado, Robert, 1980
Alves, Richard T., 1944
Amaya, Paul E., 1973
Amend, Brian, 1991
Ames, A. W., 1942
Amidon, Chester D. Jr., 1971
Amiga, Paul, 1975
Amis, William J., 1939
Ammerman, D., 1966
Ammons, Harold, 1971
Amos, D. H., 1957
Amos, L. A., 1960
Amthor, Adolph W., 1894
Anderson, B., 1966
Anderson, B. H., 1951
Anderson, B. M., 1942
Anderson, Brad, 1979
Anderson, C. W., 1940
Anderson, D. L., 1948
Anderson, D. P., 1963
Anderson, David, 1976
Anderson, E. L., 1950
Anderson, E. R., 1949
Anderson, E. S., 1945
Anderson, Eric, 1982
Anderson, Gene R., 1954
Anderson, George D., 1950
Anderson, J., 1968
Anderson, J., 1981
Anderson, James E., 1956
Anderson, Jeff, 1979
Anderson, Joe D., 1969
Anderson, John W., 1969
Anderson, Larry, 1992
Anderson, M. B., 1937
Anderson, R. G., 1954
Anderson, Randall, 1991
Anderson, Ross H., 1973
Anderson, Roy, 1977
Andrew, E. H., 1941
Andrews, C. W., 1942

Andrews, Carroll W., 1970
Andrews, Gary S., 1972
Andrews, J. G., 1953
Andrews, R., 1966
Andrews, Stacy, 1975
Andrus, George L., 1930
Andrus, Lee, 1977
Ansley, W. P., 1941
Anthony, J. M., 1944
Anthony, M. R., 1945
Anthony, Roy M., 1963
Anthony, W. E., 1958
Appeddu, Paul, 1983
Appling, G. S., 1915
Arbetter, Robert L., 1972
Arcement, Larry H. Jr., 1974
Aringdale, B. T., 1961
Arms, Robert R., 1953
Armstrong, Abbot E., 1939
Armstrong, C. Elliott, 1935
Armstrong, James, 1992
Armstrong, John W. Jr., 1957
Armstrong, K. T., 1981
Armstrong, Michael, 1990
Armstrong, R., 1957
Armstrong, R. W., 1961
Arnold, David H., 1956
Arnold, M. L., 1950
Arnold, Roy, 1982
Arnold, William, 1992
Arredondo, Rene, 1989
Arriaga, Adrian A., 1968
Arrington, R. N., 1951
Arriola, Francis, 1993
Arrison, J. R., 1960
Arthur, Harris W., 1970
Arthur, Ryan, 1992
Arvin, D. F., 1947
Ary, M. I., 1960
Asbill, Greg, 1980
Aschenbeck, Walter B., 1964
Ashbrook, D. G., 1959
Ashcraft, Audrey, 1989
Ashcroft, David P., 1951
Asher, Robert T., 1947
Ashford, Bruce F., 1971

Ashley, Rickey G., 1972
Ashley, Robert, 1975
Ashworth, M. D., 1982
Askins, J. W., 1931
Astle, Larry A., 1956
Atchley, Russell, 1975
Atkins, James R., 1981
Atkins, R. F., 1953
Atkinson, Albert, 1981
Atlee, William, 1990
Atwood, Joe V., 1949
Auberg, W. J., 1950
Aubin, Vernon, Jr. 1966
AuBuchon, Andre, 1949
August, L., 1912
Ault, Robert H., 1963
Aumann, James T., 1964
Austin, C. A., 1944
Austin, Joel, 1987
Austin, Roy, 1988
Autry, Steve, 1987
Avary, B., 1951
Averitt, J. T., 1944
Avery, D., 1966
Avery, Mack, Jr. 1993
Avery, Thomas, 1993
Axtell, C. R., 1960
Ayers, John W., 1933
Ayers, R., 1959
Ayton, Carl R., 1962
Aziz, Kevin, 1987

Babasin, Y. H., 1937
Baber, L. K., 1952
Bacchus, Kenneth R., 1970
Backloupe, J. J., 1930
Backof, Alan W., 1964
Backus, Kerby D., 1949
Bacon, Darla, 1993
Baczyk, J. E., 1954
Badders, Jeffrey A., 1978
Badgett, Robert L., 1962
Badough, Kenneth R., 1956
Bagley, Jimmie C., 1950
Bagley, Tom B., 1927
Baha, Nader, 1989

Bahlmann, Daryl, 1979
Bahlmann, G. E., 1953
Bailey, A., 1910
Bailey, Don, 1974
Bailey, Edmond I., 1957
Bailey, J. F., 1954
Bailey, J. W., 1936
Bailey, James F., 1959
Bailey, M. G., 1959
Bailey, P. A., 1911
Bailey, T. E., 1948
Baine, Steven, 1987
Bair, L. L., 1925
Baitland, Lawrence, 1992
Baker, Barry R., 1963
Baker, Cody, 1992
Baker, David, 1975
Baker, Dori, 1993
Baker, John, 1985
Baker, John, 1993
Baker, Kyle, 1992
Baker, Wilbur, 1986
Balagia, J. M., 1938
Balhorn, Charles E., 1963
Balinas, Peter Lynn, 1975
Ball, A. W., 1895
Ball, David, 1977
Ball, H. F., 1939
Ball, H. P., 1943
Ball, Patrick, 1953
Ball, R. E., 1941
Ballard, Donald, 1993
Ballard, E. E., 1910
Ballard, Stanley H. Jr., 1960
Ballerstedt, R. H., 1933
Balmer, T. A., 1936
Balmer, W. J., 1933
Banatwala, Salem, 1992
Bang, R. F., 1945
Banks, B., 1967
Banks, Gene P., 1964
Banks, J. O., 1928
Banks, J. V., 1923
Banks, M. L., 1959
Barber, D. L., 1950
Barber, G., 1966

Barber, W. J., 1945
Barefield, William E., 1953
Barfield, David R., 1971
Barfield, Larry M., 1966
Bargman, William G., 1961
Barker, David E., 1960
Barker, G. H., 1942
Barker, Robert C., 1967
Barkley, Jerry, 1977
Barnes, Harold E., 1938
Barnes, J. R., 1915
Barnes, Jackson N., 1963
Barnes, R. B., 1945
Barnes, Robert, 1975
Barnes, T. F., 1905
Barnett, G., 1938
Barnett, J. Mark, 1976
Barnett, J. W., 1951
Barnett, R. A., 1961
Barnhart, William, 1982
Barnhart, William T., 1959
Baron, Robert, 1978
Barr, Billy J., 1938
Barr, Clinal E., 1936
Barr, Dennis B., 1961
Barras, Jeff, 1980
Barrera, Carlos M. Jr., 1967
Barrera, E. G., 1945
Barrett, Charles B., 1966
Barron, Walter T., 1950
Barrows, Glyn A., 1961
Bartay, Tandy E., 1956
Bartay, Gary K., 1957
Bartels, Bryan D., 1979
Bartfield, L., 1968
Barth, H. Perry, 1984
Bartlett, Silas Conoly, 1920
Bartley, Robert, 1976
Barton, Bruce E., 1970
Barton, Henry G., 1932
Barton, Kenneth, 1980
Barton, Mauris U., 1930
Barton, Perry M., 1978
Barton, Robert, 1980
Barton, T. E., 1966
Bartsch, Ron, 1991

Bartschmid, Albert H., 1971
Barzak, R. W. "Bill," 1944
Basden, Bruce P., 1974
Basinger, James A., 1964
Bass, H. K., 1946
Bass, N. I., 1918
Bass, Ogden L., 1923
Basse, C. H., 1953
Bassett, E. L., 1927
Bassham, Clifford, 1993
Bastidas, Anthony G., 1983
Batchelor, T. L., 1908
Bateman, Alex R., 1910
Bates, Benjamin, 1988
Battenfield, Jason, 1991
Bauch, Thomas A., 1969
Bauer, Felix, 1902
Baugh, Ronald D., 1970
Bauman, M. M., 1948
Baushausen, H. V., 1931
Beach, Mark, 1977
Beach, Scott, 1976
Beall, Jonathan M., 1965
Beall, W. S. Jr., 1964
Beams, G. W., 1925
Bean, D. C., 1952
Beard, G. D., 1956
Beard, James, 1975
Beard, Norris L., 1949
Beard, P. H., 1960
Beard, R. S., 1941
Beasley, W. A., 1936
Beaty, Gary, 1988
Beauchamp, R. D., 1934
Becerril, R. H., 1963
Beck, F. E. Jr., 1962
Beck, Melvin S., 1965
Beck, S. A., 1948
Beck, W. J., 1938
Becka, John C. Jr., 1961
Becker, Arno W., 1949
Becker, F. W., 1950
Becker, Phillip, 1993
Beckes, A., 1903
Beckman, Steve, 1986
Beecroft, Bertram E., 1947

Beeman, Thomas R., 1902
Beene, Allen M., 1971
Beene, B. J., 1960
Beeson, Merle A., 1969
Beever, S. G., 1963
Behne, Michael, 1979
Behymer, M. H., 1921
Beinhom, William A. Jr., 1934
Belcher, Robert, 1983
Belew, G. N., 1941
Belile, B. M., 1957
Belinsky, Peter B., 1962
Bell, A. R., 1959
Bell, Brian, 1977
Bell, E. C., 1938
Bell, Edward H., 1957
Bell, H. C. "Dulie," 1935
Bell, J. A., 1962
Bell, J. L., 1940
Bell, J. S., 1925
Bell, Richard M., 1971
Bell, Robert, 1993
Beller, L. Steve, 1988
Belleville, Tom, 1982
Bellinger, Edwin, 1933
Bellomy, Marc T., 1970
Beloney, Charles O., 1974
Belsher, H. E., 1922
Beltz, John, 1988
Benard, J., 1924
Benavides, John, 1980
Benker, Bill, 1989
Bennet, R. M., 1933
Bennet, Richard G., 1964
Bennett, Bill, 1978
Bennett, J., 1946
Bennett, Kevin B., 1972
Bennett, Leon R., 1950
Bennett, Leon R. Jr., 1970
Bennett, W. D., 1948
Benoist, D., 1948
Benton, Michael B., 1965
Benton, R., 1965
Benton, Roger W., 1969
Berbary, Geoffrey, 1990
Beresky, Jimmy K., 1968

Berg, Erickson, 1959
Berger, W., 1981
Berger, W. F., 1942
Bergman, Louis W., 1970
Bergstrom, Paul E., 1959
Berkley, R. H., 1895
Berlakovich, Jeffrey, 1992
Bernal, L. R., 1911
Berndt, P. L., 1933
Berner, George W., 1949
Bernier, Barry, 1978
Berry, C. D., 1937
Berry, E. M., 1921
Berry, L. E., 1925
Berry, Vernon R., 1948
Bertano, Steve, 1980
Bertels, Bryan, 1978
Berthelot, P. D., 1939
Bertram, B. J., 1944
Bertrand, A. R., 1956
Bertrand, P. B., 1956
Bertrand, Steve, 1977
Bertrand, Wayne, 1985
Bess, R. C., 1959
Best, Stephen, 1983
Betten, Hans, 1992
Bettis, H. E., 1934
Betts, J., 1958
Beuershausen, Chris, 1990
Beull, Jeffrey, 1992
Beverly, G. H., 1915
Beverly, L. A., 1915
Bevers, J. T., 1942
Beyer, H. C., 1954
Beyer, M. L., 1962
Bickham, Ben W., 1946
Bickle, Leonard A., 1923
Bickley, C. E., 1940
Bielefeldt, Doulgas L., 1973
Biering, S. R., 1898
Biffen, E. D., 1930
Bigson, Kenneth E., 1949
Bilancich, D. B., 1960
Billinger, G., 1967
Bilmore, C. R., 1953
Bingham, J. H., 1956

Bingham, Ronnie, 1976
Bird, Robert, 1982
Bird, Douglas L., 1971
Bird, J. S., 1958
Bird, M. O., 1946
Birdwell, J. E., 1964
Birdwell, R. E., 1957
Birk, R. A., 1909
Birnbaum, Joe, 1933
Birt, James, 1983
Bishop, B., 1967
Bishop, C. W., 1964
Bishop, Craig J., 1972
Bishop, Glen, 1990
Bishop, Michael, 1975
Bittle, Jay, 1975
Bittle, P. B., 1894
Bittle, T. C., 1896
Bittner, R. H., 1944
Bjork, A. R., 1955
Black, A., 1981
Black, B. B., 1948
Black, H. G., 1951
Black, H. J., 1962
Black, J. R., 1964
Black, Jerry, 1980
Black, Laurin D., 1949
Black, R., 1967
Black, Rodney, 1992
Black, William, 1980
Blackburn, Arthur E., 1966
Blackburn, J. H., 1953
Blackburn, J. M., 1961
Blackmon, B. Alan, 1986
Blackmon, J. A., 1961
Blackmon, J. C., 1954
Blacksell, B. B., 1959
Blackwelder, A., 1968
Blackwell, Larry, 1978
Blackwell, Roland, 1989
Blackwell, Ronald, 1977
Blackwell, T. M., 1961
Blackwell, Thomas, 1992
Blackwell, W. A., 1897
Blair, Darren, 1993
Blair, Kelvin R., 1964

Blake, Brent, 1991
Blake, W. H., 1924
Blakemore, J. E., 1937
Blakemore, W. S., 1936
Blalock, D. G., 1956
Blalock, John, 1979
Blanchette, Lloyd, 1980
Blankenship, B. J., 1944
Blankenship, James W., 1961
Blankfield, Meyer, 1914
Blankinship, B. T., 1941
Blankinship, David, 1986
Blanton, Dennis R., 1963
Blaschke, James, 1984
Blaylock, James E., 1962
Blazek, Scott, 1989
Bledsoe, F. M., 1941
Bledsoe, J. V., 1937
Bledsoe, R. C., 1950
Bleker, Edward G., 1963
Blevins, J. C., 1957
Blevins, Jason, 1990
Blissard, E. V., 1941
Blissard, Robert J., 1947
Blochberger, Tom, 1978
Blodgett, R. W., 1931
Blodgett, W. S., 1930
Blohowiak, Charles E., 1971
Blomerth, Todd A., 1968
Bloodworth, M. B., 1962
Bloom, E. E., 1964
Bloomer, J. M. 1964
Bloomer, J. P., 1926
Blount, Floyd M. Jr., 1945
Blue, David R., 1957
Blum, Robert B., 1972
Blumberg, C. A., 1925
Blunster, Paul A., 1971
Blunt, F., 1946
Bluntzer, Paul A., 1972
Boarnet, Bernard N., 1956
Boarnet, Darren, 1988
Boatright, J. A., 1960
Bobbit, G. H., 1938
Bobbitt, Billy M., 1967
Bobick, Erica, 1992

Bobo, C. W., 1954
Bockholt, Eugene B., 1951
Bockholt, Leo B., 1949
Bockholt, Leo B., 1971
Bockhorn, Bruce F., 1970
Bocquet, P. E., 1936
Bodecker, James R., 1971
Bodemiller, H. C., 1915
Bodin, C. L., 1935
Bodine, O. H., 1961
Bodine, S., 1968
Boedecker, Thomas Jay, 1959
Boehler, E. A., 1950
Boehm, J., 1982
Boehm, Rodney J., 1974
Boeller, Karl E., 1974
Boelscher, R. A., 1922
Boerger, Weldon, 1981
Boettcher, Ernest L., 1949
Bogart, Theodore, 1959
Bogel, G. N., 1939
Bogle, R. G., 1927
Bohlmann, W. F., 1945
Bohn, H. M., 1918
Bohot, H. R., 1957
Boles, David, 1989
Bolland, E. A., 1942
Bollinger, R., 1966
Bollinger, W. J., 1948
Bollinger, Weldon T., 1964
Bolner, Clifton, 1945
Bolton, F. C., 1930
Bond, Charles J., 1951
Bond, D. G., 1942
Bond, G. M., 1938
Bond, Kyle C., 1969
Bond, Michael, 1983
Bond, Paul, 1968
Bone, G. E., 1960
Bone, J. H., 1934
Bone, R. D., 1940
Bone, Thomas R., II, 1979
Bone, W. A., 1960
Bone, W. N., 1948
Bonewitz, Roland F., 1966
Bonin, Mike, 1979

Bonker, Dwayne, 1979
Bonner, Jason, 1992
Bonnet, Steve K., 1968
Bonno, J. D., 1944
Bonny, Bill, 1980
Booker, M. M., 1945
Boone, Charles R., 1947
Boone, K., 1967
Boone, Lloyd Bates, 1920
Boothe, Bennett, 1979
Boothe, Wesley A., 1967
Borders, Daylen, 1989
Boren, B. J., 1937
Boren, Donald F., 1957
Boren, S. R., 1954
Boren, T. M., 1931
Borgfeld, Roy H., 1944
Boring, George, 1982
Bornmann, William, 1989
Bosse, E., 1943
Boswell, Noble C., 1965
Bottlinger, David, 1989
Bouas, David, 1974
Bouldin, Brett, 1978
Bounds, J. T., 1930
Bourgeois, G. G., 1951
Bourland, A. D., 1944
Bourlon, William, 1969
Boutte, Matthew, 1993
Bowden, G. M., 1962
Bowden, Karl A., 1974
Bower, J. M., 1952
Bowers, A. D., 1964
Bowles, J. C., 1913
Bowles, J. E., 1950
Box, Brian, 1989
Box, G. P., 1924
Box, R. A., 1949
Box, R. R., 1962
Boxburgh, T. B., 1944
Boyd, Christian, 1984
Boyd, Clark, 1984
Boyd, D. A., 1951
Boyd, Dean L., 1969
Boyd, Gary Don, 1971
Boyd, J. A. E., 1956

Boyd, J. S., 1927
Boyd, John, 1983
Boyd, Lawrence, 1974
Boyd, Robert J., 1969
Boykin, E. B., 1951
Boykin, G. Lester, 1919
Boykin, J. W., 1955
Boykin, Larry, 1975
Boynton, H., 1917
Boynton, H. G., 1945
Bozardt, J. M., 1957
Bracewell, J. S., 1934
Brack, T., 1945
Brackebusch, Barry, 1987
Braden, Michael W., 1967
Braden, Russell A., 1969
Bradford, J. W., 1952
Bradford, P. W., 1960
Bradford, Walter H., 1964
Bradley, Chad, 1991
Bradley, H. K., 1959
Bradley, Scott, 1976
Bradshaw, R., 1967
Brady, D. C., 1956
Brady, J. W., 1954
Brady, James, 1962
Braeuer, H. E., 1925
Brainerd, Richard W. Jr., 1978
Brall, D., 1968
Bramley, David, 1986
Branam, David K., 1970
Brand, Roderick J., 1970
Brandon, C. E., 1940
Brandon, Gary S., 1969
Brandon, R., 1966
Brandon, Scott, 1986
Brandt, H. O., 1952
Brannin, C. P., 1906
Brannon, J. R., 1950
Branscome, B. J., 1937
Branson, D. H., 1945
Brantley, Sidney B., 1974
Branyon, David, 1983
Braswell, A., 1982
Braswell, D. B., 1966
Braswell, John B., 1956

Braswell, P. K., 1973
Braunig, D. L., 1938
Braunig, F. T., 1934
Braunig, H. J., 1962
Braunig, W. A., 1936
Bravenec, Stan, 1980
Breaux, Chris, 1980
Brecher, E. R., 1913
Brehm, A. E., 1959
Brentzel, R. J., 1937
Bres, Alfonso H., 1949
Bresnen, Kenneth C., 1966
Bretchneider, W., 1894
Brevard, R., 1967
Brewer, Greg, 1977
Brewer, Hugh W., 1971
Brewer, Jay O., 1977
Brewster, H. T., 1912
Brice, Bill B., 1966
Brice, Houston A., 1907
Bridgefarmer, J. C., 1941
Bridges, James, 1964
Bridgewater, Tom, III, 1978
Bridgwater, Terri, 1980
Brieden, John A. Jr., 1968
Briggs, Charles P., 1973
Briggs, G. S., 1953
Briggs, James, 1976
Bright, Albert G., 1969
Brightman, V. E., 1924
Brimberrry, E. L., 1942
Brindle, D., 1967
Brines, David, 1993
Brinker, Phillip W., 1967
Brinker, Scott, 1981
Brinkman, Mark, 1985
Briscoe, A. C., 1939
Briscoe, Frank, 1942
Briscoe, M., 1940
Brison, E. D., 1963
Brittain, M. E., 1955
Britton, Paul D., 1984
Broad, B. C., 1925
Brock, G. A., 1935
Brock, Stephen F., 1968
Broeder, Steven, 1990

Brogden, A. C., 1938
Brogden, J. R., 1938
Brogdon, D., 1966
Brogdon, W. B., 1950
Brooks, Barry A., 1971
Brooks, C. L., 1940
Brooks, J. M., 1936
Brooks, Jack E., 1969
Brooks, John, 1991
Brooks, Joshua, 1989
Brooks, Marcus, 1989
Brooks, Morton P., 1930
Brooks, R. P., 1958
Brooks, Randy, 1982
Broome, Larry W., 1972
Brotze, Gary H., 1962
Brouer, O. A., 1921
Broussard, Edward, 1990
Broussard, J. D., 1948
Broussard, Mike, 1987
Broussard, V. L., 1946
Browder, H., 1928
Brown, A. W., 1947
Brown, B., 1944
Brown, B. M., 1908
Brown, C. E., 1962
Brown, D. S., 1959
Brown, Dean, 1973
Brown, Dwight Jr., 1952
Brown, H. B., 1945
Brown, H. L., 1953
Brown, Harry L., 1959
Brown, J. G., 1944
Brown, J. J., 1908
Brown, Jeff, 1980
Brown, Joe, 1976
Brown, Michael, 1984
Brown, Michael, 1993
Brown, Michael, 1993
Brown, Michael D., 1973
Brown, Olin W., 1956
Brown, Paul, 1979
Brown, R., 1966
Brown, R. B., 1958
Brown, R. C., 1925
Brown, R. W., 1937

Brown, Russell, 1988
Brown, S. B., 1959
Brown, S. R., 1953
Brown, T. I., 1962
Brown, Valry, 1946
Brown, W. J., 1944
Brown, W. R., 1945
Brown, W. T., 1944
Brown, William L., 1944
Browning, Robert, 1977
Broyles, J. E., 1920
Brozovick, P., 1981
Bruemiller, Preston, 1975
Brumdrette, H. M., 1911
Brumley, Jack D., 1947
Brummett, B., 1963
Brummett, J. R., 1924
Brundrett, Bruce I., 1976
Brundrett, Gale N., 1970
Brundrett, Herald M., 1912
Brundrett, Thad, 1975
Brune, Herman, 1975
Brunner, T. D., 1954
Brush, H. C., 1962
Brustein, S. H., 1941
Bryan, A. G., 1953
Bryan, C. S., 1928
Bryan, Douglas, 1975
Bryan, F. G., 1954
Bryan, F. L., 1930
Bryan, J. T., 1942
Bryan, Jeffrey, 1988
Bryan, W.W., 1954
Bryan, William J., 1974
Bryant, Craig, 1989
Bryant, Edward, 1988
Bryant, Joe E., 1950
Bryant, John, 1991
Bryant, Kyle, 1989
Bryant, Martin E., 1973
Bryant, Ned, 1988
Bryant, Steve, 1973
Bryant, Thomas, 1993
Bubela, Larry, 1993
Buchan, Frederick Emil, 1918
Buchan, R. C., 1925

Buchanan, Mark, 1978
Buchanan, Robert H., 1947
Buchannan, William, 1969
Buck, W. F., 1941
Buckellew, William R., 1961
Buckner, Fred L., 1957
Bucy, William F., 1939
Budrewicz, William P., 1972
Buell, Gregory, 1987
Buelow, James, 1946
Buenz, N. F., 1937
Buerlot, T., 1967
Buesing, Thomas, 1973
Buford, R. E., 1954
Buie, F. P., 1917
Bulgawicz, A. H., 1962
Bullard, John, 1988
Bullock, E. L., 1959
Bullock, Jon R., 1971
Bullock, Thomas, 1942
Bumpas, Hugh Jr., 1946
Bunjes, Emil H. Jr., 1947
Bunt, William D., 1969
Bunton, W., 1950
Burba, R. F., 1957
Burch, C. Austin, 1936
Burch, G. R., 1934
Burch, Voris R., 1950
Burchart, W. B., 1940
Burda, A. P., 1948
Burg, D. R., 1959
Burgin, Jonathan, 1985
Burgoon, H. T., 1927
Burgoon, Robert L., 1960
Burke, Adrian, 1980
Burkett, J. M., 1914
Burks, R. J., 1951
Burleson, Donald C., 1963
Burleson, Travis, 1988
Burnett, David, 1991
Burnett, James T., 1962
Burnett, Martin, 1973
Burnett, Naud, 1946
Burns, D., 1913
Burns, John C., 1902
Burns, Johnny, 1977

Burns, L. T., 1927
Burr, Barry, 1983
Burrow, Laurie R. Jr., 1947
Burt, Frank Otis, 1906
Burt, F. S., 1912
Burton, Donald K., 1956
Burton, H. D., 1930
Burton, H. G., 1933
Burton, M. U., 1928
Buser, Joseph J., 1955
Buser, Samuel J., 1969
Bush, William, 1988
Bushong, G. E., 1927
Bussey, Aaron, 1985
Butaud, Milton E., 1947
Butcher, C., 1935
Butler, Brian, 1986
Butler, C. L., 1959
Butler, Chester, 1946
Butler, Clifton E., 1973
Butler, M. H., 1953
Butler, M. L., 1960
Butler, W. C., 1926
Butler, W. J., 1936
Butler, William D., 1947
Byall, A. D., 1945
Byars, W. A., 1941
Byers, Brad, 1980
Byers, John, 1979
Byers, William, 1976
Byler, H. C., 1946
Bynum, L. R., 1932
Byrd, C. O., 1952
Byrd, Christopher, 1984
Byrd, F. C., 1916
Byrom, James, 1959
Byrom, Jerald D., 1965
Byrom, T. G., 1958

Caballero, P., 1912
Cabaniss, W. M., 1936
Cackrum, Ben, 1980
Cade, K. C., 1909
Cade, William "Trey," 1983
Cadens, E., 1966
Cadle, T. L., 1959

Cadwell, Larry, 1977
Cage, J., 1966
Cage, Phillip, 1991
Cage, R., 1967
Cain, D. W., 1941
Calao, Joe, 1983
Caldwell, B. G., 1951
Caldwell, C. D., 1895
Caldwell, Larry, 1975
Caldwell, Marc T., 1985
Caldwell, Richard Hanner, 1926
Caldwell, Steve, 1974
Calhoun, D. B., 1944
Calhoun, G. H., 1955
Calkins, R.R., 1957
Callaghan, G. F., 1925
Callaghan, J. B., 1924
Callahan, Michael R., 1973
Callaway, Josh B., 1952
Callaway, L. H., 1951
Callicutt, E. C., 1904
Calloway, Steve, 1987
Calogera, E. R., 1950
Calvert, J. A., 1953
Calvillo, John, 1979
Camacho, Matthew, 1991
Cambell, B. D., 1960
Cambell, G., 1966
Cambell, Randall, 1979
Cambell, Trent, 1992
Camelet, D., 1966
Camp, J. T., 1936
Camp, S. D., 1925
Campbell, B. D., 1959
Campbell, Billie J., 1952
Campbell, C. R., 1933
Campbell, Charles W., 1970
Campbell, E. V., 1951
Campbell, Jack, 1985
Campbell, Jeff, 1988
Campbell, Jimmy R., 1949
Campbell, Randy, 1978
Campbell, Robert D., 1973
Campbell, Rusty, 1980
Campbell, Trent, 1989

Campos, Jessie, 1993
Campos, Jose, 1993
Canada, J. R., 1933
Canales, Patrick, 1984
Canan, W. L., 1950
Cangelosi, V., 1957
Canizales, Olga, 1991
Cannon, J. B., 1927
Cannon, R. S., 1954
Cano, Daniel, 1974
Canon, O. B., 1945
Cantrell, T. H., 1919
Cantrell, William, 1975
Cantu, Abel, 1990
Canuteson, Alvin C., 1931
Capps, Jack D., 1970
Caramanian, Max, 1981
Caraway, Christopher, 1984
Card, L. P., 1926
Carden, Darrell L., 1973
Cardenas, Les, 1984
Carey, E., 1935
Cargile, B. L., 1953
Cargile, J. W., 1937
Cargile, R. B., 1942
Carlisle, Thomas W., 1948
Carlson, Craig L., 1973
Carlson, Katherine, 1993
Carlson, O. G., 1922
Carlton, T. A., 1944
Carol, L. P., 1929
Carothers, W. A., 1923
Carothers, W. C., 1894
Carpenter, Brian, 1985
Carpenter, C., 1965
Carpenter, L., 1967
Carpenter, Michael A., 1971
Carpenter, N. B., 1939
Carpenter, R. E., 1959
Carpenter, Timothy E., 1969
Carpenter, W. B., 1941
Carr, J., 1945
Carr, J. D., 1961
Carranco, Carlos, 1968
Carrao, J. V., 1956
Carroll, D. F., 1949

Carroll, J. G., 1908
Carroll, J. S., 1930
Carroll, Richard, 1984
Carroll, W., 1972
Carruth, W. L., 1945
Carsey, J., 1953
Carson, B. L., 1952
Carson, C. J., 1941
Carson, David, 1975
Carson, W. W., 1912
Carter, A. S., 1949
Carter, C. G., 1948
Carter, D. C., 1963
Carter, D. R., 1944
Carter, David, 1982
Carter, G. B., 1925
Carter, J. H., 1957
Carter, Michael, 1987
Carter, Richard A., 1970
Carter, S., 1951
Carter, Tommy L., 1956
Carter, W. O., 1935
Carver, J. L., 1945
Carway, Chris, 1986
Casas, Richard B., 1971
Casher, John C., 1949
Case, Joseph, 1987
Casey, Jim, 1980
Cash, Hollis, 1989
Caster, John, 1990
Castillo, Christopher, 1974
Castleberry, E., 1935
Caston, J. C., 1955
Catanach, Arthur W., 1946
Cates, C. A., 1926
Caton, John D., 1985
Catron, J. D., 1925
Catterson, Ed, 1977
Caudle, Gregory, 1991
Caudle, Michael E., 1965
Caughlin, W. C., 1945
Cave, Brice, 1988
Cavitt, George P., 1946
Cecil, Paul F., 1974
Cervenka, B. G., 1962
Cervenka, Landis, 1966

Cervenka, Lee R., 1949
Chalker, Daniel, 1978
Chamberlain, D. H., 1959
Chamberlain, Harold B., 1932
Chamberlain, N. F., 1935
Chamberlain, R. B., 1952
Chamberlain, William C., 1967
Chambers, C. L., 1940
Chambers, Edward A., 1970
Chambers, J. T., 1910
Chanceller, W. W., 1935
Chandler, Clarence R., 1957
Chandler, J. N., 1923
Chandler, Paul, 1982
Chandler, Randy, 1983
Chandler, S. P., 1914
Chaney, F. H., 1950
Chapman, Carroll B., 1949
Chapman, Dennis, 1962
Chapman, J. B., 1951
Chapman, K. T., 1939
Chapman, K. W., 1953
Chappell, R. J. Jr., 1937
Charles, H. L., 1944
Charlesworth, C. T., 1896
Chase, Mike, 1978
Chastain, J. N., 1928
Chastain, Wayne, 1993
Chatham, E. B. Jr., 1940
Chatmas, J. C., 1933
Chavez, Ruben, 1984
Cheaney, F. H. Jr., 1949
Cheek, Katherine, 1992
Chenoweth, Keith, 1988
Chenault, R. E., 1932
Cheney, R. E., 1933
Cherry, D. D., 1941
Cherry, William Paul, 1959
Cheshire, David, 1983
Chesser, J. D., 1952
Chilcoat, W. M., 1917
Childers, David, 1992
Childers, Derek, 1977
Childress, Raymond, 1969
Childs, Stephen, 1977
Chilton, Donald, 1976

Chilton, Russell, 1983
Chinske, Jesse D., 1968
Chitty, H. C., 1963
Chowning, C. H., 1920
Chrismer, Donald, 1975
Christian, Lawrence W., 1958
Christian, P., 1935
Christopher, William W., 1968
Church, Christopher, 1987
Church, W. G., 1909
Chvatal, L. A., 1955
Chvatal, James, 1984
Cisneros, Henry G., 1964
Cisneros, Robert, 1978
Clader, M. D., 1964
Clader, Timothy J., 1970
Clampffer, Blake, 1989
Clardy, Carl D., 1925
Clark, Andrew, 1992
Clark, Dawson, 1980
Clark, Dick, 1973
Clark, G. W., 1939
Clark, Jack P., 1925
Clark, Jason, 1978
Clark, Jeff, 1975
Clark, John, 1979
Clark, L. E., 1945
Clark, Lance, 1990
Clark, Mitchell, 1983
Clark, R. E., 1951
Clark, Richard A., 1972
Clark, Robert J., 1974
Clark, S. W., 1910
Clark, T. A., 1940
Clark, W. E., 1953
Clarke, John, 1978
Clarke, Julius, 1937
Clarke, L. E., 1944
Clarke, R. E., 1950
Clarke, Robert Jr., 1977
Clary, J. C., 1934
Clary, R. W., 1915
Clay, A. W., 1937
Clay, Herbert L., 1960
Clay, R. W., 1936
Claybourn, Clifton H., 1947

Clayton, Jack L., 1942
Clayton, R. Lee, 1968
Clayton, Robert Lee, 1917
Clayton, W., 1895
Clegg, A., 1968
Clem, Tommy G., 1970
Clement, C. B., 1910
Clements, B. H., 1941
Clements, J., 1981
Clements, J. R., 1944
Clements, Mike, 1980
Clements, R. B., 1945
Clements, T. H. Jr., 1897
Cleveland, W. C., 1962
Cliett, J. Q., 1957
Clifford, E. I., 1960
Clifford, N. M., 1958
Clifton, James D. Jr., 1974
Clifton, Ron, 1982
Cline, W. P., 1920
Clines, H. H., 1959
Clines, S., 1981
Clinton, S. J., 1951
Close, Fred R., 1969
Close, Michael J., 1974
Closner, G. W., 1937
Closner, J. J. Jr., 1932
Clothier, F. M., 1956
Cloud, Gay G., 1953
Cloud, Jay G., 1953
Cloud, Matthew, 1990
Cloud, W. G., 1921
Clune, Patrick, 1988
Clutter, B. A. Jr., 1927
Coale, M., 1981
Coats, Douglas B., 1975
Coats, M., 1982
Cobb, C. L., 1945
Cobb, E. R., 1942
Cobb, J. D., 1946
Cobolini, J. A., 1902
Cobolini, J. L., 1902
Cocanougher, C. M., 1949
Coch, J. R., 1958
Cocherham, W. H., 1954
Cochran, B. B., 1919

Cochran, D. M., 1942
Cochran, J. L., 1941
Cochran, Les D., 1952
Cochrcham, F. C., 1915
Cockerell, Rex A., 1971
Cockerham, William H., 1953
Cockerman, J. H., 1956
Cockrell, Bedford F., 1959
Cockrell, J., 1950
Cockrum, B., 1981
Coddou, Joseph W., 1946
Coereham, G. C., 1916
Coffman, D. H., 1937
Coffman, V. Y., 1919
Cogburn, Ronald, 1973
Cogle, R. G., 1926
Cogswell, J. W., 1942
Cohn, S. L., 1896
Coil, Carl L., 1967
Coiston, J. E., 1954
Coker, Billy F., 1947
Coker, Joel, 1987
Coker, K. R., 1936
Coker, Kyle, 1969
Coker, L. C., 1945
Coker, R. W., 1956
Cole, Charles, 1975
Cole, Dillon, 1954
Cole, N. V., 1939
Cole, W. S., 1942
Coleman, E. A., 1926
Coleman, J.D., 1950
Coleman, Samara, 1993
Collier, Curt, 1979
Collier, P. B., 1955
Collier, Robert G., 1972
Collier, W. J., 1927
Colling, Phil, 1980
Collingsworth, J., 1937
Collins, B., 1957
Collins, B. C., 1962
Collins, Charles "Chuck," 1984
Collins, Chris, 1986
Collins, George, 1977
Collins, Jennifer, 1992
Collins, Joe, 1978

Collins, Orin Russell, 1969
Collins, Robert, 1955
Collins, T. H., 1938
Collins, W. A., 1938
Collins, William, 1972
Collinsworth, Chester H. Jr.,
  1957
Collons, R. D., 1953
Collum, C. L., 1941
Colston, Daniel, 1991
Colwell, Dennis, 1992
Comley, Michael L., 1972
Compton, C. Reed, 1917
Compton, Curtis, 1984
Conally, W. L., 1926
Conant, C. M., 1959
Condeck, Wayne, 1978
Cone, Patrick L., 1971
Confoy, Joseph, 1977
Conger, Edward, 1977
Conine, B., 1945
Conlee, W. J., 1939
Conlon, Bryan, 1992
Connally, A. J., 1945
Connally, James F., 1967
Connally, T., 1953
Connally, W. L., 1924
Connell, Clint L., 1982
Connelley, Todd, 1986
Conner, Patrick, 1975
Conner, R. R., 1926
Conner, R. W., 1955
Conner, Steve, 1968
Connoley, J. T., 1951
Connolly, Craig, 1980
Connolly, D., 1953
Connolly, Dan, 1986
Connolly, Jule T., 1951
Contreras, Bianca, 1991
Conway, R. Shaw, III, 1962
Conway, Richard Y., 1949
Coody, J. R., 1928
Cook, Allen, 1979
Cook, Bryan Ray, 1976
Cook, Charles Allen, 1981
Cook, D. W., 1961

Cook, Harold Edwin, 1961
Cook, J. F., 1952
Cook, J. G., 1935
Cook, J. L., 1948
Cook, Lane, 1987
Cook, R. J., 1936
Cook, Robert, 1979
Cook, W. B., 1942
Cook, W. H., 1923
Cook, W. M., 1953
Cooke, D. H., 1958
Cooke, Russell, 1976
Cooksey, Edward, 1954
Cooley, Paul, 1989
Coombes, Jimmie L., 1958
Coon, R. W., 1945
Cooper, A. H., 1948
Cooper, Edwin H., 1949
Cooper, F. A., 1914
Cooper, J. B., 1944
Cooper, J. B., 1952
Cooper, Joseph, 1977
Cooper, Kenneth W., 1949
Cooper, R., 1966
Cooper, T. J., 1957
Cope, H. D., 1962
Copeland, E. H., 1938
Copley, Don W., 1957
Coppedge, J. L., 1906
Coquet, L. J., 1934
Corbell, Wayman K., 1947
Corbet, H., 1968
Corbett, Chad, 1985
Corbett, John, 1969
Corder, Jeff, 1981
Corder, R., 1966
Corder, Richard, 1970
Cordero, Richard, 1973
Cordes, Alfred H. Jr., 1952
Corey, Chris E., 1971
Corey, Douglas, 1965
Cornak, David, 1988
Corneille, W., 1967
Cornelius, Guillory, 1978
Cornell, Clifton C., 1983
Cornett, L. Anthony, 1976

Cornwall, J. Michael, 1953
Coronis, P. J., 1950
Corso, Tony, 1968
Corte, Frank, 1978
Cortez, E., 1960
Cory, Chris E., 1969
Cory, Doug, 1971
Cory, L. R., 1953
Cossett, R. B., 1940
Costen, Andy, 1980
Costen, John N., 1971
Costen, Peter A., 1973
Costillo, Christopher, 1973
Cottingham, C. B., 1961
Cotton, H., 1896
Couch, James R. Jr., 1957
Couey, R. H., 1941
Coulson, C. K., 1933
Coulson, D. R., 1959
Coultas, A., 1898
Coumbe, Walter B., 1975
Courim, R., 1957
Court, Frank, 1980
Courtin, Pat E., 1949
Courtney, B. H., 1937
Cousins, M. V., 1917
Cousins, R. W., 1898
Covey, R. H., 1940
Covington, H. B., 1933
Cowan, D. B., 1960
Cowan, James A., 1952
Cowan, P., 1945
Cowles, A. W., 1935
Cox, Albert G., 1957
Cox, C. H., 1938
Cox, E., 1981
Cox, G. A., 1956
Cox, G. B., 1937
Cox, G. W., 1932
Cox, Gary L., 1968
Cox, H. D., 1957
Cox, H. M., 1935
Cox, J. C., 1963
Cox, John J., 1990
Cox, L. M., 1952
Cox, Leonard C., 1971

Cox, Thomas, 1983
Cox, Thomas Arthur, 1967
Cox, W. W., 1919
Coy, Anton E., 1957
Coyle, J., 1967
Cozad, Brian, 1975
Crabbe, James, 1952
Crabtree, Frank Jr., 1958
Craddock, Joe P., 1956
Crafton, Walter P., 1970
Craig, Peter, 1987
Craig, Roger, 1965
Craig, William, 1992
Cramer, A. C., 1932
Cramer, M. B., 1933
Cranford, J. U., 1933
Crausbay, F. V., 1925
Cravey, D. O., 1945
Crawford, B. T., 1959
Crawford, J. C., 1918
Crawford, J. H., 1937
Crawford, J. N., 1962
Crawford, R. M., 1928
Crecy, Bruce, 1980
Creech, David Lee, 1960
Creider, E. G., 1962
Crews, Raymond, 1984
Crews, S. H., 1932
Crider, C. R., 1960
Crippen, W., 1917
Crislip, James Lynn, 1970
Crisp, A. S., 1920
Criswell, James W., 1964
Criswell, R. M., 1939
Crites, W. J., 1962
Crittenden, R. N., 1942
Crocker, George W., 1947
Crocker, J. R., 1964
Crockett, Dale R., 1983
Cromack, F. D., 1924
Cron, L. E., 1936
Croneberger, P. C., 1960
Crook, Bryan R., 1973
Crook, Don R., 1949
Crook, F. J., 1957
Crook, James R., 1955

Crook, James Jr., 1988
Crooker, Bruce W., 1969
Crosser, R. E., 1945
Crosswell, R. M., 1938
Crouch, J. R., 1953
Crouch, Pat K., 1958
Crouch, Zac M., 1986
Crow, Donny, 1990
Crow, G. C., 1913
Crow, S. D., 1959
Crowder, Kenneth, 1988
Crowe, James B., 1966
Crowley, J. B., 1959
Crown, Jeffery N., 1964
Crum, J. Y., 1953
Crump, J., 1966
Crutchfield, James C., III, 1960
Cude, G. A., 1954
Culberson, Jack, 1943
Culberson, O. L., 1939
Culhane, Brian, 1980
Cullers, E. W., 1936
Cullison, James E., 1974
Cullison, Steve, 1976
Culver, D., 1904
Cummings, Bruce, 1975
Cummings, David, 1976
Cummings, David, 1993
Cummings, William Bryan, 1973
Cunningham, C. L., 1932
Cunningham, Gerald W., 1944
Cunningham, T. A., 1960
Cunningham, Winston, 1976
Curd, Michael T., 1965
Curington, Dale, 1981
Currie, A. T., 1954
Curry, G. W., 1923
Curry, James, 1977
Curry, R. H., 1960
Curtino, Joseph A. Jr., 1947
Cusick, Keri, 1992
Cyrier, John, 1991

Dahlberg, F. L., 1954
Dahlgren, J. A., 1902

Dahlgren, C. B., 1910
Dahlich, J., 1895
Dahmberg, F. L., 1955
Dally, Robert W., 1973
Dammann, Jim R., 1966
Damsheen, Gerald, 1975
D'Amura, Chris, 1990
Daniel, Matt, 1989
Daniell, David, 1955
Daniels, E. J., 1959
Dantzler, J. E., 1953
Darden, Jack M., III, 1964
Darden, Kim M., 1966
Darden, Marshall Jr., 1970
Darley, R. G., 1958
Darville, R. Wayne, 1951
Davenport, Henry Swanson, 1903
Davenport, Michael, 1983
David, Brian, 1983
David, K. W., 1955
David, P. C., 1935
Davidson, A. L., 1954
Davidson, A. R., 1928
Davidson, Charles Eugene, 1917
Davidson, E. H., 1935
Davidson, F. T., 1946
Davidson, H. A., 1959
Davidson, James R., 1963
Davidson, John, 1992
Davidson, Mark, 1987
Davidson, Stephen, 1990
Davidson, Thomas A., 1974
Davidson, Troy, 1990
Davis, B., 1981
Davis, Bobby, 1992
Davis, Bob W., 1956
Davis, Brian, 1984
Davis, C. E., 1959
Davis, Craig, 1988
Davis, D., 1981
Davis, D. R., 1955
Davis, David R., 1968
Davis, F. C., 1924
Davis, Gary W., 1968

Davis, Gesna B., 1969
Davis, H. P., 1947
Davis, J., 1944
Davis, J. W., 1926
Davis, James B., 1963
Davis, Jeffery S., 1973
Davis, John F. Jr., 1981
Davis, Larry D., 1971
Davis, M., 1966
Davis, Mike, 1981
Davis, P. C., 1934
Davis, R. J., 1944
Davis, R. M., 1951
Davis, Robert, 1991
Davis, Roy, 1987
Davis, S. F., 1911
Davis, Scott, 1974
Davis, Scott, 1978
Davis, T. W., 1948
Davis, W. G., 1930
Davis, W. L., 1942
Davis, W. O., 1937
Davis, W. R., 1906
Davis, Wilson, 1924
Davison, C. E., 1918
Davison, Michael, 1990
Daws, William E., 1970
Dawson. P. P., 1949
Dawson, W. L., 1955
Day, Glen, 1986
Day, M., 1965
Day, W. C., 1956
Day, William, 1980
Deahl, W. A., 1939
Deakins, Frederik, 1989
Dealy, B., 1946
Dean, Alan A., 1970
Dean, C. V., 1952
Dean, O. G., 1939
Dean, Randy, 1980
Dean, Raymond Jr., 1941
Dean, Robert O., 1940
Dearing, R. M., 1932
Debnam, M. M., 1925
Debrecht, Doug, 1983
December, G. W., 1953

D'Echaux, H., 1894
Dees, James, 1976
De Garmo, E. B., 1936
Degelia, John, 1976
Dehl, Stanley G., 1973
Deitel, E. A., 1923
Deithloff, J. A., 1954
Delafosse, Floyd D., 1969
Delahanty, Jim, 1985
Delamater, Patrick, 1983
Delaney, Dennis, 1979
Del Bosque, Fernando, 1989
Delgado, Roger, 1980
De Lee, H. E., 1920
De Leon, Miguel, 1993
De Los Santos, Carlos, 1985
DeLuna, Kuri, 1989
DeMieri, Peter, 1987
Demke, D. D., 1937
Dempster, R. E., 1961
Dendy, C. S., 1960
Dendy, John, 1986
Denison, J. S., 1957
Dennis, A., 1966
Dennis, F. H., 1934
Dennis J. R., 1940
Dennis James R., 1971
Dennis, T., 1967
Dennis, Theodore, 1983
Dennison, C. A., 1951
Dennison, J. S., 1957
Denny, B. L., 1946
Densmore, Ralph A., 1911
Densmore, Robert E., 1911
Denton, Bruce, 1969
Denton, Murray B., 1953
Derman, M. M., 1924
De Roma, Silas, 1981
Derrington, Chris, 1992
Derryberry, G. A., 1933
Deutsch, Miklos, 1947
Devaney, D. B., 1959
De Villeneuve, Allan, 1961
De Villeneuve, Scott, 1988
Dew, Gregory A., 1976
Dew, Raleigh E., 1956

DeWeese, L. W., 1930
DeWeese, Richard M., 1973
Dexter, J. N., 1948
Dextraze, Edward, 1985
Dial, B. E., 1962
Diaz, Frank Jr., 1971
Diaz, H., 1982
Dibble, R., 1926
Dick, Erin, 1992
Dickens, R. G., 1944
Dickenson, Christopher, 1993
Dickerson, C. J., 1935
Dickey, Billy R., 1951
Dickinson, William H., 1927
Dickson, Brandon, 1992
Diedenhofen, John, 1986
Dietel, E. A., 1924
Dietert, Brandon, 1992
Dietrich, J., 1966
Digiacinto, Darren, 1992
Dillard, Joseph L., 1949
Dilley, Douglas S., 1969
Dillin, W. S., 1934
Dillon, E. M., 1934
Dillon, J. E., 1928
Dillon, Robert E., 1913
Dillon, Robert M., 1958
Dillon, W. E., 1960
Dillon, W. S., 1934
Dindy, C. S., 1960
Dinger, William, 1965
Dinsmore, J., 1936
Dixon, J. G., 1932
Dixon, William S., 1944
Doak, Joseph, 1945
Dobbs, Charley Jr., 1943
Dobbs, R. A., 1942
Docherty, Ken, 1981
Dockum, C. R., 1922
Dockum, Oscar L., 1918
Dockum, R. S., 1927
Dodd, B. A., 1921
Dodd, Bill, 1980
Dodd, C. C., 1916
Dodd, C. E., 1910
Dodd, G. C., 1912

Dodson, A. W., 1958
Dodson, C. P., 1908
Dodson, D. B., 1959
Dodson, David, 1974
Dodson, Giles L., 1957
Dodson, John David, 1976
Dodson, Larry, 1977
Doebele, Brian, 1993
Doering, Shayne, 1979
Doerr, H. L. F., 1936
Doggett, V. G., 1941
Doidge, Ken, 1983
Dolan, Michael E., 1967
Dominguez, C., 1966
Dommenge, Jeff, 1991
Dommert, Stephen, 1989
Donak, Jerry W., 1972
Donald, Randy T., 1971
Donaldson, Curtis, 1977
Donlin, C. P., 1948
Donnally, Dan, 1985
Donnell, Jeff, 1986
Donnell, L. E., 1958
Dorman, James, 1992
Dornak, David, 1986
Dornak, Jerome W., 1969
Dornak, K., 1981
Dornbusch, John F., 1951
Dorotik, J. A., 1958
Dorris, G. J., 1944
Dorris, William "Buster," 1975
Dorsey, J. W., 1922
Dorsey, Ronald B., 1968
Doss, R. P., 1939
Dotson, Gary, 1980
Dotson, John D., 1974
Douglas, C. W., 1952
Douglass, G. M., 1913
Douglass, Gene Jr., 1961
Douglass, Mark, 1986
Douphrate, William, 1951
Douthit, J. D., 1950
Dover, T. W., 1945
Downey, Russell, 1986
Downs, Garrick, 1993
Downs, Jarrett, 1988

Downs, L. H., 1924
Doyle, J., 1966
Doyle, J. F., 1930
Doyle, Patrick, 1978
Drago, R. L. Jr., 1947
Drake, Jerome E., 1949
Drake, L. L., 1951
Draper, Douglas, 1987
Drescher, K., 1968
Dreyer, M. H., 1928
Drozd, Kenneth L., 1970
Dubard, F. L., 1945
Dube, Mark, 1980
DuBois, C. N., 1932
DuBose, Chris, 1980
Dubose, Emmett Jr., 1975
DuBose, James, 1976
Duckworth, William H., 1935
Duderstadt, Perry, 1991
Dudley, Marcus G., 1971
Dudley, Michael T., 1968
Duffer, D. D., 1941
Duffield, R. F., 1926
Dugan, Jerry S., 1948
Duggan, T. B., 1894
Duke, Jim R., 1945
Duke, M. E., 1951
Dulaney, P. S., 1940
DuMar, Aaron, 1990
Dumas, Christopher, 1977
Dunavant, Eric, 1991
Dunaway, D., 1981
Duncan, D. E., 1963
Duncan, Dean, 1953
Duncan, John G., 1971
Duncan, John P., 1952
Duncan, Richard W., 1972
Duncan, William D., 1959
Dungan, A. L., 1953
Dunham, T. R., 1944
Dunks, P. A., 1905
Dunlap, A. W., 1957
Dunlap, D., 1965
Dunlap, D., 1981
Dunlap, Dale R., 1969
Dunlap, David, 1979

Dunlap, Donald D., 1954
Dunlap, R. E., 1964
Dunlap, Wayne A., 1947
Dunlevitz, H. S., 1945
Dunn, E. S., 1945
Dunn, J. C., 1951
Dunn, James D. Jr., 1967
Dunn, James M., 1949
Dunn, Jeffrey D., 1971
Dunn, M. C., 1941
Dunn, R. J., 1945
Duplissey, Keith, 1988
Dupree, T. E., 1928
Dupree, Russell, 1963
Duree, J. T., 1937
Duree, Samuel M., 1947
Durham, H. L., 1950
Durham, Wayne, 1936
Durkiss, D., 1982
Durst, L. H., 1909
Dusek, Daniel, 1978
Dutton, Jim M., 1968
Dutton, T. O., 1960
Duvall, V. M., 1949
Dye, John R., 1968
Dyer, C., 1959
Dyer, R. C., 1906
Dyer, Stanley P., 1973
Dyer, W. F., 1897
Dyson, L. R., 1964

Eads, R., 1935
Eads, Richard C., 1965
Eagleston, C. M. C., 1912
Eargle, Robert Grey, 1921
Earl, James A., IV, 1974
Earl, W. J., 1958
Early, Allen M., 1930
Easley, J. T., 1959
Easley, Ray K., 1917
Eason, J. R., 1944
Eastham, H. C., 1936
Easton, F. E., 1961
Eastwood, J. C., 1920
Eaton, D. A., 1956
Eaton, Russell, 1976

Eaves, C. C., 1936
Eberspacher, F., 1902
Eberspacher, L., 1939
Eberspacher, R., 1897
Eccard, Lawrence D., 1964
Echols, J. D., 1950
Eckert, Charles, 1946
Eckert, J. E., 1941
Eckert, William R., 1956
Eckhart, L. B., 1959
Eckles, William E., 1924
Eddleman, H. G., 1915
Edelman, Matt, 1993
Edelstein, Arthur, 1945
Edgecomb, Robert L., 1956
Edmonds, F. R., 1930
Edsell, John, 1989
Edwards, C. J., 1924
Edwards, G. R., 1945
Edwards, Joe W., 1923
Edwards, Lloyd, 1980
Edwards, M. S., 1956
Edwards, Michael, 1977
Edwards, Robin, 1977
Egglestron, M. A., 1953
Eichenour, Roger, 1989
Eichenrot, Steven L., 1979
Eichman, Frank F., 1952
Eicke, Jason, 1988
Eisenhart, Donald, 1980
Eitel, Billy B., 1956
Elder, G. P., 1935
Elder, I. J., 1927
Elenberg, Dave, 1959
Eliphant, Eric, 1992
Elkins, Aubrey C. Jr., 1957
Elkins, Irvin E., 1944
Elkins, N., 1966
Elkins, R. L., 1930
Eller, David G., 1955
Eller, James M., 1949
Ellerbrock, F. J., 1941
Ellerbrock, Joseph, 1974
Ellerbrock, William W., 1940
Ellington, Dan H., 1952
Elliot, Joseph, 1976

Elliott, Arthur L., 1921
Elliott, F. B. "Ben," 1936
Ellis, H. V., 1954
Ellis, J., 1981
Ellis, J. D., 1933
Ellis, Laurence, 1981
Ellis, Robert C., 1962
Ellisor, C. C., 1957
Ellisor, Grover C., 1948
Ellisor, James W., 1958
Elmore, L. T., 1925
Elmore, Travis E., 1968
Elmore, William E., 1947
Elmquist, Michael, 1993
Elrod, Dan, 1978
Elrod, T., 1951
Elson, M. M. Jr., 1933
Elwell, H. H., 1937
Emanuel, Walter Jr., 1956
Emmons, M. E., 1964
Emshoff, Glen, 1981
England, Arnold L., 1970
Englebert, Allen, 1979
Englebrecht, K., 1959
Engler, John, 1993
English, W. C., 1942
Engwell, Darrel, 1984
Enlow, B., 1967
Enmon, Glen, 1946
Enney, T. J., 1959
Enochs, W. A., 1944
Epperly, E. M., 1922
Eppinette, Stephen, 1992
Epps, Jim E., 1982
Epstein, S. G., 1904
Erck, A. W., 1936
Erck, C. C., 1946
Erickson, A., 1965
Erickson, David, 1987
Ermis, Kevin, 1990
Ernst, H., 1919
Erskine, Clark T., 1965
Ertle, Lori, 1992
Erwin, Jeffrey M., 1973
Eschbach, Brian, 1993
Esley, J., 1982

Esmond, Howard, 1979
Esselburn, Tom, 1977
Estes, Clifford H., 1940
Estes, Ivan G., 1962
Estes, Richard T., 1973
Estrada, Glenn, 1981
Ethridge, Bobby, 1980
Eustace, Laura, 1991
Evanoff, Nicolas, 1980
Evanoff, Stefan, 1987
Evans, Adam, 1993
Evans, B., 1953
Evans, Bethal, III, 1971
Evans, Christi, 1989
Evans, Curtis, 1978
Evans, E. C., 1902
Evans, J. A., 1955
Evans, John D., 1970
Evans, L. K., 1953
Evans, Lewis H., 1970
Evans, Murray, 1938
Evans, Paul, 1984
Evans, R. E., 1956
Evans, W. M., 1954
Evans, W. R., 1952
Everett, Malcolm O., 1970
Ewing, Hunter H., 1935

Faber, B. H., 1911
Fagan, Clifford, 1976
Fain, Bruce F., 1976
Fairbanks, Hardy, 1980
Fairbanks, Robert, 1980
Fallin, J. E., 1955
Fallin, N. Jr., 1954
Falls, J. L., 1956
Fannette, Aladan, 1990
Farley, A. R., 1959
Farlow, John R., 1952
Farmer, James E., 1948
Farmer, Larry, 1966
Farmer, Larry W., 1972
Farr, R. S., 1897
Farrar, Thomas, 1984
Farrington, David E., 1956
Faseler, S., 1981

Faterkowski, Kenneth, 1993
Faubion, M., 1966
Faucette, Robert C., 1973
Faudy, Fayze, 1944
Faught, A. H., 1904
Faulk, H. G., 1940
Faulkner, Frank, 1966
Faulkner, J., 1982
Faust, W., 1895
Faw, Stephen, 1988
Feagan, R., 1966
Feagin, Frank Joe, 1930
Fehler, Edward, 1964
Feldman, H. J., 1942
Felmmons, Kacy, 1992
Feltz, D. E., 1951
Fennald, W. F., 1961
Fenton, M. E., 1961
Fereday, B. E., 1948
Fergus, David L., 1971
Fergus, Mark V., 1966
Ferguson, A. O., 1953
Ferguson, G. Woody, 1940
Ferguson, J. L., 1956
Ferguson, J. N., 1896
Ferguson, R., 1968
Ferguson, Robert A., 1976
Ferhart, Rob, 1975
Fernald, William R., 1961
Fernandez, Guy J., 1952
Ferrell, Dennis, 1971
Ferrell, L. C., 1939
Ferrell, Mark, 1975
Ferris, George P., 1971
Ferris, John, 1990
Fess, D. W., 1955
Fest, Stephen E., 1963
Feuerbacher, David, 1989
Feuerbacher, Kirk, 1989
Fickey, L. T., 1951
Field, Albert F., 1946
Field, E. A., 1940
Field, John, II, 1977
Fielder, R. L., 1946
Fields, Charles, 1977
Fields, Eugene, 1942

Fields, H., 1981

Fields, J. W., 1948

Fields, John, 1980

Fields, Robert L., 1975

Fields, Scott, 1986

Figueroa, Pete, 1991

Files, Stephen B., 1968

Files, W. Frank, 1970

Fimble, C. W., 1956

Fimble, David, 1990

Fink, W. L., 1960

Finkelstein, Leon, 1930

Finkleman, Gary, 1979

Finkler, J. T., 1944

Finley, Jimmy C., 1958

Finley, W. K., 1937

Finn, J. W., 1961

Finney, John F. Jr., 1951

Finney, Roy, 1986

Fischer, Alfred O., 1938

Fischer, Donald L., 1968

Fischer, Heidi, 1988

Fischer, Jeffrey, 1975

Fischer, Maurice D., 1958

Fischer, R. C., 1950

Fischer, R. M., 1918

Fischer, Richard, 1977

Fischer, Richard H., 1953

Fischer, Robert E., 1969

Fischer, Rodney, 1974

Fischer, Stephan, 1984

Fischer, Tut, 1978

Fischer, Walter D., 1967

Fish, Edward W., 1952

Fisher, A. O., 1939

Fisher, D., 1968

Fisher, D. C., 1946

Fisher, Duke, 1991

Fisher, H. M., 1952

Fisher, Jeff, 1975

Fisher, Patrick, 1987

Fisher, R. C., 1948

Fisher, R. M., 1919

Fisher, Richard, 1978

Fisher, Robert L., 1970

Fisher, Rodney, 1975

Fitzgerald, Daryl, 1977

Fitzgerald, Willie L., 1970

Fitzpatrick, Patrick, 1975

Flanagan, A. C., 1951

Flaniken, F. M., 1937

Flatt, Clint, 1987

Fleitman, Don, 1982

Fleitman, James, 1987

Fleitman, Mike, 1981

Fleming, Evan L., 1969

Fletcher, C. M., 1952

Fletcher, K., 1974

Fletcher, Ken, 1983

Flocke, Robert A., 1964

Floore, E. L., 1937

Florence, David M., 1952

Flores, Anthony H., 1944

Flores, Joe, 1979

Flores, Octavio E., 1950

Flores, Roger, 1987

Flowers, J., 1951

Flowers, Jeffrey D., 1984

Floyd, Ben, 1991

Floyd, Brad, 1992

Fluker, Thomas S., 1946

Fly, Robert P., 1944

Flynt, J., 1966

Focke, John, III, 1965

Focke, J. H., 1937

Foerster, A. E., 1954

Folbre, F. S., 1953

Foley, J., 1965

Follis, John, 1983

Follis, William, 1987

Folmar, David, 1993

Folton, Mark, 1987

Fomby, D. P., 1955

Fong, Harry M., 1967

Fonteno, Michael R., 1972

Foote, V. A., 1930

Foran, William J., 1937

Ford, Cecil, III, 1986

Ford, Cleve, 1993

Ford, Creed L., 1948

Ford, Kimberlie, 1993

Ford, L., 1953

Ford, Rance, 1992

Ford, Ryan, 1993

Foreman, Walter "Skip," 1985

Foretich, R. B., 1952

Forney, Bruce, 1942

Forney, Mark, 1967

Forrest, H. L., 1941

Forshee, Ronald Jr., 1947

Forste, F. P., 1944

Forston, B. W., 1942

Forsythe, William, 1944

Fort, M. G., 1940

Fortson, B. W., 1943

Foshee, Ronald E., 1947

Foster, Kyle, 1983

Foster, L. R., 1951

Foster, R. J., 1942

Foster, Russ, 1984

Foster, Stephen, 1989

Foster, Todd, 1991

Foulk, A. R., 1951

Fowler, J. G., 1962

Fowler, N. D., 1944

Fowler, Wayne, 1983

Fox, Donald, 1978

Fox, R. L., 1934

Fox, Sean, 1981

Fox, Steven, 1981

Foxworth, L., 1966

Foy, Bryan, 1977

Foy, Dana Ray, 1974

Foy, H. F. Jr., 1904

Foy, Stephen, 1979

Fraga, Daniel, 1976

Fraiser, John, 1983

Fraley, Michael, 1979

Frame, B., 1946

Frame, William De Vere, 1918

Francis, A. J., 1908

Francis, J. W., 1914

Francis, K., 1966

Francis, Kirk W., 1973

Frank, John H., 1959

Franke, Leland B., 1983

Franklin, B., 1956

Franklin, Chad, 1992

Franklin, J. E., 1955
Franklin, Leland Jr., 1968
Franklin, Levi Jr., 1984
Franklin, Theodore, 1987
Franz, James F., 1951
Fraser, John W., 1959
Frasley, Mike, 1980
Frauenheim, Larry, 1991
Frazier, Marshall, 1981
Frazier, Robert, 1975
Frederickson, Knude C., 1948
Freeman, A., 1964
Freeman, C. D., 1959
Freeman, Charles H., 1960
Freeman, J., 1946
Freeman, J., 1961
Freeman, J. S., 1956
Freeman, R., 1966
Freeman, R. S., 1944
Freeman, Robert A., 1972
Freeman, William, III, 1970
Freeman, William C., 1967
Freemeyer, Mark, 1984
Freitag, Derwood J., 1969
Fremming, Richard A., 1947
French, L. Rene, 1968
Fresca, Steve, 1980
Frey, Brian, 1977
Frey, Walter, 1930
Frieburg, J. L., 1942
Friedrich, A. L., 1956
Friedrich, Don H., 1953
Friemel, G. J., 1946
Frierson, Ervin Eugene, 1947
Frietag, D., 1968
Friley, C. E., 1910
Friley, C. E., 1931
Frome, W. D., 1917
Fruman, Mark, 1976
Fryar, Wilson, 1966
Fugger, E. F., 1960
Fulgham, George S., 1950
Fuller, J. R., 1919
Fuller, Stephen A., 1972
Fuller, William G. Jr., 1966
Fullwood, C. E., 1962

Fulton, George W., 1935
Fulton, Mark, 1985
Funke, Robert, 1976
Funn, Roam A., 1970
Furgueron, J. D., 1950
Furman, M. E., 1920
Furness, John, 1991
Furney, Mark A., 1969
Fuschak, Kim, 1980
Fuselier, Joseph, 1990

Gabriel, Kacey, 1990
Gaeke, Robert G., 1970
Gage, Phillip, 1990
Gager, D. L., 1960
Gaida, E. M., 1934
Gaines, H. C., 1922
Gaines, M. E., 1951
Gaines, R. H., 1921
Gaines, Robert V., 1972
Gaither, Timothy P., 1976
Gallaher, Richard, 1983
Gallimore, L. D., 1964
Gallomore, Jeff, 1987
Galloway, B. G., 1954
Galloway, F. C., 1943
Galloway, G. G., 1942
Galloway, Guy, 1987
Galloway, J. D., 1944
Galloway, Robert E., 1972
Galpin, James, 1993
Galvin, Daniel L., 1960
Galvin, Larry J., 1971
Galvin, Raymond E., 1949
Galvin, T. J., 1951
Galzener, Keith, 1976
Gamble, Arthur, m, 1979
Gamble, N. D., 1955
Gamertsfelder, Joe, 1988
Gamez, Jose, 1989
Gandara, Joseph, 1983
Gandy, Jason, 1993
Gandy, L. M., 1926
Gant, G., 1968
Gantt, R., 1982
Garb, Forrest, 1947

Garbade, C. J., 1896
Garbee, Thomas, 1985
Garber, John, 1991
Garcia, Arthur G., 1984
Garcia, Bobby L., 1973
Garcia, Gavin, 1984
Garcia, J., 1961
Garcia, Jeff, 1991
Garcia, Joseph, 1992
Garcia, L. R., 1951
Garcia, Leonard R., 1969
Garcia, Lionel G., 1952
Garcia, Rafael, 1992
Garcia, Ray, 1989
Garcia, Richard, 1984
Garcia, Richard R., 1969
Garcia, Steven, 1987
Garcia, Veronica, 1991
Gardenas, Alfred H., 1947
Gardenour, Rusty, 1991
Gardner, J. B., 1933
Gardner, Mark, 1981
Gardner, N. E., 1913
Gardner, O. C., 1937
Gardner, T. H., 1963
Gardner, William W., 1943
Garibald, J. B., 1951
Gamer, A. M., 1950
Gamer, C. C., 1940
Garner, David A., 1974
Garner, Taylor S., 1967
Garnett, R. H., 1958
Garrett, C. I., 1930
Garrett, E. G., 1936
Garrett, Grady B., 1974
Garrett, J. N., 1952
Garrett, R. J., 1940
Garrett, Richard D., 1966
Garrett, Russell, 1986
Garrett, V. L., 1919
Garrison, Robert G., 1970
Garth, Dennis J., 1984
Gartrell, J. W., 1954
Gary, E., 1966
Gary, Jordan, 1967
Garza, Andreas, 1984

Garza, Armando, 1993
Garza, D. M., 1956
Garza, Eduardo H., 1952
Garza, Hector, 1993
Garza, M. F., 1912
Garza, M. L., 1953
Garza, Mario Jr., 1981
Garza, N. G., 1964
Garza, Robert, 1988
Gates, Edmund L., 1973
Gatewood, Herman, 1970
Gatlin, Jay P., 1956
Gatrell, J. W., 1956
Gaudara, J., 1982
Gaul, Roy, 1951
Gault, Tony, 1991
Gawlick, J., 1981
Gay, R. A., 1959
Gay, William D., 1967
Gayer, H. C., 1955
Gaytan, Rodolfo, 1993
Gearreald, T. N., 1930
Geddie, Steven G., 1971
Geese, Jeffrey, 1975
Geistweidt, J. A., 1959
Gentes, Scott, 1993
Gentry, Paul E., 1951
Georgandis, Simon, 1966
George, I. C., 1944
George, Kenneth G., 1952
George, Larry, 1968
George, R. W., 1954
George, W., 1931
Gerald, Thomas S., III, 1965
Gerber, James, 1984
Gerhart, Robert A., 1975
Gerick, Anthony, 1979
Gerlach, Ed, 1937
Gerlach, Eric, 1965
Gerling, Frank, 1977
Germain, Michael, 1991
German, Donn L., 1961
German, John, 1958
Germany, Joseph A., 1937
Gersch, Daryl W., 1970
Gersch, James A., 1973

Gersteman, O., 1894
Geurra, David, 1990
Gharis, F. L., 1956
Gheen, William, 1991
Gibbens, J. Michael, 1968
Gibbons, Patrick C., 1973
Gibbs, Andy M., 1983
Gibbs, Jack, 1981
Gibbs, Jeffrey, 1989
Gibson, Daniel Jr., 1961
Gibson, Daniel M., 1949
Gibson, E. W., 1950
Gibson, James M., 1970
Gibson, K. E., 1950
Gibson, Mark, 1992
Gibson, R. B., 1936
Gibson, R. L., 1961
Gibson, S. P., 1935
Gibson, T. E., 1941
Gideon, H. W., 1928
Giese, Art Jr., 1949
Giesecke, D. B., 1905
Giesecke, Leonard F., 1932
Giesecke, M. C., 1908
Giessing, William, 1981
Giesweidt, J. A., 1959
Giffen, Emmett D., 1927
Giffin, H. A., 1921
Gilberry, Scott, 1989
Gilbert, Richard, 1965
Gilbreath, W. W., 1930
Gill, Chuck, 1982
Gill, Ellis C., 1962
Gill, Hugh, 1949
Gill, Michael, 1954
Gillette, L. D., 1934
Gilley, Alan R., 1974
Gilliam, Lacy C., 1972
Gilliand, E., 1945
Gillikin, B. B., 1960
Gillis, T. O., 1962
Gillman, Thomas A., 1971
Gilmore, C. R., 1952
Gilmore, H. A., 1894
Gilmore, W. C., 1951
Gilmore, Wiley, 1977

Gilpin, Lendon, 1966
Gimarc, Charles E., 1971
Gimarc, J. D., 1946
Gimarc, John A., 1969
Ginder, James, 1986
Gipe, G. W., 1961
Gipson, William H., 1971
Gist, A. M., 1950
Gist, Byron, 1906
Gist, Wilbert, 1988
Givens, Robert, 1987
Gjerstad, Gunnar E., 1972
Glanz, Mark, 1990
Glaser, James, 1959
Glass, Joe, 1945
Glass, Martin E., 1971
Glazener, Keith L., 1973
Glendenning, F. B., 1940
Glenn, Wayborn, 1966
Glessing, Bill, 1984
Glezen, H. N., 1916
Glick, F. Scott, 1970
Glidden, J. D., 1934
Glockzin, A. P., 1957
Glover, Jim, 1988
Glovier, Kevin R., 1969
Godwin, J. S., 1981
Godwin, Z. A., 1913
Goen, Clyde M., 1964
Gold, B. G., 1951
Goldapp, E. E., 1944
Golden, E. A., 1945
Golden, E. W., 1945
Golden, J. Y., 1945
Golden, Ray M., 1946
Golenterner, J., 1930
Golladay, C. S., 1952
Gombeski, William R., 1968
Gomez, Jose, 1990
Gomez, Rolando A., 1973
Gondeck, Wayne, 1976
Gonzales, Henry, 1969
Gonzales, Henry Jr., 1976
Gonzales, Julian, 1990
Gonzales, Richard, 1976
Gonzales, Richard, 1988

Gonzalez, Elizabeth, 1993
Gonzalez, Jerry, 1989
Gonzalez, Julian, 1990
Gonzalez, R. J., 1963
Gooch, Charles O., 1902
Gooch, R. B., 1913
Good, J. O., 1956
Goodgame, David, 1973
Goodman, Robert L., 1942
Goodrich, H. P., 1940
Goodrich, T. B., 1930
Goodrich, T. T., 1961
Goodson, J. H., 1942
Goodson, J. R., 1963
Goodson, Mark, 1974
Goodwin, Gary, 1939
Goodwin, M. R., 1959
Goodwin, Richard L., 1947
Goppert, C. W., 1950
Goppert, J. G., 1939
Gordon, C. R., 1947
Gordon, D.S., 1959
Gordon, J. F., 1939
Goss, V. A., 1959
Gossett, R. B., 1938
Gottlich, Robert P., 1973
Gough, A. B., 1908
Gougler, Philip O. Jr., 1976
Goulden, S., 1981
Goulding, John, 1992
Gower, Daniel, 1966
Gowin, G., 1968
Grady, K. G., 1957
Grady, R. E., 1941
Grady, T., 1968
Graeber, Michael D., 1969
Graesser, John, 1976
Graf, K. E., 1962
Grafton, Michael B., 1962
Graham, C. B., 1960
Graham, C.R., 1960
Graham, Chris, 1986
Graham, David E., 1962
Graham, Gary, 1974
Graham, J. S., 1959
Graham, James, 1984

Graham, Lloyd W., 1974
Graham, M. F., 1955
Graham, Oscar D., 1954
Graham, Paul D., 1939
Graham, Paul S., 1971
Graham, Rick J. W., 1963
Graham, S. R., 1957
Graham, Tim, 1985
Grahman, Mark, 1975
Grainger, John, 1968
Grammer, R. B., 1934
Granger, Gregory, 1982
Grant, B. W., 1959
Grant, C., 1967
Grant, Gillian, 1986
Grantham, A. H., 1954
Gras, E. H., 1940
Grassman, J. M., 1932
Graves, W. E., 1938
Graves, William G., 1976
Gray, Brian, 1978
Gray, David, 1978
Gray, G., 1981
Gray, J., 1967
Gray, J. Earle, 1932
Gray, J. T., 1931
Gray, Kenneth H., 1973
Gray, Phillip, 1977
Greaney, D. E., 1949
Greaney, Gordon, 1983
Greek, J. A., 1926
Green, Brian M., 1972
Green, Charles J., 1967
Green, D., 1966
Green, David, 1985
Green, George E., 1963
Green, J., 1966
Green, J., 1968
Green, J. E., 1945
Green, Jedd H., 1951
Green, L. A., 1954
Green, M. D., 1895
Green, R. J., 1948
Green, Robert, 1980
Green, Tim S., 1982
Greenberg, Todd, 1984

Greene, O. W., 1911
Greenhaight, R. A., 1935
Greenlee, C. H., 1959
Greenslade, V. R., 1921
Greenwade, Bill C., 1971
Greenwade, Ronald A., 1975
Greenwald, Thomas, 1984
Greenwall, J. P., 1954
Greenwood, Robert, 1980
Greer, D. C., 1919
Greer, J. A., 1925
Greer, Lee, 1952
Greer, W. A., 1926
Greg, Ross, 1991
Gregg, C. S., 1960
Gregg, Donald, 1951
Gregg, Guy, 1992
Gregg, Russell, 1989
Gregory, M. L., 1964
Gregory, P. R., 1938
Gregory, Raymond, 1988
Gresham, W. O., 1904
Greunke, James H., 1973
Grewe, Christopher, 1977
Grice, R. T., 1965
Griffin, C. E., 1953
Griffin, D. G., 1924
Griffin, G. A., 1953
Griffin, Joe, 1977
Griffin, Kirk, 1977
Griffin, Russell, 1987
Griffin, W. R., 1910
Griffis, Allen, 1989
Griffis, Yale B., 1926
Griffith, E., 1945
Griffith, Rodney S., 1957
Griffith, S. K., 1962
Griggs, Ray, 1977
Grigsby, F., 1951
Grigsby, John D., 1979
Grimes, B. L., 1924
Grimes, Frank W., 1959
Grimsinger, C. E., 1960
Grisghtitan, V. E., 1926
Grohman, Mark, 1974
Groover, Frank Jr., 1941

Gross, B., 1964
Gross, Don, 1980
Gross, E. B., 1950
Gross, John, 1979
Gross, L., 1930
Gross, W. S., 1964
Gruben, Raymond, 1975
Gruber, G. A., 1949
Gruenke, James H., 1973
Gruetzner, Eric, 1990
Grun, Joe, 1975
Grun, William J., 1974
Gruss, Lucius R., 1947
Grygar, Robert, 1990
Guenther, E. O., 1904
Guenther, Gary, 1979
Guerra, Cesar R., 1959
Guerra, David, 1989
Guerra, Luis, 1992
Guerrero, Enrique, 1975
Guevara, A. E., 1953
Guford, R. E., 1955
Guidry, Brian, 1990
Guillory, Warren, 1975
Guinn, J. L., 1955
Guinn, Stephen, 1993
Guinn, W. B., 1903
Gulledge, Leslie D., 1967
Gulledge, M. Layne, 1966
Gullette, T. W., 1947
Gunn, Roam, 1971
Gunter, L., 1965
Gurevich, Alan H., 1969
Gurley, A. M., 1925
Gustafson, Robert H., 1963
Gustine, J. E., 1962
Guthrie, Sampson C., 1949
Guthrie, Russell, 1989
Gutierrez, Robert, 1990
Guy, Andy, 1976
Guzman, Jesse, 1990
Gwin, Holmes, 1989

Haag, Larry W., 1975
Haas, Philip Jr., 1953
Habner, F., 1945

Hackbart, Kristie, 1986
Hackney, Don V., 1940
Hadder, Roderick, 1987
Haddon, J. L., 1927
Hadeler, R. B., 1953
Haenel, A. W., 1935
Hafner, J. L. 1963
Hagemeyer, Michael W., 1973
Hagerty, Joseph, 1993
Haies, Raymond, 1940
Hail, Ewen D., 1954
Haines, R. L., 1940
Hajovsky, Charles J., 1956
Hakemack, David Glen, 1979
Halbig, W. B., 1940
Hale, David, 1977
Hale, H. C., 1948
Hale, Melvin, 1970
Hale, Ray, 1970
Hale, Tom, 1982
Haley, David L., 1970
Hall, Albert C., 1932
Hall, C. Richard, 1958
Hall, E. C., 1944
Hall, H. D., 1932
Hall, J. J., 1928
Hall, James J., 1965
Hall, N., 1968
Hall, Steven, 1984
Hall, T. M., 1951
Hall, Tommy G., 1949
Hallaron, Ferrick, 1976
Hallaron, J. Dennis Jr., 1975
Hallaron, Michael, 1984
Halling, Clint, 1990
Halling, T. Derek, 1990
Hallmark, Joseph J., 1969
Halpain, Richard T., 1960
Halstead, Herbert L., 1957
Halstead, Nathan, 1984
Haltom, Guy T., 1902
Haltom, J. H., 1960
Haltom, Robert, 1967
Hamilton, Clay, 1978
Hamilton, Dale R., 1956
Hamilton, Daniel J., 1934

Hamilton, Edward A., 1935
Hamilton, H. J., 1957
Hamilton, Horace C., 1925
Hamilton, John R., 1957
Hamilton, Joseph Bruce, 1974
Hamilton, R. R., 1960
Hammer, Brian, 1986
Hammer, Jeffrey, 1987
Hammers, James T., 1953
Hammond, Ryan, 1992
Hancock, C. E., 1915
Handley, Chris, 1987
Handley, Robert Jr., 1981
Haney, Joe T., 1944
Haney, Randy, 1982
Haney, Scott, 1984
Haney, W. F., 1950
Hankamer, H. J., 1957
Hanks, Steven, 1986
Hanna, Daniel N. Jr., 1949
Hanna, Wayne W., 1962
Hanneman, Otto L., 1973
Hanneman, Paul, 1972
Hanning, Charles M., 1964
Hansberger, Mark, 1990
Hansen, C. M., 1948
Hansen, Christopher, 1993
Hansen, Eric, 1991
Hansen, S., 1968
Hanson, G. B., 1913
Hanson, W. K., 1913
Hantz, Kyle, 1978
Hanzalic, A., 1960
Hapman, Gary, 1984
Harbers, L. H., 1953
Harbin, J., 1981
Harborth, N. B., 1948
Harbour, Ronald W., 1974
Hard, Mike, 1977
Hardcastle, Erich S., 1969
Hardcastle, George W. Jr., 1947
Hardesty, T. M., 1960
Hardin, David P., 1969
Hardin, Michael R., 1967
Hardin, Phillip R., 1964
Hardin, W. Ross, 1939

Harding, L. R., 1952
Hardy, Mark, 1980
Hare, Steve, 1986
Hargrove, B. M., 1944
Hargrove, M. H., 1922
Hargrove, T. D., 1944
Harkey, J. D., 1950
Harkrider, G. L., 1948
Harlan, Mark, 1978
Harle, Robert M., 1937
Harle, R. P., 1945
Harling, Charles W., 1969
Harmel, Lawrence W., 1937
Harmon, R. F., 1956
Harmon, Ross, 1978
Harp, James F., 1953
Harp, Michael R., 1976
Harp, T., 1966
Harper, B. E., 1927
Harper, Jack, 1988
Harper, R. A., 1953
Harper, T., 1966
Harrell, B. J., 1952
Harrell, Billy B., 1970
Harrington, Ira H., 1951
Harrington, T. W., 1941
Harris, B. J., 1952
Harris, Claude Jr., 1950
Harris, David, 1989
Harris, Dustin, 1991
Harris, Harold F., 1946
Harris, J. D., 1909
Harris, Kevin, 1979
Harris, Marc, 1982
Harris, Patrick, 1966
Harris, R. E., 1955
Harris, Raymond Jr., 1978
Harris, Scott, 1957
Harris, Terrance J., 1988
Harrison, A. A., 1930
Harrison, Bedford "Scoot," Jr.,
    1944
Harrison, C. B., 1944
Harrison, D. W., 1938
Harrison, F. Brad, 1971
Harrison, Guy F., 1936

Harrison, J. L., 1957
Harrison, Jerome, 1898
Harrison, Tom R., 1937
Harrison, W. A., 1895
Harrison, W. P., 1933
Harriss, G. B., 1953
Harsdoff, G., 1968
Hart, J., 1956
Hart, Jim, 1983
Hart, M. S., 1959
Hartfield, J. M., 1951
Hartgroves, O. E., 1953
Hartney, Daniel C., 1974
Hartsfield, R. J., 1955
Harvey, Gary L., 1972
Harvill, Luther E., 1950
Harville, W. E., 1953
Harwell, Howard W., 1953
Harwood, Thomas, 1965
Hastings, Ricky, 1986
Haswell, H. M., 1926
Haswell, Henry M., 1956
Haswell, Henry Matthew, 1929
Haswell, Matt, 1989
Hatch, G., 1966
Hatch, K. J., 1934
Hatcher, John L., 1951
Hathaway, William, 1965
Hathorn, J. B., 1964
Hatton, James R., 1961
Hauser, Bill, 1944
Hausmann, Alan, 1984
Havard, Jeffrey, 1990
Havenot, Russell, 1983
Hawes, L. C., 1945
Hawes, Steve, 1982
Hawes, W. H., 1946
Hawkins, B. M., 1927
Hawkins, John, 1991
Hawkins, Joseph, 1980
Hawkins, William S., 1972
Hawks, Joe W., 1935
Hawley, Alfred D., III, 1970
Hawthorne, James R., 1967
Hay, James C., 1946
Hay, Richard, 1989

Hay, T. E., 1928
Hayes, S. B., 1957
Haygood, Ronald L., 1971
Hayhurst, Karl, 1978
Hays, H. R., 1922
Hays, Michael, 1993
Haywood, Ronald L., 1973
Hazlewood, R. M., 1917
Head, J. B., 1958
Head, Rene, 1984
Heard, J. A., 1953
Heard, Robert W., 1970
Heard, W. H., 1953
Heam, D. L., 1942
Heam, Larry Charles, 1964
Heam, T. L., 1951
Hearnsberger, Jason M., 1990
Heath, David, 1983
Heath, Roy, 1987
Heathman, Ben L., 1949
Heatley, M. D., 1962
Heaton, Randy, 1980
Hebert, August J., 1944
Hebert, August J. Jr., 1974
Hebisen, E. E., 1939
Hebner, Frank Jr., 1946
Hebner, Frank, 1977
Hecox, Carl D., 1966
Hecox, Glen D., 1964
Hecox, Orlin D., 1969
Hedges, H. D., 1928
Heeter, Brandon, 1993
Hegar, Joseph, III, 1974
Heider, A. W., 1952
Heilscher, Charles, 1929
Heimm, J. L., 1925
Heinroth, Michael, 1992
Helcamp, J. F., 1963
Helm, G. H., 1948
Helm, J. I., 1924
Hembree, Calvin S., 1953
Hembree, Gene, 1964
Hembrey, Mark, 1975
Hemphill, N. R., 1951
Hendershot, Gary, 1987
Hendershot, Simon, III, 1981

Henderson, B. L., 1927
Henderson, H., 1965
Henderson, H. C. Jr., 1962
Henderson, John W., III, 1936
Henderson, T. F., 1942
Henderson, Trey, 1980
Hendrick, Andrew J., 1939
Hendrick, Kyle, 1991
Hendrick, R. J., 1937
Hendricks, John, 1975
Hendricks, Rohn H., 1972
Hendricks, Sam, 1982
Hendrickson, C. F., 1951
Hendrickson, W. R., 1950
Hendrix, A. E., 1958
Hendrix, C. Dale, 1962
Hendrix, Ernest E. Jr., 1934
Hendrix, Lowell D., 1967
Hengst, Dwayne, 1977
Henicke, Charles J., 1957
Henley, John, 1992
Henley, John K., 1967
Henley, R. C., 1969
Henneberger, A. E., 1930
Henneberger, Dwight, 1973
Henneberger, Kenneth, 1957
Hennecke, J. D., 1955
Hennigan, James K., 1950
Henry, James W., 1941
Henry, Jason, 1983
Henry, Michael M., 1974
Henry, P. D., 1925
Henry, T. M., 1944
Henry, Thomas W., 1972
Hensley, C. W., 1959
Hensley, W. W., 1946
Hensley, William M., 1963
Henson, Bobby, 1974
Henson, J. H., 1940
Henson, Michael, 1992
Herblin, L., 1907
Herbst, Clinton, 1984
Herbst, K. C., 1957
Herigan, S., 1982
Hering, Michael D., 1972
Herley, R. Craig, 1970

Herman, Paul A., 1974
Herman, W. A., 1940
Hermann, Gary, 1987
Hernandez, Maximino Y., 1969
Hernandez, Raymond, 1986
Hernandez, Rudolfo, 1952
Herrera, Antonio, 1949
Herrera, Ernest, 1966
Herrera, Jess, 1944
Herring, Donald, 1987
Herring, Michael D., 1973
Herring, Richard, 1975
Herring, Tom, Sr., 1944
Herrington, David E., 1966
Herrington, H. W., 1958
Herrington, John M., 1972
Herrington, Mark, 1975
Herrington, Paul C., 1969
Herrmann, F. D., 1923
Herrmann, Gary, 1988
Herrmann, T. D., 1922
Hervey, Brian, 1989
Herzik, Gus R. Jr., 1930
Herzik, M. C., 1933
Hess, Allan, 1985
Hess, Michael, 1985
Hess, Robert, 1988
Hester, R., 1968
Hester, R. R., 1957
Hetherington, Frank, 1983
Hevenor, Russell, 1982
Hewett, Billy C., 1951
Hey, Don, 1984
Heye, W. J., 1916
Heyerdahl, H. E., 1934
Heyne, D., 1950
Hickerson, R. C., 1915
Hickey, Mark, 1993
Hickman, K., 1950
Hicks, Bruce W., 1964
Hicks, Charles, 1988
Hicks, David C., 1971
Hicks, Kenneth D., 1964
Hicks, L. S., 1921
Hicks, Vernon T., 1935
Hieatt, Robert, 1928

Hielschen, C. N., 1930
Higgins, P. H., 1960
Higgins, W. S., 1937
Higgs, F. E., 1930
Hightower, H. N., 1954
Hightower, James Christopher, 1989
Hilburn, Benny M., 1961
Hilburn, H. Spence, 1968
Hill, D., 1974
Hill, Daniel, 1980
Hill, David, 1989
Hill, Edward H., 1948
Hill, E. V., 1941
Hill, F. C., 1952
Hill, F. M., 1958
Hill, Frank G., 1970
Hill, J., 1967
Hill, J. H., 1958
Hill, Jimmy, 1979
Hill, John M., 1964
Hill, John Rutledge, 1909
Hill, K. W., 1951
Hill, Phillip, 1987
Hill, Robert, 1983
Hill, T., 1966
Hill, W. G., 1924
Hiller, Scott, 1976
Hilley, W. G., 1933
Hilliard, H. A., 1937
Hilliard, William, 1976
Hillier, C. R., 1933
Hilsmeier, D. P., 1958
Hinds, A. M., 1938
Hinds, Frank, 1993
Hines, G. L., 1951
Hinnant, Robert, 1993
Hinnant, Robert G., 1972
Hinojosa, Javier, 1992
Hinojosa, John, 1976
Hinshaw, Conrad S., 1935
Hinton, J. O., 1922
Hinze, Victor L., 1949
Hipp, Charles R., 1955
Hirncir, F., 1982
Hitschel, Roy, 1982

Hix, Charles Jr., 1943
Hixson, John, 1992
Hobison, E. E., 1942
Hobson, G. O., 1957
Hoch, John J., 1945
Hoch, Kurt, 1975
Hodges, McCloud B. Jr., 1935
Hodges, R. S., 1925
Hoecker, L. L., 1926
Hoelscher, Richard, 1976
Hoelscher, Thomas R., 1972
Hoephner, John, 1967
Hoff, W. C., 1957
Hoffer, Temple B., 1902
Hoffland, Eric, 1986
Hoffland, Marc, 1991
Hoffman, Buren W., 1958
Hoffman, R. G., 1961
Hoffman, Rudolf A., 1949
Hoffmeister, Gary W., 1973
Hogan, Bill, 1972
Hogan, Michael E., 1972
Hogan, Theodore W., 1942
Hogan, Thomas C. Jr., 1941
Hogan, V. E., 1939
Hohn, J. Y., 1955
Hoke, Greg, 1971
Hoke, Will, 1987
Hokom, Michael, 1986
Holbrook, Ray Jr., 1944
Holbrook, Gray, 1974
Holcomb, R., 1899
Holder, Barry, 1975
Holderness, B. C., 1939
Holderness, H. G., 1943
Holick, E. W., 1912
Hollabaugh, C., 1945
Holland, Christopher, 1989
Holland, Daryl L., 1969
Holland, Greg, 1993
Hollar, Gene, 1946
Holleman, Asa, 1946
Holleman, C., 1981
Holley, Cyrus H., 1953
Holley, J. T., 1944
Holley, John Jr., 1960

Holley, M. W., 1961
Holliday, E. S., 1945
Holliman, C., 1982
Holliman, C. I., 1928
Holliman, Joe L., 1973
Holling, Derek, 1990
Hollis, R., 1981
Holloway, Everette N., 1944
Holloway, R., 1966
Hollowell, Jeffery R., 1971
Holly, J. L., 1959
Holmes, David, 1973
Holmes, David L., 1963
Holmes, Lowell A., 1948
Holmes, Marion Lee, 1981
Holmes, Scott, 1980
Holt, M. Wayne Jr., 1968
Holthouser, Kenneth, 1985
Holubec, Melton G., 1950
Homan, A. C., 1895
Homes, Lee, 1983
Homeyer, Bruno C., 1949
Homeyer, F. C., 1961
Honeycutt, W. H., 1960
Hood, C., 1936
Hood, Thomas, 1980
Hoopers, -----, 1959
Hoover, LaRoy, 1985
Hope, Stephen A., 1973
Hopewell, C. Alan, 1967
Hopkins, B., 1946
Hopkins, P. R., 1931
Hoppers, R. G., 1958
Hopson, Fred A., 1956
Hopson, M. W., 1939
Hopson, William B., III, 1952
Horchler, Mike, 1986
Horn, Alexander, 1979
Horn, E. S., 1930
Horn, J. Y., 1958
Horn, W. J., 1924
Hornickel, Edward P., 1938
Hornsby, C. W., 1941
Homsey, Joseph, 1988
Horrell, J. W., 1946
Horton, L. P., 1952

Horton, Roger, 1979
Horvitz, Aaron, 1993
Hostetler, William, 1984
Hottenroth, James R., 1960
House, David, 1983
House, David L., 1971
House, George W., 1968
House, W., 1945
Houseworth, Steven, 1992
Houwen, Stephen, 1977
Howard, D. R., 1945
Howard, David M., 1965
Howard, Jack, 1980
Howard, Lawrence E., 1951
Howard, Mark, 1975
Howard, Scott, 1988
Howell, David R., 1944
Howell, Daniel D., 1949
Howell, Hulen W., 1952
Howell, J. B., 1922
Howell, J. Brian, 1982
Howell, J. G., 1958
Howell, William R., 1965
Howen, Steve, 1980
Howes, Ralph C., 1956
Hoyer, Richard G., 1969
Hoyle, K. R., 1956
Hrabal, Richard, 1980
Hryhorchuk, Fred, 1985
Hubbard, Clinton L., III, 1968
Hubby, T. E., 1920
Huber, W., 1966
Hubert, A., 1922
Huck, Dan A., 1973
Huckaby, W., 1958
Huddleston, W. A., 1950
Hudson, A. L., 1956
Hudson, Glenn, 1986
Hudson, Kris, 1975
Hudson, Matthew, 1985
Hudson, Matthew, 1993
Hudson, Michael, 1993
Hudson, Patton C., 1949
Huerth, Alan, 1973
Huff, Arthur. W., 1921
Huff, C. R., 1920

Huffaker, Robert, 1955
Huffman, Mahlon B., 1936
Huffman, Robert, 1947
Huffmeyer, Andrew, II, 1987
Hufford, E. S., 1923
Hufford, Paul, 1950
Hufhines, Bobby R., 1962
Huggins, J. E., 1927
Huggins, J. E., 1964
Hughes, F., 1925
Hughes, Gaylon E., 1961
Hughes, James H. Jr., 1978
Hughes, R. F., 1924
Hughes, R. L., 1925
Hughes, Robert, 1978
Hughes, Roy N., 1944
Hughes, W. L. Jr., 1926
Hulan, Henry D., 1949
Hulsey, Jeremy, 1992
Humble, George A., 1944
Humphrey, A. F., 1944
Humphreys, Shawn, 1978
Humphreys, T. E., 1924
Hunt, Matthew, 1987
Hunt, Z., 1958
Hunter, Homer A., 1922
Hunter, M., 1966
Hunter, R. F., 1955
Hunter, R. L., 1928
Hurdt, Cody B., 1983
Hurley, Robert, 1945
Hurst, Don L., 1927
Hurta, Thomas L., 1949
Hurta, Valerie, 1987
Huskey, William L. 1952
Hutchins, R. W., 1956
Hutchinson, Daniel M.
    "Marty," 1974
Hutchinson, John, 1993
Huttman, B., 1945
Hutto, Donald A., 1956
Hutto, Earl L., 1978
Hyatt, John, 1984
Hybarger, Charles D., 1972
Hyde, Michael W., 1961

Hyltin, Leroy G. Jr., 1954
Hynds, C. L., 1938

Ibanez, Jose, 1992
Ihms, O. L., 1960
Ihms, R. G., 1964
Ikard, Donald G. Jr., 1968
Iley, Don, 1983
Imperal, David, 1980
Inglehart, J. E., 1938
Inglis, T. N., 1940
Ingram, R. L., 1961
Inmon, W. G., 1946
Insall, Jerry, 1988
Inzer, R., 1966
Irby, L., 1965
Irish, Shawn, 1980
Irvin, Daniel L., 1974
Irwin, I., 1926
Isaacs, Myron, 1989
Isbell, B. B., 1942
Isbell, H. L., 1941
Isbell, James, 1989
Israel, G., 1959

Jack, Robert Williams, 1947
Jacks, Kemp, 1978
Jacks, W. V., 1962
Jackson, Eric, 1985
Jackson, Kelly, 1985
Jackson, Leland, 1991
Jackson, Mark L., 1970
Jackson, Michael, 1988
Jackson, R. E., 1936
Jackson, Royce L., 1973
Jackson, Scott, 1987
Jackson, Thomas H., 1938
Jackson, William T., 1972
Jackson, William W., 1971
Jacobs, D. W., 1959
Jacobs, William, 1993
Jaffe, Stephen H., 1963
Jageler, Charles D., 1962
James, C. L., 1945
James, Charles, 1991

James, Edgar L., 1953
James, Forrest C., 1925
James, Howard, 1976
James, K., 1960
Jamieson, Warren S., 1967
Jamison, Pete, 1977
Jamison, William C., 1957
Janak, Clarence, 1942
Janak, Frank A., 1940
Janak, Larry F., 1968
Janak, Mark Alan, 1974
Janak, Michael, 1983
Janals, C., 1946
Janals, F., 1946
Jancik, Edward C., 1925
Janik, Frank C., 1982
Japhet, H., 1899
Japp, Jack W., 1949
Jarboe, Kristafer, 1992
Jarmon, J. K., 1924
Jarrard, N. E., 1933
Jarratt, David, 1979
Jarrell, Freeman J. Jr., 1963
Jarrett, E. B., 1946
Jarrett, Ed Lee, 1911
Jarrett, James T., 1942
Jarrett, L. R., 1948
Jatzlau, Michael J., 1968
Jay, Billy Joe, 1971
Jay, Chris, 1993
Jay, Daniel Brent, 1974
Jechow, Michael, 1975
Jefferson, J. R., 1924
Jeffery, T. D., 1942
Jeffrey, Clark R., 1977
Jeffries, Armstead, 1938
Jeffus, Mac, 1930
Jemison, Howard B., 1983
Jenke, Ralph K., 1967
Jenkins, Arthur, 1894
Jenkins, J. B., 1948
Jenkins, Jerry G., 1949
Jenkins, W. L., 1939
Jennings, C. M., 1955
Jenson, Charles, 1978

Jephson, J. D., 1942
Jernigan, Jack W., 1952
Jetton, Jeffrey, 1981
Jetton, Ronald C., 1969
Jinks, J., 1927
Joachim, Kyle B., 1982
Joachim, Scott, 1981
Jobson, H. H., 1904
Jobson, W. A., 1906
John, J. Y., 1955
John, Michael M., 1984
Johns, Monroe F., 1945
Johns, Wade, 1991
Johnson, A. G., 1933
Johnson, Arnold R., 1928
Johnson, Bruce B., 1956
Johnson, C., 1932
Johnson, C., 1964
Johnson, C. A., 1895
Johnson, David, 1981
Johnson, Douglas, 1976
Johnson, Ernest B., 1974
Johnson, Ernest E., 1967
Johnson, Frank A., 1953
Johnson, Greg, 1978
Johnson, Guy, 1939
Johnson, J., 1955
Johnson, J. M., 1948
Johnson, James E., 1961
Johnson, James K., 1980
Johnson, James L., 1980
Johnson, Kevin, 1983
Johnson, Lige B., 1972
Johnson, Mark, 1980
Johnson, Mark, 1985
Johnson, Michael D., 1973
Johnson, R., 1966
Johnson, R. Doyle, 1961
Johnson, Roland H., 1945
Johnson, Randy, 1981
Johnson, S. L., 1945
Johnson, S. W., 1942
Johnson, Samuel, 1978
Johnson, Scott, 1986
Johnson, T. L., 1942

Johnson, Timothy, 1985
Johnson, Troy, 1987
Johnson, W. E., 1944
Johnston, A. S., 1948
Johnston, David, 1979
Johnston, Jason, 1990
Johnston, John P., 1970
Johnston, K. M., 1959
Johnston, Russell, 1987
Johnston, Walter E., 1956
Joiner, J. R., 1990
Jones, A. P., 1931
Jones, Aaron, 1988
Jones, Allen, 1982
Jones, B. H., 1944
Jones, B. W., 1941
Jones, C. L., 1925
Jones, Clay, 1915
Jones, David, 1985
Jones, David S., 1960
Jones, Felix B., 1956
Jones, Glenn M., 1942
Jones, J. K., 1938
Jones, J. R., 1955
Jones, Jeffrey, 1974
Jones, John P. Jr., 1950
Jones, Kevin, 1987
Jones, Leonard B., 1928
Jones, M. H., 1930
Jones, Marion L., 1942
Jones, Norbon Clay, 1974
Jones, P., 1931
Jones, Pat L., 1928
Jones, R. G., 1948
Jones, Robert C., 1949
Jones, Robert G., 1954
Jones, Stephen C., 1968
Jones, Teresa, 1987
Jones, Vidal, 1987
Jordan, D. J., 1945
Jordan, Eric, 1989
Jordan, H., 1968
Jordan, J. E., 1937
Jordan, J. Irwin Jr., 1949
Jordan, Kevin, 1991

Jordan, M. D., 1964
Jordan, Sam P., 1970
Jordan, W. D., 1944
Jourdan, H., 1913
Joyce, Claude, 1976
Joyce, John, 1984
Joyce, R. E., 1956
Jozwiak, P. L., 1961
Judd, Travis, 1993
Juenke, Glenn, 1986
Julich, Scott, 1993
Juren, Patrick, 1984
Justice, J. E., 1952

Kaczmarek, Tom, 1981
Kahlden, James, 1969
Kahn, M. S., 1897
Kahn, S. D., 1907
Kainer, V. R., 1954
Kallina, Tom, 1980
Kaminar, John, 1981
Kana, Philip A., 1969
Kane, P. W. Jr., 1957
Kanz, Randolph A., 1951
Kapple, Brian, 1990
Kaptchinskie, Partick, 1979
Karrer, David L., 1959
Karsteter, Burton W., 1928
Karsteter, Robert B., 1954
Kasper, E. L., 1953
Kast, Paul, III, 1974
Kaufman, Melody, 1988
Kaulback, E. A., 1904
Kearney, C. E., 1949
Keating, Jerry, 1989
Keck, William, 1977
Keelan, Richard F., 1971
Keen, E. M., 1922
Keen, James, 1965
Keen, L. S., 1918
Keeney, W., 1968
Keenum, Michael, 1988
Keeter, Homer Jr., 1943
Keirn, Jimi, 1991
Keith, D. H., 1921

Keller, C. R., 1950

Keller, Gordon D., 1947

Keller, Michael, 1988

Keller, W. W., 1949

Kelley, J. L., 1953

Kelley, J. T., 1939

Kelley, M. C., 1922

Kelley, Mark, 1973

Kelley, Michael, 1985

Kelley, R. T., 1960

Kelley, Rodney, 1993

Kelley, Tim, 1975

Kelly, Earnest E. Jr., 1969

Kelly, G. R., 1934

Kelly, H. Dennis, 1969

Kelly, J. H., 1960

Kelly, J. W., 1958

Kelly, Jerome, 1980

Kelly, M., 1966

Kelly, Patrick, 1993

Kelly, R. P., 1958

Kelly, Rodney W., 1957

Kelly, Timothy L., 1974

Kelso, L. R., 1960

Kemp, J. R., 1950

Kendall, Sigurd S., 1967

Kendall, Steven C., 1970

Kendrick, Katherine, 1992

Kendrick, M. R., 1917

Kendrick, T. J., 1959

Kenedy, G., 1951

Kenedy, A. B., 1926

Kennady, K., 1981

Kennedy, Alvin B., 1944

Kennedy, Billy B., 1944

Kennedy, D. D., 1942

Kennedy, Daniel, 1988

Kennedy, Dean S., 1949

Kennedy, G. D., 1948

Kennedy, H. B., 1938

Kennedy, K. H., 1961

Kennedy, K. Robert, 1952

Kennedy, Matthew R. Jr., 1959

Kennedy, R. M., 1958

Kennedy, William G., 1970

Kennemer, Larry C., 1962

Kennerly, A. B., 1923

Kent, Karl, 1987

Kent, W. D., 1953

Keough, Scott, 1988

Kerber, Mike, 1977

Kerby, Joel, 1979

Kerby, Tim, 1982

Kerchner, Cody, 1986

Kersh, Michael, 1992

Kesse, Jana, 1990

Kessie, Charles, 1965

Ketchen, William, 1993

Key, J. R. Jr., 1933

Kidd, James H. Jr., 1948

Kierum, Calvin, 1977

Kiker, L. W., 1946

Kiley, Sean, 1992

Killebrew, John G., 1946

Killingsworth, A. E., 1961

Killingsworth, E. L., 1935

Killion, Kenneth G., 1951

Killough, David T., 1961

Killough, J. M., 1927

Kilman, Kevin, 1985

Kilpatrick, Freeman A. Jr., 1983

Kinard, Charles S., 1953

Kinard, L. C., 1946

Kincaid, John A., 1971

Kincaid, John W., 1952

Kincl, Louis J., 1938

Kindrick, Stephen, 1990

King, A. L., 1916

King, David G., 1958

King, Donald R., 1972

King, J. D., 1926

King, Jack L., 1937

King, Jim, 1986

King, Jon B., 1960

King, Kirk, 1984

King, Kyle, 1990

King, Robert, 1917

King, Robert C., 1950

King, W. C., 1918

King, W. D., 1951

King, William, 1993

Kirberg, Emil W., 1970

Kirby, Ronald, 1986

Kirchner, Cody, 1987

Kirk, Paul, 1992

Kirk, T. R., 1948

Kirkland, James M., 1971

Kirkpatrick, Donovan J., 1958

Kirksey, Cecil T. Jr., 1954

Kirksey, Warren P., 1952

Kissman, Bridance R., 1957

Kitchens, Clyde B., 1945

Kitley, D. R., 1934

Kitterman, J. R., 1956

Kittlitz, J. N., 1946

Kitzman, Oliver Stanley, 1984

Klatt, Fred Jr., 1947

Kleibrink, Ricky, 1983

Kleinfield, J. F., 1957

Kleinsmith, E. A., 1903

Klemm, Mark, 1977

Klett, George E., 1952

Klett, Wes, 1977

Klingman, C. J., 1956

Klossner, Robert H., 1931

Klossner, Roy O., 1934

Klunkert, William M., 1973

Knape, B. W., 1960

Knapp, C. R., 1926

Knapp, F. E., 1941

Knapp, Robert, 1991

Knauth, Joseph, 1954

Knesek, Jerome J., 1968

Knight, Rex, 1978

Knight, Van, Jr. 1969

Knight, W., 1967

Knowles, Robert, 1979

Knox, Kenneth, 1979

Knox, Thomas M., 1944

Kobs, Ernest C., 1946

Kocen, Bradley, 1978

Kocian, David Arlen, 1963

Kocian, James, 1952

Koeck, William, 1992

Koehler, C. C., 1953

Koehler, James, 1975

Koehler, Steve, 1980

Koen, J. J., 1955

Koenig, Michael, 1965
Koenig, Victor L., 1937
Koenig, William Thomas, 1963
Koerth, Robert L., 1927
Kohler, David, 1990
Kohn (also spelled Cohn), S., 1894
Kohutek, Gordon L., 1970
Kohutek, Kenneth J., 1967
Kojak, L. E., 1930
Kolb, Charles R., 1974
Koliba, E. L., 1964
Komm, Richard, 1976
Konvicka, Michael, 1993
Kooken, R. A., 1927
Koonce, David F., 1985
Koontz, James, 1973
Koontz, James L., 1949
Koop, O. W., 1953
Kopecky, Mike, 1981
Korenek, Stephen, 1964
Korman, John G., 1939
Kornegay, Dean, 1973
Korpanty, R., 1966
Kosh, J. M. Jr., 1957
Kosub, Philip B., 1946
Kosub, Phillip S., 1970
Koszewski, Martin, 1980
Kotwal, Russell, 1981
Kowalski, Bernard, 1904
Kraatz, Jonathan, 1993
Kracmer, V. E., 1960
Kramer, E., 1966
Kramer, Martin D., 1969
Kraulik, H. J., 1902
Krause, Kenneth K., 1980
Krauss, Theodore, 1977
Krawetz, Howard M., 1951
Krebbs, Arno W., 1960
Kreipe, Mark, 1984
Kret, Rodger, 1978
Kret, Rodney, 1978
Kretzschmar, Gilbert E., 1961
Kriedler, H. M., 1942
Kriss, S., 1944
Krobot, Rodney, 1975

Krochell, F. M., 1898
Krueger, Douglas W., 1951
Krueger, Doyle E., 1949
Krueger, F. P., 1956
Krueger, Roy, 1993
Krugler, Paul E., 1968
Krumholz, E. P., 1930
Kruse, Ken E., 1971
Kruse, Robert F., 1963
Kubin, R. L., 1941
Kubitz, J. R., 1950
Kuehne, Oscar A., 1934
Kuenemann, Charles L., 1960
Kuetemeyer, Scott, 1986
Kuhl, Kurt, 1990
Kuhn, E. W., 1934
Kunath, G. W., 1954
Kursteter, B. W., 1931
Kurth, D., 1967
Kyle, Karl D., 1970
Kyle, Stanley K., 1973
Kyle, Steven K., 1973

Laake, E. W., 1908
Laas, William A., 1968
Labatt, Louis, 1993
Labruyere, James, 1986
Lack, Jack, 1984
LaCour, Damon, 1988
Lacy, James, 1940
Ladd, K. L., 1959
Lagow, Ralph, 1988
Lagow, Samuel C., 1956
LaGrone, David R., 1969
Laird, Jeff, 1993
Lake, Miguel, 1983
Laky, Stephen, 1977
Lamb, E. A., 1945
Lambert, Burton, 1945
Lamkin, John T., 1972
Lamm, Edwin, III, 1966
Lamm, James R., 1968
Lamm, Michael E., 1961
Lamners, Jimmie L., 1971
Lamping, Charles, 1988
Lampley, G. H., 1951

Lamprecht, William O. Jr., 1959
Lancaster, J., 1982
Lancaster, Robert D., 1969
Lancaster, Thomas D., 1956
Landers, Fritz E., 1953
Landers, J., 1951
Landers, John Brooks, 1959
Landers, Roger Q. Jr., 1950
Landreth, Gordon, 1963
Landua, C., 1966
Landua, O. H., 1937
Lane, Chris, 1979
Lane, George Jr., 1951
Lane, H. Radford, 1955
Lane, J. W., 1903
Lane, Mark, 1988
Lane, Stephen, 1964
Lanford, Don M., 1972
Lang, Brian, 1990
Lang, Bryce, 1991
Lang, C., 1955
Lang, George H., III, 1947
Lang, Joel, 1991
Lange, Aubrey K., 1961
Langford, Charles, 1985
Langford, J. D., 1922
Langham, D. O., 1957
Langley, B., 1946
Langley, William D., 1944
Langlotz, W. E., 1923
Langowski, Faustyn, 1980
Langston, Charles, 1968
Langston, David P., 1970
Langston, Gordon George, 1931
Langston, Laurence W., 1967
Langston, Michael A., 1968
Lanier, D., 1981
Lankin, L. G., 1923
LaQuey, Lindsey E., 1972
LaReau, Glen C., 1946
Larkin, Frank E., 1953
LaRoche, Paul F., 1941
LaRoche, William E., 1944
Larroca, Antonio E., 1945

Larsen, Victor, 1978
Lasater, E. T., 1953
Lash, John D., 1966
Lassberg, Osbert M. Jr., 1973
LaStrapes, Kevin, 1984
Latch, L. R., 1948
Latham, J. D., 1950
Latta, Edwin, 1958
Latta, John S., 1957
Lattimore, Charles E., 1944
LaTurne, E. H., 1932
Lauderdale, John R., 1943
Lauderdale, Tony, 1974
Lauderdale, William R., 1948
Laudermilk, Neal, 1993
Laughbaum, Kevin G., 1983
Laurence, J. E., 1944
LaVail, M. M., 1937
LaVergne, Kevin, 1993
Law, Morris C., 1932
Law, W. E., 1939
Lawhon, L. F., 1928
Lawhorne, C. O., 1944
Lawler, Robert W., 1946
Lawless, D., 1966
Lawrence, James L., 1940
Lawrence, Oscar V. Jr., 1936
Lawrence, W. F., 1931
Laws, D. A., 1962
Lawson, Arnold L., 1973
Lawson, David A., 1949
Lawson, Randy D., 1974
Lawson, Whitney, 1992
Lax, W. W., 1946
Lay, Billy G., 1949
Lay, Richard I. Jr., 1948
Layman, Robert E. Jr., 1940
Layton, Robert E., III, 1970
Leach, David, 1976
Leach, R. P., 1961
Leach, Richard S., 1964
Leal, Ramon, 1949
Leal, Robert A., 1968
Leavitt, John T., 1957
Ledbetter, Cynthia, 1993
Ledbetter, James P., 1937

Ledbetter, R. W., 1940
Ledbetter, William R., 1936
Ledlow, James C. Jr., 1972
Ledlow, Jeff, 1974
Ledlow, John, 1980
Ledlow, Joseph, 1975
Lednicky, H. F., 1958
Lednicky, W. E., 1961
Lee, Calvin E. Jr., 1974
Lee, David, 1976
Lee, Fitzhugh, 1921
Lee, Hung, 1992
Lee, Ira F., 1968
Lee, J. A., 1922
Lee, J. D., 1936
Lee, Michael, 1979
Lee, R. V., 1958
Lee, Samuel Dwight, 1919
Lee, W. B., 1927
Leffel, Robert C., 1914
Legler, Billy M., 1942
Legler, Joyle D., 1945
Legler, Lee O., 1940
Lehman, George, 1971
Lehman, James, 1986
Lehman, L. M., 1948
Leigh, J. B., 1908
Leigh, Mack F. Jr., 1971
Leigh, Scott, 1984
Leighman, James, 1989
Leininger, Thomas, 1982
LeMessurier, Allen, 1981
Lemley, Foster L., 1939
Lemley, Joe R., 1939
Lemmon, Paul, 1977
Lempert, Lewis H., 1905
Lenart, Bernard H., 1967
LeNoir, Blanchard L., 1951
Leonhardt, Curtis G., 1972
Leopold, Philip, 1980
LePori, Brian, 1984
LePori, David, 1977
LePori, Firmin G. Jr., 1952
LePori, Kenneth, 1978
Lesh, Tack B., 1933
Letty, L. O., 1944

LeVelle, M. E., 1948
Levin, Marvin L., 1947
Levine, Dennis C., 1970
Levine, Jack H., 1940
Levy, Hertsel, 1977
Levy, Robert H., 1942
Lewi, Jack, 1949
Lewi, Kenneth E., 1948
Lewis, Chad, 1992
Lewis, Dudley Joe, 1932
Lewis, Edward, 1949
Lewis, J. C., 1961
Lewis, James, 1991
Lewis, James Nolan Jr., 1974
Lewis, Keith, 1973
Lewis, Larry, 1979
Lewis, R., 1967
Lewis, Russell, 1987
Lewis, Stan, 1984
Lewis, W. T., 1904
Libby, Billy W., 1954
Libby, Michael, 1984
Lienhard, Leon Victor, 1909
Light, William, 1976
Lightfoot, Larry R., 1951
Lightner, Larry F., 1924
Lightsey, John R., 1964
Lightsey, K. L., 1955
Liles, B. G., 1957
Lilly, J., 1967
Lime, Bruce F., 1972
Lincecum, R. L., 1944
Lincoln, L. J., 1956
Lindig, Michael, 1985
Lindner, M. J., 1952
Lindsey, G. J., 1955
Linn, George E., 1923
Linskie, George A., 1934
Lipe, John A., 1961
Lippke, Hagen, 1955
Lippke, Lawrence A., 1965
Lippke, Rolf R., 1958
Lipscomb, Patrick C., 1921
Lipsey, D., 1974
Lipsey, Douglas, 1979
Litchfield, W. H., 1930

Little, Alfred E., 1941
Little, Don D., 1939
Little, Thomas, 1967
Littlejohn, Jack H., 1931
Littlejohn, Thomas M., 1935
Littleton, Bradley, 1993
Litvin, R., 1951
Lively, Robert, 1985
Livengood, W. L., 1944
Livingston, Jeffrey, 1992
Livingston, Kenneth B., 1952
Lloyd, J., 1981
Lobrecht, Morris, 1963
Lochte, Keith, 1981
Lochte, Paul, 1984
Lockard, Marcus, 1968
Locke, Howard W., 1928
Locke, Kevin, 1980
Lockett, T. Wayne, 1972
Lockey, Edwin, 1964
Lockridge, James, 1980
Lockwood, R. B., 1960
Loesch, Russell, 1971
Loflin, Ed M., 1944
Loftin, J. H., 1941
Lokey, Ted Y., 1946
Lomax, Everit, 1935
Lomax, K. H., 1934
Lombard, Steve, 1986
Long, B. M., 1920
Long, J. H., 1955
Long, James G., 1944
Long, Matthew, 1986
Long, Michael, 1965
Long, N. E., 1930
Long, Robert M., 1949
Long, Scott, 1983
Long, Timothy, 1988
Long, W. B., 1922
Longley, A. J., 1947
Longley, O., 1946
Loomis, Stephen M., 1964
Loper, J. F., 1930
Lopez, O., 1954
Lopez, P., 1981
Lopez, Tomas L., 1971

Lord, H. R. Jr., 1931
Lord, Sidney C., 1937
Loughborough, Henry, 1978
Love, Stephen L., 1951
Love, William F., 1924
Loveless, R. W., 1926
Lovett, Steven, 1978
Loving, Frank A., 1937
Loving, Robert O., 1932
Lowe, J. F., 1955
Lowe, Joseph D., 1984
Lozano, Ruben P., 1970
Lucas, Mark, 1980
Lucas, O. W., 1936
Lucas, Paul, 1985
Lucey, Durwood C., 1934
Lucius, David A., 1971
Luckenbach, Carl A., 1963
Luddeke, Henry, 1965
Luedke, Edward, 1982
Luggerio, Nicholas, 1988
Luikens, Jonathan, 1992
Luitwieler, Mark, 1988
Lund, Jena, 1992
Lund, Walter J., 1952
Lundelius, Charles R., 1946
Lundell, Kenneth, 1934
Lunsford, Kevin, 1984
Lunsford, Ray P., 1958
Lunsford, Robyn, 1989
Lurie, L. M., 1952
Lusk, Leon, 1902
Luter, Robert, 1977
Luton, John H., 1968
Lutz, F. K., 1955
Lykins, Forrest Jr., 1980
Lyles, William, 1981
Lyles, S., 1981
Lynch, Billie, 1977
Lynch, Lane C., 1973
Lyons, Keith, 1982
Lyssy, Bryan, 1989
Lyssy, Walter Jr., 1981

Mabry, Frank M., 1924
McAdams, R. C., 1957

McAfee, W. R., 1936
McAleer, Raymond C., 1970
McAlister, Greg, 1983
McAnally, Dan G., 1940
McAnelly, Ray L., 1972
McBride, Martin Jr., 1932
McBride, Patrick, 1968
McBride, R. B., 1916
McCaleb, Craig, 1979
McCall, Maurice W., 1937
McCall, Richard H., 1933
McCamy, I. L., 1940
McCargo, F. W., 1940
McCarroll, J. C., 1931
McCartney, Michael, 1975
McCarty, Sean, 1990
McCarty, William Jr., 1954
McCary, J., 1895
McCaskill, Michael C., 1969
McCaskill, S. E., 1938
McCaslin, Jonathan, 1991
McChord, W. C., 1945
McClain, C. L., 1950
McClanahan, J., 1966
McClanahan, R., 1967
McClelland, Michael, 1988
McClendon, Evard W., 1939
McClendon, H. D., 1953
McClish, B. M., 1939
McClothing, H., 1953
McClung, J. E., 1962
McClure, Donald H., 1949
McClure, G. B., 1950
McConnell, Donald, 1965
McConnino, S. F., 1898
McCord, William, 1945
McCown, R. L., 1927
McCoy, H. W., 1961
McCoy, James M., 1971
McCracken, D. W., 1953
McCrary, Guy R., 1971
McCravy, Dewey, 1986
McCrea, W. W., 1924
McCready, Ross D., 1945
McCrory, J. H., 1942
McCulley, David A., 1972

McCullough, F. D., 1939
McCullough, J. W., 1959
McCune, D. M., 1955
McCurry, Mark, 1992
McDaniel, James, 1980
McDaniel, James A., 1963
McDaniel, Jerrold W., 1969
McDaniel, Jimmie H., 1954
McDaniel, Kenneth, 1979
McDaniel, Kenneth A., 1973
McDaniel, Stephen W., 1967
McDaniel, T. P., 1957
McDaniel, W. R., 1922
McDaniel, William N., 1955
McDaniels, Jerry D., 1971
McDonald, J. L., 1903
McDonald, James, III, 1965
McDonald, Jayson, 1993
MacDonald, John G., 1949
McDonald, Mark A., 1971
McDonald, W. H., 1899
McDougald, Bruce, 1987
McDowell, David H., 1961
McDowell, F. O., 1906
McEwen, Mike, 1973
McFarland, Clay, II, 1952
McFarland, J. R., 1958
McFarland, K., 1959
McFarlane, A. S., 1945
McFarlane, W. D., 1944
McGarr, John P., III, 1964
McGee, Leroy C., 1935
McGee, Russell, 1981
McGhee, C., 1967
McGilberry, Scott, 1989
McGill, Manley, 1958
McGilvray, David H., 1966
McGilvray, Lester K., 1974
McGinnis, Charles T., III, 1962
McGinnis, Scott, 1982
McGolthin, L. H., 1951
McGoughey, J. H., 1921
McGowan, John R., 1935
McGraw, Montgomery C., 1970
McGregor, Alexander, 1942
McGregor, J. B., 1940

McGuffin, Don, 1980
McGuill, David, 1980
Macha, John M., 1966
Machemehl, Gary, 1979
Machemehl, William P., 1930
Machett, R. L., 1957
McHoughton, A. H., 1917
Macik, E. J., 1958
McIntire, Scott, 1992
McJohnson, Robert B., 1956
Mack, Richard B., 1964
McKain, Michael, 1980
McKay, David E., 1958
McKay, G., 1908
McKechnie, James, 1980
McKelvey, E. A., 1941
McKenna, K., 1968
Mackenson, Otto, 1921
McKenzie, Eric, 1993
McKenzie, Gilbert, 1978
McKenzie, J. G., 1922
McKenzie, Oak, 1934
McKenzie, Sam, 1977
McKerall, William C., 1975
McKinney, O. N., 1951
McKinnon, E., 1895
McKirahan, George Jr., 1967
McKnight, Michael, 1985
McKnight, Steven Keith, 1984
McLain, David W., 1954
McLain, N. A., 1938
McLane, Derek, 1991
McLarty, Michael A., 1978
McLaughlin, Joel R., 1971
McLaughlin, Lester A., 1960
McLaughlin, Robert H., 1950
McLellan, D., 1967
McLennan, Stuart G., III, 1973
McLester, C., 1958
McMahan, A. G., 1925
McMahan, Harry, 1990
McMahan, Michael E., 1974
McMahon, Joel, 1986
McMains, Lewis W. "Pete," 1952
McMasters, W. W., 1937
McMillan, Scott, 1984

McMullen, T. C., 1908
McMurray, David W., 1960
McMurray, Robert D., 1961
McNair, C. L., 1917
McNair, Dixon Jr., 1966
McNair, Doug, 1980
McNair, Howard, 1941
McNair, Sean, 1989
McNair, Timothy D., 1975
McNees, R. G., 1959
McNeill, K. F., 1944
McNess, George, 1923
McNew, James, 1985
MacNutt, John G., 1962
McPhee, Rolin, 1987
McQueen, Dennis, 1978
McRae, John, 1980
McReynolds, Charles S., 1969
McReynolds, John H., 1934
McReynolds, Oliver B., 1970
McReynolds, Weldon M., 1938
McVeigh, Andrew, IV, 1980
McVey, Stanley A. Jr., 1960
McWhirter, Charles O., 1938
Macy, W. S., 1922
Madden, Joseph, 1979
Maddux, Joe T., 1954
Maddux, Thomas J., 1973
Madeley, Gerald R., 1960
Madeley, Neil S., 1940
Madeley, Philip C., 1960
Madison, William F., 1933
Maedgen, C. E., 1902
Maffitt, T. S., 1940
Magee, Mark, 1990
Magee, W. L., 1948
Magruder, Jay, 1983
Mahan, P. E., 1944
Maher, Mark, 1974
Malanga, John, 1985
Maldonado, Edward R., 1958
Malina, Frank J., 1930
Malinak, James, 1970
Mallory, C. F., 1926
Malone, Clem, 1964
Malone, T. M., 1945

Malone, Vernon, 1910
Maloney, J. M., 1919
Maloney, Zachary, 1991
Maltsberger, Mark, 1993
Manes, Archie, 1946
Manfield, B. J., 1908
Mangold, Larry R., 1944
Mangum, C. V., 1910
Manley, Jim M., 1972
Manlove, R. E., 1924
Mann, J. A., 1913
Mann, J. T., 1939
Manning, Charles R., 1935
Manning, Edgar C., 1970
Manning, Grady W., 1973
Manning, Jeffrey, 1979
Manning, R. T., 1963
Manning, William Jr., 1940
Mannix, John, 1967
Manor, W. R., 1940
Manry, B. L., 1955
Mansfield, B. J., 1908
Mapes, W. R., 1949
Maple, Lenwood G., 1964
Maples, Herron N., 1936
Maples, J. D., 1956
Maples, J. G., 1939
Maples, Loran E., 1939
Marburger, A., 1907
Marburger, B. D., 1902
Marcotte, Shoshanna, 1991
Marek, E. L., 1903
Marek, J. W., 1931
Marek, Larry, 1979
Marek, S. J., 1935
Marek, William Craig, 1978
Maresh, Mike, 1975
Marion, David P., 1961
Marion, Paul, 1985
Marks, A. R., 1945
Marquardt, Kent, 1980
Marquez, J. S., 1961
Marron, Paul, 1976
Marrs, John T., 1968
Marsh, Curtis W., 1971
Marshall, D. O., 1920

Marshall, M. D., 1958
Marshall, W. H., 1944
Martel, J. G., 1933
Martin, A. G., 1961
Martin, C. D., 1946
Martin, C. E., 1943
Martin, D. S., 1959
Martin, D. W., 1955
Martin, David, 1943
Martin, E. L., 1955
Martin, F. W., 1928
Martin, G. W., 1960
Martin, Gary J., 1967
Martin, H. S. 1940
Martin, James, III, 1979
Martin, M., 1981
Martin, Manuel, 1988
Martin, P. L., 1927
Martin, R. A., 1964
Martin, R. L., 1950
Martin, Robert, 1940
Martin, S., 1982
Martin, T. G., 1936
Martin, Timothy, 1988
Martin, Vernon Z., 1948
Martinets, Bret, 1983
Martinez, Carlos, 1986
Martinez, J. L., 1958
Martinez, Joseph, 1984
Martinez, Manuel Jr., 1987
Martinez, Marc, 1988
Martinez, Michael, 1993
Martinez, Ramiro, 1946
Marvin, Paul D., 1982
Marwil, Stanley J., 1938
Marx, J. B., 1942
Mask, Donald, 1980
Mason, Craig, 1980
Mason, Steve, 1974
Massey, C. G., 1948
Masters, John R., 1969
Mata, V. H., 1948
Matchett, R. L., 1958
Matchett, Robert K., 1920
Mathias, Donald P., 1961
Mathis, David, 1989

Mathis, F. M., 1953
Mathis, J., 1967
Mathis, T. F., 1942
Mathis, W. N., 1894
Matlock, John, 1988
Matney, David, 1980
Matthews, D. B., 1959
Matthews, Gregory, 1983
Matthews, J. M., 1939
Matthews, Phillip, 1949
Matthews, W. F., 1953
Matthews, William P., 1961
Mauldin, David, 1980
Mauldin, Donald, 1988
Mauldin, H. S., 1945
Mauldin, Leslie, 1980
Maurer, John Jr., 1936
Maurer, Kim, 1971
Maurer, W. E., 1942
Maxfield, Lawrence G., 1947
Maxson, T. E., 1918
Maxwell, E. P., 1948
Maxwell, Robert William Jr., 1932
May, A. L., 1959
May, Dwayne E., 1964
May, Larry, 1975
May, M. U., 1933
May, Roy Louis, 1962
Mayer, James, 1986
Mayer, Max F., 1902
Mayer, Ralph W., 1945
Mayes, Gary, 1993
Mayes, J. C., 1942
Mayes, O. L., 1958
Mayfield, J., 1946
Mayfield, James H., 1984
Mayfield, Ramon B., 1958
Mayo, H. B., 1938
Mays, Brian Keith, 1978
Mays, John K., 1981
Mays, Wesley, 1977
Maze, Shawn, 1993
Mazur, Edward, 1963
Mazzella, Patrick, 1989
Mazzu, J. G., 1948

Meadors, C. K., 1928
Meadows, C. D., 1958
Mebane, Wallace C., 1944
Medford, Michael, 1993
Medlin, E. L., 1960
Medlock, Landrum L., 1933
Meece, George Frank, 1947
Meek, Robert W., 1901
Meier, W. F., 1934
Meiller, John, 1964
Meininger, Douglas C., 1969
Meissler, Ray, 1978
Mejia, J. M., 1951
Melcer, J. D., 1945
Melcher, David, 1991
Melcher, Fred W., 1949
Melcher, Max A., 1937
Mellinger, Dale D., 1974
Melton, James, 1978
Melton, S., 1968
Melton, Samuel, 1976
Menchaca, Arnold H., 1959
Meneghetti, Louis, 1982
Menger, Charles, 1979
Meninger, Dale, 1975
Menville, E. R., 1958
Meredith, David D., 1969
Meredith, John L. Jr., 1949
Mergen John A., 1969
Mergen, Richard J., 1963
Meriwether, J. B., 1945
Merka, Gary, 1978
Merka, S., 1981
Merrick, Keith H., 1972
Merrill, W. C., 1938
Merrill, W. H., 1937
Mertz, James, 1943
Messer, C. R., 1961
Metcalf, Mark, 1984
Meyer, Alvin H., 1955
Meyer, B., 1966
Meyer, Kenneth W., 1971
Meyer, M. W., 1957
Meyers, C. G., 1919
Meyers, E. V., 1953
Meyers, P. C., 1961

Meyers, R. W., 1955
Meyerson, D. W., 1931
Michalka, E. F., 1930
Michalka, Rudolph E., 1936
Michaud, Eric, 1989
Middlebrook, D., 1966
Middleton, Paul, 1988
Midgley, W. E., 1945
Miears, Thomas, 1961
Miessler, Ray, 1975
Miessler, Tom O., 1982
Migliaccio, Louis, 1993
Mikel, James, 1989
Miles, C. L., 1961
Miles, Edward P. Jr., 1946
Millar, Andrew A., 1970
Millegan, H., 1966
Millender, Kirk, 1987
Miller, A. D., 1951
Miller, A. O., 1928
Miller, B., 1939
Miller, B., 1946
Miller, B. W., 1956
Miller, Barry, 1987
Miller, Bert Jr., 1963
Miller, C. L., 1913
Miller, C. N., 1959
Miller, David, 1981
Miller, David C., 1961
Miller, Donald C., 1941
Miller, Gregory S., 1972
Miller, H. C., 1909
Miller, J. L., 1935
Miller, James N., 1970
Miller, Jeffrey, 1989
Miller, John, 1976
Miller, John K., 1948
Miller, Joseph, 1976
Miller, Joseph H., 1926
Miller, Keith, 1976
Miller, L., 1927
Miller, Lane, 1988
Miller, M. M., 1940
Miller, Mike G., 1969
Miller, R., 1968
Miller, R. H., 1909

Miller, R. M., 1942
Miller, R. M., 1959
Miller, Robert, 1962
Miller, Stanley R., 1960
Miller, Travis M., 1964
Miller, Walter L., 1954
Miller, Wesley L., 1962
Miller, William, 1962
Miller, William, Sr., 1943
Miller, William C., 1945
Millican, Bradley, 1989
Millican, Michael Brent, 1986
Milligan, L. E., 1960
Mills, D., 1981
Mills, H. E., 1969
Mills, R. A., 1949
Mills, R. L., 1959
Mills, Shannon E., 1968
Millsap, George W., 1951
Milsapp, Keith, 1985
Mims, James W., 1941
Mims, Jim, 1943
Minden, P. J., 1928
Minix, Richard W., 1969
Minnock, Edmund, 1937
Minor, Joseph E., 1955
Mintor, Bruce, 1983
Minyard, James C., 1959
Minze, Lonnie Jr., 1988
Mires, A. A., 1922
Mitchell, Christopher, 1980
Mitchell, Howard, 1922
Mitchell, Joe, 1980
Mitchell, Kyle, 1987
Mitchell, M. H., 1955
Mitchell, Robert, 1975
Mitchell, W. T., 1922
Mittag, Michael, 1982
Mittank, E. A., 1913
Mittendorf, Ehrhard, 1940
Mize, J. H., 1950
Mobley, Melvin K., 1945
Mock, Richard E., 1963
Moellenberndt, A. W., 1906
Moeller, A., 1946
Moffett, E. A., 1945

Moffett, Hamilton, 1941
Moffett, Paul A., 1973
Moffitt, D. C., 1946
Mahle, Paul H., 1948
Mohn, Howard, 1976
Mollgard, J., 1955
Mollinary, Beau, 1992
Molteni, George C., 1946
Monfort, Kenneth A., 1974
Monnich, C. David, 1970
Monroe, J. S., 1897
Monroe, Kenneth W., 1949
Monroe, Stephen P., 1973
Monson, Donald R., 1945
Monson, Donald R., 1971
Montalvo, Eugene, 1969
Montemayor, F. I., 1945
Montemayor, Oscar A., 1970
Montgomery, C. A. Jr., 1931
Montgomery, Clemon, 1969
Montgomery, James C., 1974
Montgomery, M. B., 1933
Montgomery, S., 1913
Moody, J. T., 1942
Moon, Ronald P., 1959
Moore, A. B., 1932
Moore, Alan, 1988
Moore, Arthur J., 1922
Moore, B. R., 1950
Moore, Bill, 1986
Moore, Brandt, 1991
Moore, Carl, 1978
Moore, Charles O., 1972
Moore, David, 1970
Moore, Doug, 1980
Moore, Franklin D., 1957
Moore, Gary R., 1970
Moore, H. M., 1939
Moore, J. E., 1953
Moore, J. W., 1955
Moore, James G., 1974
Moore, James O., 1954
Moore, John W., m, 1959
Moore, Ladnore, 1983
Moore, Lester, 1992
Moore, M. A., 1949

Moore, M. S., 1946
Moore, Marbert G. Jr., 1962
Moore, Marbert G., III, 1984
Moore, Philip, 1976
Moore, R., 1968
Moore, R. C., 1952
Moore, R. R., 1952
Moore, S. W., 1959
Moore, Scott, 1990
Moore, Steven C., 1970
Moore, W. D., 1948
Moore, William, 1988
Moore, Z. A., 1937
Moorhead, Charles R., 1968
Moreau, B. J. Jr., 1952
Moredock, S. K. Jr., 1945
Morefield, Bradley, 1992
Moreno, Gilbert, 1992
Morgan, B., 1966
Morgan, Chris, 1993
Morgan, D., 1981
Morgan, Garth R., 1983
Morgan, J., 1967
Morgan, James M., 1960
Morgan, James W., 1973
Morgan, John F., 1970
Morgan, Robert, 1979
Morgan, Robert T., 1950
Morgester, K. M., 1952
Moriarity, Kenneth R., 1970
Morita, Akitomo, 1989
Morris, A. E., 1933
Morris, B. C., 1951
Morris, C. S., 1946
Morris, David V., 1974
Morris, Don, 1964
Morris, Douglas R., 1962
Morris, G. C., 1916
Morris, J. M., 1956
Morris, James, 1968
Morris, James, 1981
Morris, James L., 1970
Morris, P. P., 1964
Morris, Rebecca, 1993
Morris, Thomas Kyle, 1912
Morris, W. C. Jr., 1924

Morrison, Dave, 1980
Morrison, Ronald, 1987
Morriss, Stephen L., 1969
Morrow, J. M., 1950
Morrow, T. H., 1953
Morse, H. A. "Calfornia," 1894
Mortensen, James, 1944
Mortensen, John A., 1946
Morton, Michael C., 1985
Morton, Scott, 1980
Morua, Martin, 1986
Moseley, J. J., 1935
Moseley, Victor A., 1952
Moser, F. A., 1940
Moses, Dave, 1987
Moses, Kenneth, 1976
Moss, Kennard S. Jr., 1951
Mote, John K. Jr., 1980
Motheral, Paul H., 1948
Maughan, George N., 1924
Mounce, H. Wendell, 1952
Mrazek, L. G., 1951
Mueller, Frederick W., 1928
Mueller, Harold A., 1931
Mulanax, Charles, 1989
Mulanax, Virgil E., 1956
Mullino, G. A., 1951
Mullins, Bert D., 1963
Mullins, Hal, 1944
Muncey, Terry, 1957
Munn, W. Burton, 1940
Munoz, Randall, 1992
Munroe, Thomas W., 1973
Munske, R. E., 1951
Munson, A. H., 1939
Murata, Ryan, 1992
Murdoch, L., 1966
Murphy, J. A., 1959
Murphy, M. H., 1953
Murphy, William T., 1941
Murrah, F. V., 1915
Murrah, Thomas A., 1934
Murray, Charles E., 1942
Murray, Henry J., 1969
Murray, W. H., 1936
Murto, Thomas, 1984

Musey, Mitchell Jr., 1946
Musser, Tommy W., 1962
Myers, Andrew, 1987
Myers, E. V., 1954
Myers, J., 1945
Myers, Jack E., 1963
Myers, L. W., 1934
Myers, P. C., 1960
Mylius, Maurice F., 1937
Myres, W. J., 1921

Nabb, B., 1965
Nabors, William A., 1985
Nachlinger, Harvey, 1966
Nagle, John W., 1941
Nail, Frank M., 1954
Nail, Ronald, 1977
Nail, W. W., 1950
Naler, E. R., 1928
Namendorf, Robert M., 1976
Nash, J. F., 1911
Nash, James C., 1930
Nast, P., 1981
Natho, James E., 1965
Nauck, Marshall H., 1981
Nava, Juan, 1991
Ne, Andrew, 1990
Neal, Carl, 1947
Neale, J. L., 1921
Neander, Robert Todd, 1991
Nedbalek, A. G., 1926
Nedbalek, Ben W., 1926
Nedbalek, George E., 1952
Nedbalek, L. E., 1926
Neeley, Charles H., 1947
Neeley, J. E., 1962
Neeley, R. E., 1941
Neeley, Thomas, 1993
Neely, J., 1982
Neely, Matt, 1990
Neely, Richard, 1963
Neelz, R., 1981
Neeson, William, 1983
Neff, A. J., 1899
Neff, Monroe C., 1944
Neff, W. D., 1925

Nehlson, Bruce, 1983
Neill, Gary B., 1971
Nelson, David, 1982
Nelson, J. Dean, 1975
Nelson, Jack, 1937
Nelson, Kevin, 1978
Nelson, R. E., 1938
Nelson, Randal L., 1977
Nelson, Richard W., 1974
Nelson, T. M., 1937
Nelson, Wayne, 1975
Nelson, Will, 1986
Nentwich, Brian, 1987
Nentwich, Karl, 1981
Ness, Christopher, 1988
Ness, L. P., 1938
Nethery, Jimmy C., 1960
Neuberger, F. A., 1946
Neuenfelt, Brian, 1975
Neuenschwander, J. B., 1993
Neumann, Larry D., 1964
Nevins, J. B., 1935
New, B. L., 1962
New, Noah E. Jr., 1958
Newberry, James, 1982
Newbury, B. O., 1933
Newlin, Borah P., 1949
Newlin, T. M., 1955
Newman, Gene W., 1957
Newman, J. G., 1953
Newman, Jason, 1991
Newman, Mark, 1974
Newman, Richard, 1965
Newman, V. J., 1927
Newsoroff, Paul, 1993
Newton, Chartier C., 1951
Newton, Larry, 1977
Newton, Thomas, 1944
Newton, W. J., 1956
Neynaber, A. C., 1918
Nguyen, Rick, 1986
Nicholas, Daniel, 1986
Nicholas, Donald H., 1959
Nicholas, R. W., 1961
Nicholas, Terry, 1964
Nicholl, Elden C., 1932

Nicholl, W. H., 1928
Nichols, Bobby E., 1955
Nichols, E. C., 1930
Nichols, J. D., 1952
Nichols, Jim, 1980
Nichols, L. G., 1919
Nichols, Richard H., 1945
Nichols, Robert, 1987
Nicholson, William, 1942
Nicklin, R. L., 1957
Nicks, P. B., 1964
Nicol, B. J., 1939
Nicol, Elizabeth, 1991
Nicola, C., 1966
Niehaus, Thomas, 1988
Niera, Carlos, 1990
Nimocks, Mark, 1984
Nisbet, R. E., 1937
Nix, J. K., 1955
Nixon, Willie J., 1969
Nobiling, William Jr., 1944
Noble, M. J., 1953
Noel, P. C., 1937
Noell, Alan, 1985
Noell, Douglas, 1987
Nogueras, Robert, 1988
Nohrn, Robert, 1977
Nolte, E. R., 1951
Nolte, H., 1914
Noonan, Michael D., 1964
Noone, E. J., 1961
Nordin, N. David, 1970
Norman, Nicholas L., 1970
Norris, Joe W., 1947
Norris, T. E., 1956
North, W. G., 1935
Northcutt, D. L., 1960
Northcutt, William Davis Jr., 1917
Northrup, L. L., 1910
Norton, C. P., 1936
Norton, P. G., 1922
Noster, Manford Freeman, 1930
Noster, Wayne M., 1960
Novak, Andrew, 1972
Novak, James R., 1970

Novak, Kelly, 1975
Nowell, Alan L., 1985
Nowlin, Robert, 1978
Nowotny, Berthold E., 1927
Noxon, Jon E., 1962
Nuckles, J. F., 1954
Nuckles, S. J., 1952
Nuckles, W. A., 1954
Nugent, D., 1965
Nuhn, A. D., 1956
Nutt, Erich, 1987
Nutt, M. L., 1957
Nutt, Michael, 1992
Nutt, Steve, 1989
Nuzzaco, Jeffrey, 1978
Nyberg, Jeff, 1992
Nye, Ira B., 1935
Nyman, Stephanie, 1993

Oakes, Donald D., 1954
Oas, H., 1968
Oates, Oscar K., 1969
O'Bannon, R. A., 1923
O'Berg, Jeffrey, 1981
Obergfell, E. A., 1928
O'Brien, M. D., 1950
O'Brien, P. D., 1953
O'Brien, Patrick J., 1969
O'Bryan, J. B., 1957
O'Callahan, R. L., 1917
O'Conner, R., 1911
Odneal, C. E., 1928
Odom, R. M., 1951
O'Donnell, W. G., 1945
Ofcarcik, Ralph, 1962
Ogle, Scott, 1989
O'Grady, -----, 1965
Oho, C. Jim, 1969
Oliphant, Eric, 1991
Oliphant, L. N., 1910
Oliphant, W. C., 1924
Olivar, John B., 1972
Olivarez, Samuel O., 1967
Olive, Philip, 1992
Oliver, C., 1927
Oliver, John, 1975

Oliver, Mark, 1977
Oliver, Paul R., 1961
Olschner, Paul Q., 1941
Oltmann, Callan D., 1965
Omez, Rolando A., 1974
Oncken, R. H., 1960
O'Neal, Ronald, 1973
O'Neal, W. B., 1945
Onken, Blake M., 1978
O'Quinn, Danny, 1975
Orem, A. B., 1925
Organ, Charles B., 1958
O'Rourke, H. E., 1899
O'Rourke, Leo J., 1964
Ortiz, J., 1967
Orton, Ed, 1978
Orton, O. J., 1930
Osborne, Bill, 1945
Osbourn, Larry C., 1959
Osburn, Monte C., 1983
Osburn, Wesley, 1977
Oser, G. A., 1948
Osteen, David L., 1969
Otken, Jay, 1984
Ott, Kenneth W., 1970
Otte, John, 1992
Ottesen, Craig L., 1972
Otto, Calvin J., 1968
Otto, John C. Jr., 1966
Oualline, John A., 1968
Oughton, Stephen, 1973
Outley, Norman, 1987
Outwin, Christian P., 1970
Overstreet, James L., 1971
Overton, J. F., 1914
Owen, James, 1985
Owens, Burton T., 1971
Owens, Mark D., 1974

Pace, Charles J., 1942
Paddenburg, John, III, 1988
Padilla, Israel, 1987
Padilla, Marcell S., 1984
Padilla, William, 1977
Page, E. T., 1941
Painter, Graham, 1966

Paletta, Frank, 1945
Palmer, Daniel W., 1962
Palmer, Kenneth A., 1969
Palmie, A. G., 1944
Panico, Kevin, 1989
Pannkuk, Tyrone, 1990
Pappas, G. F., 1936
Parden, Jim L., 1971
Pare, Alan, 1983
Parish, H. F., 1930
Parish, Thomas H., 1949
Parish, Thomas L., 1918
Park, J. W., 1938
Park, James F., 1941
Parker, Clarence C., 1934
Parker, Eric, 1978
Parker, Gerald A., 1954
Parker, H. B., 1928
Parker, J. R., 1951
Parker, J. V., 1960
Parker, K. B., 1959
Parker, Randy K., 1970
Parker, Robert, 1943
Parker, W. V., 1927
Parkman, Michael, 1977
Parks, Don M., 1967
Parks, George B., 1936
Parrett, N. A., 1965
Parris, Robert, 1989
Parrish, Dennis Roy, 1964
Partain, Morris D., 1952
Partheymiller, Elizabeth, 1986
Partlow, Ray D., 1951
Paschall, J. C., 1908
Paschetag, Mark, 1978
Pasher, Brian, 1974
Pate, Craig, 1986
Pate, Michael, 1978
Pate, R. Wesley, 1977
Pate, Robert, 1988
Pate, S. B., 1960
Pate, William, 1985
Patrick, Danny, 1971
Patrick, Dennis B., 1971
Patrick, J. H., 1922
Patterson, Buddy D., 1952

Patterson, Chris, 1989
Patterson, Craig, 1985
Patterson, Earl F., 1921
Patterson, Jason, 1990
Patterson, Jerome, 1991
Patterson, N. H., 1934
Patterson, W. E. 1960
Patton, C. E. Jr., 1934
Patton, David, 1990
Patton, Gary, 1972
Patton, Gery, 1966
Patton, J. L., 1961
Patton, Layne, 1973
Patty, Howard, 1974
Paul, J., 1982
Pauler, Donald L., 1974
Paulus, Mike, 1975
Pawlik, Daniel, 1946
Paxson, J. B., 1942
Payne, Michael, 1977
Payne, W. L., 1953
Pearce, Clifton R., 1974
Pearce, Homer L., 1931
Pearce, Jerry, 1976
Pearce, Marcellus M., 1949
Pearce, Reginald B., 1934
Pearce, Rufus B. Jr., 1938
Pearce, Terry A., 1968
Pearson, Craig H., 1968
Pearson, Jacquy C., 1964
Pearson, Philip R., 1949
Peavy, H. L., 1934
Pechacek, Damien, 1989
Pedigo, Edward M., 1933
Pedigo, Maxie Smith, 1912
Peeler, A. M., 1958
Peeler, Jennifer L., 1985
Peeples, L. M., 1915
Peeples, R. R., 1924
Peeples, Rufus R., 1949
Pehl, Jeff, 1985
Pehl, Stanley, 1970
Pellerin, John, 1982
Pellerin, Leopold, 1943
Pelt, Phillip, 1962
Peltier, P. C., 1960

Pena, E. V., 1961
Pena, Steve, 1979
Penick, Michael E., 1970
Pennington, David R., 1973
Pennington, Patrick A., 1973
Pennington, Robert, 1965
Pennington, William R., 1973
Pennington, William T., 1972
Pense, Brad, 1986
Pepkin, Danny, 1975
Perales, David, 1977
Percifield, J. M., 1959
Percifield, J. Michael, 1988
Peret, Max M., 1933
Perez, Joe F., 1969
Perez, Jonathan, 1978
Perez-Cantu, Rafael J., 1990
Perkins, A. B., 1942
Perkins, F. D., 1894
Perkins, J. B., 1950
Perkins, J. M., 1916
Perkins, M. F., 1937
Perkins, Paul Richard, 1914
Perkins, Sean, 1992
Perritt, Mikeual, 1966
Perry, Charles M., 1969
Perry, Clayton H., 1974
Perry, David, 1981
Perry, Dirk, 1978
Perry, Edwin B., 1939
Perry, O. M., 1945
Perryman, J. C., 1933
Persohn, Lee, 1985
Peter, Kevin, 1985
Peters, M. J., 1964
Peters, Robert L. Jr., 1951
Peters, Sean, 1982
Petershagen, Andy, 1993
Peterson, Jennyth, 1993
Peterson, Jimmy, 1978
Peterson, L. L., 1936
Peterson, M. G., 1961
Peterson, Ralph E., 1956
Peterson, Richard H., 1959
Petree, Ernest L. Jr., 1965
Petteway, G. N., 1956

Pettit, Jonathan R., 1981
Pettit, Morris W., 1936
Petty, D., 1982
Petty, Howard, 1975
Petty, Lawrence O. Jr., 1946
Pevoto, C. A., 1952
Peyton, T. J., 1937
Pfeil, James W., 1978
Pfeil, R., 1981
Pfeil, Richard, 1984
Pfeuffer, F. R., 1909
Philippus, Hugh Jr., 1950
Philippus, Mike, 1979
Phillips, B. G., 1953
Phillips, Bobby W., 1955
Phillips, C. E., 1941
Phillips, C. H., 1911
Phillips, Charles C., 1949
Phillips, J. A., 1959
Phillips, James, 1980
Phillips, Larry A., 1961
Phillips, Mike W., 1970
Phillips, Pat L., 1970
Phillips, Patrick, 1992
Phillips, Paul H., 1957
Phillips, Vaughn Hill, 1917
Phipps, Charles, 1975
Phipps, K. C., 1917
Pichotta, M., 1981
Pickle, Durwood, 1951
Piehl, James, 1979
Piehl, Pat, 1950
Piehl, Patrick, 1982
Pierce, W. E., 1939
Pierson, Edwin G., 1953
Pierson, Jeffrey, 1980
Pike, Earl L. Jr., 1951
Pike, Joe V., 1945
Pilcher, William, 1979
Pillittere, Leonard, 1979
Pimentel, D. E., 1961
Pingenot, John, 1983
Pinion, Douglas M., 1972
Pink, Jack L., 1925
Pinnell, A. B., 1952
Pipes, John F., 1974

Pipkin, C. H., 1936
Pipkin, M., 1975
Pipkin, Steve, 1973
Pipleen, Steve, 1975
Pippen, Charles J., 1949
Pitts, L. A., 1942
Pitts, Randall, 1985
Piwonka, Donald, 1965
Pixley, P. T., 1957
Pixley, Roy A. Jr., 1946
Pizzini, Larry G., 1971
Place, J. S., 1944
Placke, F. O., 1949
Placke, Fred, 1992
Planeaux, Chris, 1985
Plato, J. C., 1953
Platt, Frank, 1975
Plattsmier, D. C., 1961
Pleasant, Kevin, 1980
Pleasant, Richard, 1975
Pless, Steven, 1985
Poahler, L., 1961
Poe, F. E., 1944
Poe, John Jr., 1965
Pointon, David W., 1974
Poitevint, Carl R., 1970
Polasek, Bill E. Jr., 1945
Polen, Lloyd L., III, 1971
Poling, Richard, 1965
Polinski, Stephen, 1990
Pollard, James, 1965
Pollard, James, 1975
Pollard, John N., 1959
Pollard, Jonathan, 1977
Pollock, Kevin, 1979
Pollock, Randall, 1981
Pomeramtz, Melvin N., 1941
Ponder, Richard, 1973
Pontelandolfo, Frank J., 1965
Pool, Dana, 1974
Pool, Lance B., 1973
Pool, Scott, 1989
Pool, Thomas, 1992
Pope, John A., III, 1948
Pophin, Daniel R., 1973
Porter, D. A., 1963

Porter, John, 1958
Porter, Kenneth L., 1973
Porter, R. G., 1950
Porter, R. N., 1952
Porter, Robert S., 1970
Porter, Ronald C., 1970
Porter, Walter L. Jr., 1935
Posey, Daniel, 1965
Post, C., 1946
Post, C. W., 1939
Post, Gerald G., 1945
Post, Jerry V. Jr., 1950
Post, Lynn, 1961
Poston, Billy M., 1947
Poteet, W. D. Jr., 1937
Potter, Clarence H. Jr., 1959
Potter, D. J., 1960
Potthast, H. C., 1900
Potts, Charles Bruce, 1919
Potts, John Jr., 1959
Potts, John T., 1967
Potts, L. B., 1922
Potts, Mike, 1971
Pouete, G., 1953
Poulter, Charles J., 1937
Poulter, George A., 1940
Pouzar, Jeff, 1984
Powell, Donald B., 1952
Powell, Douglas, 1974
Powell, T. S., 1961
Power, Michael, 1974
Powers, E. C., 1944
Pradel, Tom, 1990
Prague, T., 1950
Prasek, Paul E., 1952
Prater, Felix D., 1941
Prater, Tracy J., 1974
Prather, Otto A., 1949
Prather, W. H., 1960
Prather, William, 1963
Prather, William, 1965
Pratlow, William, 1979
Pratt, Carl, 1934
Pratt, John T., 1967
Pratt, Michael, 1990
Preecs, Charles, 1984

Prentiss, Thomas, 1965
Preslar, Paul, 1976
Presnal, Jeffrey, 1976
Preston, C. W., 1896
Preston, C. W., 1964
Prestridge, K. K., 1913
Prewitt, Robert, 1991
Price, C., 1950
Price, Harry H., 1957
Price, J. L., 1960
Price, Jeff, 1991
Price, Phil, 1978
Price, Richard M., 1970
Price, W. B., 1950
Price, W. S. Jr., 1922
Price, W. W., 1903
Price, William S. Jr., 1947
Prideaux, R. O., 1932
Pridgen, James E., 1935
Priesmeyer, Troy, 1983
Prim, C. J., 1944
Prince, Preston O., 1947
Prince, R., 1966
Prinz, Eric, 1982
Pritchard, Allan N., 1958
Procter, David, 1984
Procter, William S., 1934
Proctor, Keith, 1975
Protas, R., 1968
Prutzman, Forrest G. Jr., 1933
Pryor, James, 1944
Puckett, James, 1977
Pugh, Bruce, 1983
Pugh, F., 1967
Purkiss, David, 1981
Purkiss, J., 1974
Purkiss, Jeffrey, 1980
Pustejovsky, A. A., 1955
Pustejovsky, Mark, 1980
Putz, Richard E., 1956
Putz, Richard Jr., 1984
Putz, Robert Jr., 1979
Pyle, Bryan, 1983
Pyle, Joe, 1949

Quaglino, C. A., 1957
Qualline, John A., 1968
Qualtrough, Henry M., 1932
Quarles, P., 1938
Quast, Don C., 1950
Quast, Fredrick, 1992
Quayle, Steven, 1978
Quesenberry, W. B., 1944
Quinn, Gary G., 1971
Quintana, Arnnulfo, 1983
Quintana, Greg, 1985
Quintana, Michael, 1991
Quisenberry, Sean, 1987
Quist, Paul, 1990

Raab, Quinton J., 1951
Rabel, A. B., 1958
Rabel, William H., 1959
Rackley, Kyle, 1985
Ragsdale, J. W., 1950
Rahlamn, G. E., 1953
Railey, R. S., 1934
Raines, Jeff, 1978
Rainey, J. Rogers Jr., 1940
Rainey, J. Rogers, Sr., 1902
Rambo, James E., 1952
Ramirez, Alexander, 1992
Ramirez, Joe E. Jr., 1975
Ramsay, M., 1935
Ramsey, Nathan James Jr., 1973
Rand, Scott, 1978
Rand, William M., 1976
Randle, Robert M., 1970
Randolph, Alvin G., 1970
Raney, A. D., 1953
Raney, Matthew, 1976
Rankin, J. M., 1941
Rankin, L. G., 1922
Raphael, H. R., 1898
Rasco, Charles W., III, 1953
Rasco, David T., 1971
Rascoe, W. M., 1940
Rasmussen, Richard A., 1962
Rathbone, Pembroke T., 1951
Rather, J. B., 1904
Rauhut, J. B., 1945

Rawlins, H. E., 1895
Ray, A. M., 1960
Ray, C. Fount, 1944
Ray, C. L., 1955
Ray, Henry H., 1953
Ray, Larry D., 1958
Ray, O., 1926
Ray, William A., 1942
Ray, William C., 1947
Rayfield, Richard M., 1976
Rayfield, Robert S. Jr., 1971
Raynaud, Joseph B., 1949
Raynaud, Walter L., 1953
Rea, Robert H., 1952
Ready, John F., 1947
Reagan, Franklin, 1972
Reavis, D. H., 1950
Reber, W. C., 1964
Recio, Orlando L., 1949
Redd, W. E., 1945
Redding, Robert W., 1985
Reder, Daniel G., 1969
Redfern, P. R., 1924
Redford, Thomas D., 1949
Redi, David R., 1972
Redi, Robert, 1977
Redmon, Agile H. Jr., 1942
Redmond, F. C., 1956
Redwine, R. M., 1948
Reece, G. E., 1960
Reed, Alfred, 1974
Reed, Archie E., 1953
Reed, B. K., 1953
Reed, David, 1979
Reed, E., 1967
Reed, J. W., 1941
Reed, Matthew, 1979
Reed, Michael T., 1973
Reed, P. M., 1927
Reed, R. D., 1948
Reed, Roger R., 1952
Reed, Ronnie, 1967
Reed, Russell M., 1951
Reed, S. M., 1958
Reed, Tom, 1975
Reed, William A., 1972

Reeder, R. C., 1952
Reedy, W. N., 1921
Reese, Brian, 1976
Reese, Charles H., 1960
Reese, George E., 1961
Reese, H. L., 1941
Reese, K. Hoffman, 1940
Reese, W. N., 1960
Reeves, Cullen S. Jr., 1966
Reeves, J. E., 1964
Reeves, J. M., 1952
Reichert, Andrew, 1986
Reicherzer, Gary W., 1961
Reid, D. J., 1957
Reid, David R., 1973
Reid, J. H., 1952
Reid, James W. Jr., 1940
Reid, Joe R., 1950
Reid, Michael, 1991
Reid, R., 1953
Reid, Robert, 1977
Reid, Sherry, 1990
Reid, Stephen M., 1955
Reid, W. R., 1952
Reininger, Terrance Paul, 1991
Reinke, S. T., 1960
Reitzer, Joel V. Jr., 1964
Renn, David F., 1971
Rennels, J. C., 1940
Repino, Thomas A., 1984
Resendez, Charlie, 1981
Retta, Edward, 1973
Reuter, E., 1937
Reyes, Julio, 1949
Reyna, A. E., 1964
Reyna, Mike, 1983
Reyna, R., 1968
Reynaud, B., 1951
Reynolds, Andrew, 1984
Reynolds, D. R., 1956
Reynolds, G. D., 1955
Reynolds, Gene B., 1970
Reynolds, Harry G., 1968
Reynolds, Mark, 1980
Reynolds, R. W., 1946
Reynolds, W. M., 1953

Rheinlander, Thomas E., 1976
Rhodes, J. W., 1958
Rhodes, Lawrence W., 1968
Rhodes, R. E., 1930
Rhodes, S. F., 1958
Ribble, B. J., 1954
Rice, C. M., 1954
Rice, John D., 1948
Rice, W. W., 1923
Rich, D. A., 1959
Richard, William, 1992
Richards, Harry L., 1948
Richards, Kirk, 1989
Richards, Ronald, III, 1989
Richards, Ronald R., 1960
Richards, Russell, 1963
Richards, W. Q., 1957
Richards, William H., 1971
Richardson, B., 1967
Richardson, Clyde P. 1966
Richardson, D. M., 1961
Richardson, Dan, 1975
Richardson, David P. Jr., 1949
Richardson, G. C., 1942
Richardson, Gary H., 1972
Richardson, J. L., 1951
Richardson, J. S., 1913
Richardson, L. V., 1963
Richardson, Michael L., 1968
Richardson, O. L. Jr., 1941
Richardson, Stan, 1985
Richardson, T. F., 1955
Richardson, W. D., 1939
Richbourg, Glenn, 1980
Richers, Emil, 1945
Richmond, J. R., 1937
Richmond, M. E., 1960
Richmond, Steve, 1976
Richmond, Steven, 1981
Richmond, William, 1977
Richter, Randal, 1977
Riddle, Neal, 1987
Ridgeway, Jim, 1982
Ridgway, Billy, 1975
Ridgway, Scott, 1987
Ridley, Jennifer, 1992

Ridley, R. L., 1960
Riebschlager, Gary, 1974
Ried, R., 1952
Riedel, W. Taylor, 1940
Rieger, Shawn, 1992
Ries, Lee, 1985
Riewe, Brian, 1975
Rigelsky, James, 1990
Riggs, Jimmy, 1977
Riggs, L. P., 1937
Riggs, Robert, 1993
Rihn, Doug, 1978
Riley, Matt, 1993
Riley, Vance, 1979
Rinehart, James O., 1938
Rinn, Calvin A. Jr., 1973
Rinn, Ralph E., 1929
Ripley, John F., 1981
Risien, George Wilson, 1902
Risley, C. G., 1921
Ritchie, Mark, 1978
Rivas, Luis, 1991
Rix, C. C., 1939
Roach, Chris J., 1973
Roach, John B. Jr., 1969
Roach, L., 1981
Roach, Robert G., 1973
Roarck, Kevin, 1974
Roark, Randy, 1980
Roark, Robin, 1974
Robbins, Cooper P., 1924
Robbins, J. J., 1939
Roberson, Barry, 1981
Roberson, Billie C., 1939
Roberson, H. D., 1944
Roberson, John "Trey," 1979
Roberson, K. T., 1953
Roberts, David W., 1949
Roberts, Edward, 1983
Roberts, James T. Jr., 1955
Roberts, John, 1975
Roberts, Kevin, 1985
Roberts, Landon K., 1949
Roberts, P. O., 1953
Roberts, Roy, 1976
Roberts, Roy G. Jr., 1937

Roberts, Vernon K., 1949
Robertson, Britt, 1991
Robertson, D. W., 1951
Robertson, Dayton, 1980
Robertson, Early G., 1948
Robertson, F. E., 1908
Robertson, Joey, 1989
Robertson, Sammie Jr., 1980
Robertson, Stephen, 1985
Robichaud, R., 1967
Robinett, W. G., 1908
Robinson, Barry P., 1972
Robinson, F. H., 1955
Robinson, Gerald E., 1968
Robinson, H. P., 1957
Robinson, J. D., 1948
Robinson, K. F., 1932
Robinson, Louie, 1948
Robinson, Olen, 1992
Robinson, P., 1945
Robinson, R. C., 1944
Robinson, R. L., 1949
Robinson, Steve, 1977
Robinson, Thomas W., 1970
Robson, William S., IV, 1970
Rocholl, Bruce M., 1970
Rockwell, Carol, 1985
Roderick, C. F., 1928
Rodgers, Charles W., 1947
Rodgers, David, 1980
Rodgers, J., 1981
Rodgers, J. F., 1960
Rodgers, R. J., 1930
Rodgers, Randall, 1988
Rodgers, William L., 1956
Rodriguez, Arnold, 1980
Rodriguez, D., 1904
Rodriguez, Edward C. Jr., 1947
Rodriguez, Gilbert, 1969
Rodriguez, Guillermo, 1990
Rodriguez, Landon, 1984
Rodriguez, Larry W., 1972
Rodriguez, Rosaura, 1993
Roeder, Erich, 1983
Roeder, G. A., 1934
Roesler, Adolph Jr., 1966

Roesner, Robert H., 1956
Roff, C. S., 1905
Rogers, B., 1980
Rogers, B. C., 1939
Rogers, Charles, 1946
Rogers, Craig, 1974
Rogers, David, 1977
Rogers, J. F., 1959
Rogers, J. L., 1948
Rogers, J. M., 1923
Rogers, James W., 1949
Rogers, Judson, 1964
Rogers, L. R., 1955
Rogers, Mark, 1981
Rogers, Robert C. Jr., 1947
Rogers, Robert L., 1979
Rogers, Sam Jr., 1942
Roland, C. A., 1925
Roland, George W., 1968
Roland, Steve, 1975
Rollins, Jack Lee, 1971
Romberg, Conrad J., 1920
Rooks, Louis M., 1947
Rooth, R. L., 1950
Roper, Don, 1971
Rosaire, Caroll, 1979
Roscoe, W. M., 1938
Rose, Donald H., 1935
Rose, Douglas, 1984
Rose, Paul P., 1935
Rose, Theron, 1986
Rosenbaum, John F., 1970
Rosenbaum, Julius, 1975
Rosenbaum, Ken, 1974
Rosenburg, M. L., 1918
Rosenfield, M., 1966
Rosenstein, Daniel, 1965
Rosenstein, Thomas W., III, 1963
Ross, David, 1978
Ross, G. W., 1926
Ross, P. L., 1954
Rothweiller, R. W., 1944
Row, V. E., 1940
Rowe, Bradford, 1993
Rowe, C., 1967

Rowin, C. H., 1948
Rowley, Shane, 1989
Roxburgh, T. B., 1946
Royall, John N. Jr., 1953
Royar, Kenneth D., 1954
Raycroft, R. E., 1954
Rozspyal, Chris, 1992
Rubano, Joseph, 1969
Rubenstein, M. S., 1932
Rucker, Desiree, 1993
Ruiz, Dan, 1975
Rumset, Kells F., 1976
Runge, H. E., 1914
Rupnow, Scott, 1985
Rush, L. C. Jr., 1971
Rush, Scott, 1993
Rushing, Mark A., 1975
Russek, Victor B., 1948
Russell, Bob, 1992
Russell, Carson Jr., 1941
Russell, Robert R., 1938
Russell, W. R., 1963
Rust, J. C., 1936
Rutherford, E. E., 1933
Rutherford, Joe E., 1947
Rutherford, Richard M., 1972
Rutherford, Ross, 1979
Rutland, C. J., 1909
Rutzman, F. G., 1936
Ryan, Robin, 1980
Rydell, Dwayne, 1984
Rydell, Edwin, 1982
Rylander, Halley G., 1928
Ryle, Thomas A., 1970

Sablatura, Leon H., 1954
Sabol, Donald E. Jr., 1972
Sacco, J. N., 1957
Saegert, Jesse J., 1935
Saenz, Eloy J., 1971
Saenz, F., 1953
Saenz, Mark, 1983
Sahol, J. R., 1940
Saibara, Paul E., 1966
St. Mary, John, 1978
Sais, Alonzo, 1986

Saleh, Michael, 1978
Saldana, Stephen, 1987
Saldana, Thomas, 1981
Salema, Abraham, 1986
Salinas, Albert, 1987
Salinas, Louis B., II, 1972
Salley, R., 1968
Saloma, David, 1991
Saloma, Rafael Ricardo, 1987
Sam, Titus, 1993
Samford, C., 1923
Sammis, Mark, 1986
Sammis, Michael, 1986
Sammons, J. E., 1959
Sammons, R. J., 1937
Samples, Jack, 1922
Sampson, W. E., 1906
Sampson, Whitney, 1982
Sams, T. G., 1941
Sanchez, Aniado, 1989
Sanchez, Romulo B., 1953
Sanchez, Richard G., 1966
Sanckey, H. R., 1948
Sandars, George W., 1956
Sander, Dennis W., 1958
Sanders, J. C., 1951
Sanders, R. N., 1939
Sanders, Shaun, 1986
Sanders, Sheldon, 1982
Sandilands, E. B., 1904
Sandlin, Joe F., 1951
Sandoval, E. J., 1948
Sandoval, Edmund, 1992
Sandoval, Joseph, 1980
Sandridge, David L., 1981
Sandridge, Douglas, 1979
Sanfilippo, C. J. Jr., 1952
Sanfilippo, Mike, 1980
Sanford, T. C., 1924
Sansom, Jaye, 1992
Santana, Jaime, 1991
Santos, Rolando H., 1974
Sartain, James E., 1960
Sartor, Christopher, 1993
Sasse, Fredric W., 1961
Sasse, Scott A., 1969

Satoro, Anthony, 1993
Satterwaite, Ryan, 1993
Saulter, Catherine, 1988
Saunders, J. R., 1923
Saunders, W. K., 1897
Saurette, Gregory, 1987
Savage, Carl H., 1911
Savage, Francis E., II, 1963
Savage, Francis I. Jr., 1956
Savage, Thomas J., 1948
Savell, J. F., 1951
Sawers, William, 1984
Sawey, Robert, 1984
Sawyer, Greg, 1989
Sawyer, Michael, 1991
Saxton, Randy M., 1968
Sayers, A. L., 1957
Scaggs, William, 1958
Scamardo, J. E., 1961
Scannell, J. J., 1951
Scarborough, C. D., 1953
Scarborough, John R., 1952
Scarbough, L., 1967
Schader, Rick A., 1974
Schaedel, Charles T. Jr., 1941
Schaefer, Daniel, 1989
Schaefer, Doug, 1978
Schaeffer, Charles A., 1937
Schaeffer, J. E., 1964
Schaeffer, Jimmie F., 1963
Schaeffer, Seley Eugene, 1909
Schaer, Robert W., 1970
Schafer, John S., 1949
Schaffer, Derek, 1983
Schaffer, S. L., 1952
Schaper, S., 1981
Schara, Monte, 1976
Schattel, F. B. A., 1913
Schaub, Peter G., 1982
Schell, J. H., 1936
Schellinger, William, 1968
Schemmelpfennig, W. H., 1913
Schiavo, J. S., 1964
Schiller, C. A., 1954
Schiller, R. E., 1903
Schlegel, Thomas R., 1970

Schleider, Ben H. Jr., 1939
Schlicher, Rex, 1969
Schlueter, Daniel J., 1966
Schlueter, David A., 1964
Schmid, Ben, 1954
Schmidt, C. O., 1927
Schmidt, Milton, 1965
Schmidt, Paul, 1975
Schmidt, Raymond W., 1985
Schmitt, David, 1981
Schneider, Dean, 1978
Schneider, Frederick C., 1971
Schneider, Neal, 1985
Schneider, Russell G., 1947
Schoen, David, 1980
Schoolcraft, Alan L., 1970
Schott, Paul, 1982
Schottie, Phillipe, 1975
Schroeder, E. F., 1902
Schroder, William H., 1955
Schubert, Jeremy, 1989
Schubert, Joseph A., 1987
Schubert, Rudy C., 1955
Schuller, Jerome A. Jr., 1973
Schuller, Michael, 1976
Schultz, A. W., 1950
Schultz, Chris, 1992
Schultz, E. C., 1899
Schultz, E. F., 1941
Schultz, Mark, 1989
Schultz, R. L., 1940
Schultz, W., 1946
Schultze, James Marbrooks,
   1988
Schulz, Harvey, 1965
Schumpert, M. C., 1931
Schuricht, Hans, 1991
Schuster, Mike, 1989
Schwank, Ronald H., 1963
Schwarz, Dean B., 1972
Schwarz, Duane, 1978
Schwarz, G. A., 1944
Schwarz, Kirk F., 1949
Schwennsen, William P., 1973
Scibetta, Salvatore, 1993
Scoggins, Gary R., 1971

Scoggins, Harold G., III, 1970
Scoggins, Terry, 1991
Scoggins, William Curtis, 1970
Scogin, James, 1975
Scott, C. B., 1952
Scott, C. W., 1937
Scott, D. L., 1950
Scott, David, 1965
Scott, David A., 1984
Scott, Donald F., 1970
Scott, Douglas, 1965
Scott, Eldon D., 1948
Scott, H. A., 1910
Scott, Hugh M. Jr., 1947
Scott, J. C., 1952
Scott, Lee, 1982
Scott, Leon, 1947
Scott, Mike, 1989
Scott, Morgan, 1975
Scott, Parker H., 1969
Scott, Paul, 1977
Scott, Steven, 1977
Scott, Tommy J., 1955
Scott, Ward, 1986
Scrivener, L. A., 1944
Scroggins, John, 1987
Seago, Joe, 1987
Seale, Michael R., 1963
Sealy, T. R., 1925
Searer, G. E., 1961
Sears, E. T., 1941
Sears, William, 1985
Seay, Jefferson, 1946
Sebesta, W. A., 1925
Sechrist, Robert J., 1930
Seefeldt, H. R., 1925
Seely, Thomas Russell Jr., 1961
Segal, N. V., 1957
Segrest, James C., 1963
Segzl, N. J., 1955
Seiter, David, 1979
Seiter, Thomas W., 1975
Seitz, David, 1975
Seitz, David, 1992
Seitz, Earl G., 1982
Seiwell, Robert, 1964

Self, Stanley A., 1946
Seligman, D. M., 1942
Sellars, B. B., 1895
Sellen, J. M., 1944
Sellman, Wayne S., 1958
Semands, Everett D., 1944
Sennette, Wilbert J., 1973
Sepesi, Zachary, 1985
Sepolio, Anthony F. Jr., 1969
Sergesketer, Robert, 1982
Sergest, C., 1966
Sergi, David, 1978
Sexton, Brian, 1980
Seydler, Joseph M. "Jody," 1975
Shadle, Stephen, 1987
Shaffer, Derek, 1983
Shanks, Homer K. Jr., 1954
Shanks, John L., 1951
Shannon, I. M., 1923
Shannon, J., 1943
Shannon, James A., 1969
Shannon, K., 1981
Shannon, Michael P., 1969
Shannon, Pat J., 1971,
Shannon, Paul, 1975
Sharon, Gary A., 1967
Sharp, Daniel, 1980
Sharp, G. K., 1958
Sharp, Harry R., II, 1956
Sharp, J. B., 1940
Sharp, James M., 1936
Shaw, Conway R., III, 1959
Shaw, H. L., 1958
Shaw, J. B., 1919
Shaw, L. W., 1961
Shaw, S. L., 1956
Shea, Jeff, 198 7
Shea, Stephen, 1980
Shea, Thaunia, 1989
Sheara, Don, 1984
Sheets, Michael, 1965
Shegeta, K. Y., 1952
Sheiker, W. G., 1956
Sheiness, Hershel L., 1960
Sheiness, Marc A., 1964
Shelburn, James R., 1904

Shelby, Stephen, 1992
Shell, R. K., 1935
Shelton, Charles, 1979
Shelton, Clifford, 1978
Shelton, Larry H., 1969
Shelton, Richard, 1986
Shenkir, William G., 1956
Sheppler, William, 1992
Sherman, F. H., 1925
Sherrou, Mark, 1979
Sherwood, H. J., 1894
Sherwood, Sidney, 1973
Shieldes, Lee, 1993
Shields, R. J., 1961
Shiers, Robert, 1978
Shiffrin, Cullen, 1977
Shiller, E. V., 1941
Shiller, R. E., 1902
Shindler, H., 1907
Shipley, Grady D., 1959
Shipley, Robert W., 1947
Shipp, B. G., 1947
Shires, Irwin, 1984
Shivers, Robert, III, 1975
Shives, John, 1976
Shives, Mark, 1978
Shives, William B., 1953
Shockley, Albert Lee, 1975
Shone, Louis, III, 1960
Short, Taylor J., 1936
Short, Tommy W., 1952
Shortle, Wayne, 1977
Shoultz, James C., 1936
Showers, Wayne A., 1949
Shubel, Kyle, 1989
Shults, Curtis, 1977
Shults, T. Mark, 1988
Shults, William, 1976
Shumate, Bruce E., 1931
Siecke, Paul, 1927
Siegert, Robert W., III, 1970
Siegmund, Eric D., 1970
Siem, Michael, 1992
Sikes, Samuel L., 1964
Siller, George C. Jr., 1969
Siller, Michael G., 1972

Silvernale, P. B., 1946
Silvernale, Paul, 1976
Simmang, Clifford L., 1972
Simmons, L. B., 1949
Simmons, R. B., 1944
Simms, G. M., 1959
Simms, L. A., 1903
Simon, Haskell L., 1949
Simon, Robert J., 1985
Simon, Timothy A., 1973
Simonds, F. H., 1903
Simpson, Donald G., 1946
Simpson, James H. Jr., 1945
Simpson, O. R., 1932
Simpson, Scott, 1974
Sims, Craig, 1982
Sims, Milton W., 1970
Sims, Vance, 1978
Sinclair, E. E., 1965
Sinclair, W. G., 1944
Singletary, Ricky L., 1965
Singleton, J. R., 1933
Sipe, D. M., 1958
Sisler, Carlton E. Jr., 1939
Sisson, J. E., 1955
Sivilich, Luke, 1989
Skaggs, R. L., 1961
Skaggs, William J., 1955
Skelton, J. A., 1921
Skelton, Jack, 1987
Skinner, L., 1924
Skinner, R. H., 1931
Skipworth, Kevin, 1978
Skolaski, W., 1981
Skrivanek, William, 1984
Slack, Gregory L., 1975
Slack, Joseph L., 1949
Slack, Michael L., 1969
Slack, Steve, 1975
Slack, T. E., 1938
Slackmon, Alan, 1989
Slatten, D. A., 1951
Slaughter, David C., 1961
Slaughter, Ernest Jr., 1944
Slaughter, John K., 1984
Slay, J. F., 1910

Slay, J. R., 1915
Slay, Samuel Houston, 1910
Slayton, J. C., 1947
Slicker, Edward, 1986
Slider, W. H., 1908
Sligh, David, 1976
Sloan, Scott, 1978
Slocker, Ed, 1989
Slover, George W., 1972
Sluck, Stephen Jr., 1973
Sluder, F. B., 1945
Smahlik, Henry J., 1968
Small, John F., 1966
Small, William W., 1935
Smart, F. P., 1937
Smedburg, Barry A., 1962
Smith, Albert R. Jr., 1971
Smith, Austin, 1992
Smith, B. A, 1963
Smith, Bruce D., 1954
Smith, Byron, 1977
Smith, C., 1982
Smith, C. B., 1956
Smith, C. E., 1952
Smith, C. G., 1939
Smith, C. O., 1921
Smith, C. W., 1959
Smith, Chris, 1983
Smith, Clinton D., 1969
Smith, D., 1965
Smith, D. G., 1932
Smith, David, 1987
Smith, David H., 1948
Smith, Donn W., 1944
Smith, E. F., 1944
Smith, E. J., 1950
Smith, Edwin, 1983
Smith, Edwin B. Jr., 1957
Smith, Eric, 1983
Smith, G. W., 1962
Smith, Garland P., 1949
Smith, George W., 1936
Smith, H. L., 1956
Smith, Harris Jr., 1946
Smith, Jay, 1977
Smith, Jerry D., 1956

Smith, Joe, 1955
Smith, John D., 1933
Smith, John Douglas Jr., 1961
Smith, Judson, 1955
Smith, Kevin, 1980
Smith, Kyle, 1992
Smith, L. C., 1959
Smith, L. N., 1934
Smith, Lloyd, 1980
Smith, Luttrell, 1979
Smith, Malcolm C. Jr., 1953
Smith, Mark, 1976
Smith, Max A., 1969
Smith, Merrill, 1936
Smith, Michael, 1984
Smith, Mike, 1977
Smith, Niley J., 1935
Smith, Paul M., 1959
Smith, R., 1981
Smith, R. C., 1959
Smith, R. D., 1961
Smith, R. E., 1958
Smith, R. L., 1944
Smith, R. Michael, 1983
Smith, R. S., 1945
Smith, R. W., 1944
Smith, R. W., 1958
Smith, Randy K., 1973
Smith, Ray, 1983
Smith, Richard A., 1968
Smith, Richard W. Jr., 1971
Smith, Robert, 1987
Smith, Robert A., 1965
Smith, Ronald T., 1959
Smith, Roy E., 1935
Smith, Ryan, 1993
Smith, S., 1981
Smith, Samuel P., 1964
Smith, Sidney V., 1940
Smith, Stephanie, 1991
Smith, Stephen, 1975
Smith, T., 1981
Smith, Timothy, 1975
Smith, V. G., 1959
Smith, Virgel, 1980
Smith, W. J., 1955

Smith, W. P., 1933
Smith, W. S., 1955
Smith, William Hiram Jr., 1945
Snead, Edwin D., 1947
Snearly, R. C., 1906
Sneed, Phillip, 1976
Snell, D., 1981
Snell, Keith, 1978
Snider, R. A., 1930
Snow, Joseph M. Jr., 1968
Snow, Michael, 1983
Snowden, Jonathan D., 1984
Snyder, B., 1967
Snyder, Bob, 1977
Soderquist, Markus K., 1938
Soles, Allan, 1977
Solomon, R. W., 1927
Sonnenburg, Jay, 1992
Soope, R., 1907
Sorensen, A. H., 1959
Sorenson, Daniel D., 1972
Soule, W. W., 1965
Sousares, Teddy, 1944
Sowden, M. S., 1961
Spacek, J. F., 1960
Spadafora, E. V., 1962
Spalti, H. D., 1924
Spann, Joseph Alan, 1974
Sparks, Don B., 1947
Sparks, Fred, 1963
Spaw, Steven, 1978
Speakerman, Wayne, 1975
Speed, J., 1968
Speed, T. L., 1930
Speer, Philip R., 1953
Speery, A. L., 1943
Speights, Stephen, 1966
Spence, Dan, 1990
Spence, David, 1993
Spencer, Byron, 1983
Spencer, Fred D., 1935
Spencer, G. L., 1939
Spencer, Robert F., 1982
Spencer, W. S., 1906
Spencer, W. W., 1908
Spense, Tyler, 1986

Spiars, Russell, 1978
Spiekermann, Wayne, 1975
Spikes, J. A., 1957
Spiller, H. S., 1954
Spiller, Robert E., 1973
Sponberg, D. E., 1921
Spoonts, P. R. A., 1936
Sprague, Denton, 1933
Sprague, R. D., 1958
Spreen, Carey R., 1974
Spreen, K., 1981
Springer, C. R., 1948
Springer, Joy V., 1947
Sprinkle, David, 1991
Sprinkle, Nathan, 1973
Sprinkle, William, 1989
Sprouls, James C., 1964
Sprouls, Scott M., 1969
Spruiell, W. L., 1956
Srygley, David, 1987
Stacell, H. Glen, 1963
Stacey, J. H., 1917
Stacey, Rodger D., 1969
Stack, Jon, 1980
Stack, T. L., 1958
Stackhouse, W. E., 1943
Stacy, J. G., 1959
Stacy, Kris, 1989
Stacy, Roger, 1967
Stadler, Erik, 1987
Staff, Jeffrey, 1985
Staffel, Gerald Jr., 1949
Stafford, David, 1975
Stafford, Roger, 1964
Stafford, T. O. M., 1962
Stafford, W. M., 1957
Staggs, F. M., 1944
Stagner, Q. P., 1945
Stahl, Billy J., 1949
Stahl, J. H., 1952
Stahl, John R., 1970
Stainback, Floyd Lee, 1947
Stalcup, J. K., 1940
Stalcup, James F., 1902
Stalcup, Louis H., 1924
Stallworth, Willett R., 1956

Stalting, Robert A., 1969
Stambaugh, Paul, 1988
Stamm, Scott, 1991
Stamps, Alton D., 1978
Stamps, David, 1975
Stanaland, Cody, 1992
Stanaland, S. I., 1963
Standefer, J. L., 1942
Standefer, John A., 1944
Standefer, Matthew, 1987
Standtman, L. V., 1941
Stanford, George, 1965
Stanford, R. W., 1958
Stanford, Richard B., 1944
Stanford, William D., 1972
Stanford, William J., 1937
Stanish, Albin Jr., 1976
Stanish, Jay, 1978
Stanley, G. C. "Pete," 1942
Stanziola, Alejandro, 1979
Staples, Stanley, 1986
Starckey, Sam, 1940
Starr, Jeffrey, 1985
Starr, L. B., 1936
Startz, Steven, 1974
Stearns, Claude R., 1962
Stearns, Reginald H., 1958
Steck, H. H., 1942
Steel, Tommy R., 1950
Steele, J. L., 1930
Steele, Robert M., 1974
Steen, D. R., 1954
Steen, James, 1992
Stehle, D. R., 1956
Stein, A. E., 1927
Stein, Julius A., 1922
Steinhoff, R. G., 1930
Steinle, F. W., 1957
Stell, Cyrus, 1977
Stelle, B. J., 1939
Stephens, David W., 1972
Stephens, Gregory, 1981
Stephens, J. M., 1940
Stephens, Karl A., 1953
Stephens, R., 1981
Stephens, R. L., 1939

Stephenson, Sidney F., 1958
Stepp, R. A., 1955
Sterenberg, E. H., 1895
Sterling, Benjamin G., II, 1972
Sterling, James, III, 1967
Sterling, James B. Jr., 1934
Sterling, Tommy M. Jr., 1957
Stevens, Mark, 1980
Stevens, Mark R., 1971
Stevens, Morris H., 1938
Stevens, R. S., 1959
Stevens, Richard, 1976
Stevens, W. M., 1946
Stevenson, Dewie, 1956
Steward, W. Cecil, 1952
Stewart, Alvin R., 1968
Stewart, Claude C., 1938
Stewart, Donald R., 1964
Stewart, Mark D., 1969
Stewart, Michael A., 1968
Stewart, T. G., 1951
Stickle, Dwight, 1977
Stickle, George, III, 1976
Stigall, Don V., 1947
Stiles, Andy, 1984
Stiles, Edwin L., 1947
Stiles, J., 1944
Still, Charles E., 1957
Stilson, David, 1988
Stindt, William H., 1957
Stockard, David M., 1969
Stocks, A. B., 1920
Stockstill, Jess E., III, 1956
Stockton, B. A., 1928
Stoddard, H. L., 1941
Stoelu, Richard A., 1969
Stoerkel, Walter, 1986
Stoffregen, Glen E., 1961
Stokes, M. R., 1956
Stoll, J. F., 1955
Stolle, R. M., 1953
Stolting, Robert A., 1968
Stone, Garrett M., 1937
Stone, Richard B., 1969
Stone, Stephen P., 1972
Stone, T. J., 1945

Stout, Kenneth E., 1974
Stout, M. C., 1960
Stover, Curt, 1980
Stover, Kenneth A., 1976
Stover, Terrance, 1978
Stracke, Sam L., 1940
Strain, C. E., 1897
Strandtman, L. V., 1939
Strange, J. R., 1958
Street, Jerry N., 1964
Stribling, S. R., 1911
Stricklin, Steven, 1972
Strieber, A. L., 1922
Strieber, C. A., 1924
Strieber, F. E., 1924
Stringer, Timothy, 1985
Strom, Earl, 1976
Stroman, William J. Jr., 1964
Stroud, James W., III, 1971
Stroud, W. F., 1957
Strauhal, Paul, 1978
Struck, Carl, 1985
Studebaker, Shannon, 1991
Stuessy, Eugene, 1958
Stumberg, Richard K., 1978
Stuntz, P., 1981
Stuntz, Richard A., 1973
Sublett, Stephen W., 1973
Suerth, Michael, 1989
Sullivan, Daniel A., 1973
Sullivan, L., 1967
Sullivan, Michael Q., 1988
Sullivan, Steven T., 1968
Sullivan, W. B., 1941
Summers, John W., 1968
Supak, Gene, 1963
Surlet, Steve, 1976
Surovik, William L., 1936
Suter, Tom, 1976
Suttle, Courtney, 1977
Suttles, James C., 1970
Sutton, B. K., 1926
Sutton, John, 1977
Sutton, Robert, 1993
Suvarnapruska, Tony, 1988
Swann, William A. Jr., 1952

Swanson, Robert, 1976
Swayne, Royce B., 1967
Swayze, C. D., 1917
Sweaney, Richard H., III, 1966
Swearingen, Lawrence C., 1968
Swearingen, W. Oren, 1948
Sweatman, R. H., 1925
Sweatman, R. Q., 1958
Sweeney, R., 1966
Swinford, Orr K., 1971
Swingle, D., 1968
Swinnea, Joe, 1981
Swinney, Jack O., 1973
Swinney, R., 1980
Swinney, Tim, 1977
Sykes, S. Lee, 1964
Syler, John T., 1951
Symm, Mark, 1992

Tabor, S. H., 1922
Tagert, David, 1974
Taglavore, Patrick, 1985
Taite, Timothy, 1984
Takacs, J. E., 1936
Talbott, J. R., 1962
Taliaferro, W. E., 1958
Talk, E. M., 1941
Talk, W. A., 1942
Talley, David, 1965
Tallman, J. D., 1957
Tallworth, W. R., 1956
Talmadge, B. E., 1927
Taniguchi, Kim, 1976
Tanner, Carrol B., 1949
Tanner, Shane, 1993
Tarrant, James R., 1949
Taru James, 1988
Tarver, Jason, 1988
Tarver, Robert, 1983
Tarver, Sean, 1988
Tarwater, Paul, 1985
Tate, Darrell L., 1968
Tate, Jeff, 1986
Tate, Tim, 1984
Tatum, R. G., 1951
Tavu, Tan, 1987

Taylor, Glenn E., 1923
Taylor, James, 1989
Taylor, John, 1976
Taylor, M. D., 1953
Taylor, Mark, 1986
Taylor, Randy, 1980
Taylor, Robert, 1985
Taylor, Robert E. Jr., 1949
Taylor, W. U., 1940
Tea, Charles, 1987
Teague, Keith, 1979
Teal, Randy, 1989
Teas, Joseph P., 1952
Teems, D. M., 1954
Teer, B. D., 1953
Teinert, Mark, 1982
Tejeda, Patrick, 1988
Teller, H. M., 1956
Tempio, Bryan, 1981
Temple, James, 1992
Templeton, J. B., 1946
Terrell, Cloyce M., 1944
Terrell, David, 1976
Terrell, Glenn, 1982
Terrell, Jere D., 1971
Terrell, Rodney, 1982
Terrell, Ronald, 1982
Terrell, T. H., 1957
Terrell, Thomas H., 1931
Terrell, Toby, 1992
Terrell, William Jr., 1981
Terry, C., 1966
Terry, P., 1981
Terry, William L., 1960
Tetsch, F. L., 1953
Teurpe, E. C., 1919
Thacker, Eric, 1990
Thacker, Ike C., 1971
Thaxton, E. A., 1939
Theole, Todd, 1989
Thiberville, Andy, 1977
Thiberville, Philip, 1983
Thiberville, Robert, 1976
Thiers, J. L., 1950
Thiessen, Mark A., 1974
Thigpen, Ben B., 1944

Thimas, Kim, 1975
Thoele, Todd, 1987
Thomas, Allan, 1976
Thomas, Bill, 1978
Thomas, D. W., 1949
Thomas, E. E., 1897
Thomas, Ed, 1986
Thomas, Edward E., 1950
Thomas, Edwin F., 1938
Thomas, F. L., 1936
Thomas, G. G., 1930
Thomas, H. J., 1948
Thomas, James H., 1949
Thomas, James, 1977
Thomas, Jason, 1988
Thomas, Jerry, 1974
Thomas, Jesse, 1993
Thomas, John, 1986
Thomas, John C., 1964
Thomas, Joseph, 1989
Thomas, K., 1981
Thomas, Karl W. Jr., 1970
Thomas, Kent, 1985
Thomas, Kim, 1975
Thomas, Kirk F., 1972
Thomas, Mike, 1975
Thomas, Richard O., 1943
Thomas, Robert S., 1949
Thomas, Stanley, 1950
Thomason, Wayne E., 1928
Thompson, Bruce F., 1947
Thompson, David, 1982
Thompson, Douglas Jr., 1987
Thompson, G. A., 1931
Thompson, H. Durwood, 1929
Thompson, J., 1981
Thompson, J., 1982
Thompson, J. M., 1925
Thompson, J. R., 1962
Thompson, Jeffrey, 1978
Thompson, John, 1944
Thompson, Jon, 1991
Thompson, Kenneth I., 1971
Thompson, Larry M., 1970
Thompson, Mike, 1975
Thompson, R. N., 1925

Thompson, Richard B., 1970
Thompson, Roy W., 1958
Thompson, Stanley W., 1947
Thompson, Steven, 1981
Thompson, Thomas, 1986
Thompson, W., 1967
Thompson, William F., 1946
Thomsen, P. W., 1952
Thomson, Donald B., 1984
Thomson, Jack W., 1973
Thomson, R. J., 1951
Thom, Donald C., 1947
Thom, J., 1966
Thornhill, Otto M., 1923
Thornton, Lloyd D., 1944
Thorpe, Edwin H., 1954
Thorpe, Gary, 1978
Thorpe, Robert C., 1969
Thorpe, Sam T., 1971
Thorpe, Wix C., 1942
Thrash, Thomas Jr., 1979
Threadgill, A. R., 1920
Threadgill, Edwin G., 1950
Thrusher, J. E., 1933
Thurman, Jack E. Jr., 1962
Thurman, N. D., 1940
Thurman, Richard, 1980
Tice, Francis, 1964
Tienert, M., 1982
Tierce, J., 1950
Tiffin, David B., 1973
Tigner, Thomas Jr., 1975
Tijerina, Albert, 1985
Tijerina, Albert A. Jr., 1961
Tijerina, Andrew A., 1963
Timmons, Mitchell J., 1967
Tingle, Jeff, 1987
Tinsley, Malcolm W., 1958
Tippett, Ross, 1942
Tipton, L., 1926
Tittle, James D., 1946
Toland, Albert D., 1936
Toland, Clinton J., 1938
Toles, Tommy, 1984
Tolley, Terry H., 1974
Tolson, L., 1981

Tolson, W. A., 1917
Tom, Hal H., 1938
Tomkins, Kurt, 1985
Tomlinson, Howard M., 1973
Tomme, Curtis R., 1974
Tomscha, Jason, 1993
Tooley, Terry H., 1973
Toone, Roy C. Jr., 1968
Torgerson, Donald T., 1973
Torrence, Glenn R., 1945
Torres, Arturo, 1988
Torres, Judith, 1993
Tovar, G. F., 1950
Towery, Kendall, 1986
Townsend, F. H., 1924
Townsend, Robert N., 1972
Townsend, W. M., 1951
Townsley, David W., 1973
Tracy, H. H., 1895
Transclair, John, 1975
Travis, Robert O., 1928
Travis, Robert S., 1949
Treadway, James, 1980
Treat, Russell, 1976
Trefry, W. H., 1904
Treude, Karl, 1979
Trevino, R. P., 1954
Trevino, Rey Jr., 1986
Tribaldos, Santiago, 1958
Triche, Gary J., 1974
Trimble, B. B., 1952
Trimble, D. W., 1956
Trimble, Harry B., 1936
Tromblee, Douglas B., 1975
Trosclair, John, 1975
Trosper, Paul D., 1971
Trotter, J. M., 1951
Trotter, Richard, 1989
Trousdale, W. B., 1951
Troxell, David, 1977
Trudell, John, 1988
Truscott, John, 1984
Trusty, Kenneth, 1991
Tschirhart, Cary, 1989
Tschirhart, John E., 1969
Tschirhart, Mike, 1977

Tsesmelis, John G., 1946
Tuccori, F. E., 1938
Tucker, D. L., 1955
Tucker, Joe, 1952
Tucker, P. M., 1953
Tucker, Thomas, 1957
Tuerpe, Ellis R., 1911
Tuerpe, Elmer C., 1917
Tumulty, Matthew, 1989
Turbeville, Arthur Ray, 1926
Turbeville, B. F., 1923
Turley, Edward V., 1969
Turner, Aric, 1979
Turner, C. M., 1957
Turner, Daniel, 1992
Turner, John, 1986
Turner, Michael, 1988
Turner, N. P., 1922
Tyson, Charles, 1977

Udell, Marlon D., 1973
Udemi, Joseph, 1975
Ulmer, J. A., 1957
Ulmer, James F., 1944
Ulrich, Joseph W., 1970
Umbach, Daniel, 1986
Undenstock, J., 1967
Underwood, Max, 1976
Uniz, F., 1949
Upchurch, John P., 1960
Urbani, Pompeo, 1949
Urbanic, Charles E., 1957
Urbanosky, Thomas F., 1957
Ussery, Ryan, 1991
Uzzell, B. R., 1951

Vabry, Brown, 1949
Vacek, Rudolph, 1988
Vader, Kevin, 1993
Vaille, Kevin, 1980
Valadez, Tim, 1991
Valdez, Mario, 1987
Valdez, Vincent, 1993
Valenciano, Carlos, 1989
Valverde, Frank W., 1965
Van Boskirk, Scott, 1987

Van Buskirk, Brian, 1993
Van Heerde, Christopher, 1993
Vance, P. A., 1917
Vandezande, Paul S., 1972
Vanderbilt, Carl, 1976
Vanderbilt, David, 1977
Vandermiller, G. R., 1951
Van Dom, A. L., 1961
Van Dyke, Eric, 1992
Van Dyke, Steven, 1987
Van Ermen, William C., 1962
Vannoy, C. P., 1939
Vannoy, Thomas R., 1940
Van Slambrouk, D., 1981
Van Wie, William, 1985
Vanzandt, H. R., 1951
Varvel, Kenneth G., 1940
Varvil, Mark, 1987
Vaughan, John M., 1944
Vaughn, Billy M., 1946
Vaughn, Charles H., 1946
Vaughn, D., 1968
Vaughn, Richard, 1979
Vaughn, Richard W., 1964
Vaughn, Virgil A., 1927
Vega, Antonio, 1987
Veien, John A., 1943
Velasquez, D., 1981
Vellenga, D. D., 1960
Venable, Harold K., 1971
Venzey, M. M., 1915
Veren, J. A., 1942
Vester, S. H., 1948
Vick, J. E., 1959
Vickery, Eric, 1985
Vickrey, R. L., 1937
Vickroy, Stephen C., 1974
Viera, Robert, 1989
Vierling, Theodore, 1993
Villanueva, A. F., 1952
Villareal, Juan A., 1970
Villarreal, Miguel, 1988
Vinson, J. M., 1935
Vinson, R. N., 1935
Vinz, Frank L., 1949
Visoski, Steven B., 1951

Vittrup, John B., 1948
Vizza, Albert F., 1947
Vladyka, Boyd, 1983
Voelkel, Tyson, 1992
Voelter, C., 1928
Voelter, Charles E., 1953
Voelter, David L., 1957
Vogel, E. Neal, 1986
Vogel, Morris, 1965
Vogeli, Mike, 1990
Vogelsang, John W., 1967
Voinis, Michael, 1993
Volcik, Douglas, 1991
Volk, Donald, 1978
Volts, E. E., 1940
Von Roeder, G. L, 1936
Von Rosenberg, Leslie Austin,
  1914
Von Schoeler, Waldemar Jr.,
  1944
Vrla, Daniel E., 1972
Vrla, Stanley E., 1945

Waak, Kyle, 1980
Wackwitz, Donald, 1980
Wacusek, G., 1944
Wade, R. C., 1922
Wadley, B. N., 1910
Wadley, C. M., 1924
Wagener, G. H., 1932
Wagenfuehr, R. H., 1925
Waggoner, Thomas B., 1949
Waggoner, William, 1980
Wagner, G. P., 1946
Wagner, Laddie F. Jr., 1971
Wahle, Malcolm M., 1972
Wahrmund, Henry O., III,
  1970
Wait, Russell E., 1972
Wakefield, James, 1988
Waldie, Alan D., 1946
Waldroup, M., 1965
Wales, Curtis, 1985
Wales, Philip A. Jr., 1971
Wales, Scott, 1988
Walford, Daniel, 1987

Walker, B. J., 1941
Walker, Charles E., 1949
Walker, D., 1981
Walker, Dalan, 1991
Walker, David, 1993
Walker, Frank E. Jr., 1937
Walker, H., 1967
Walker, Howard C., 1940
Walker, J. C., 1904
Walker, J. C., 1958
Walker, J. G., 1948
Walker, Jordan A., 1914
Walker, Luther A., 1949
Walker, Matt, 1980
Walker, Naomi, 1990
Walker, P. E., 1939
Walker, R. D., 1950
Walker, W. R., 1950
Wall, Brandon, 1993
Wall, T. A., 1934
Wallace, David, 1987
Wallace, Dennis, 1966
Wallace, G. D., 1942
Wallace, Marc, 1985
Wallace, W. V., 1926
Wallin, S. P., 1962
Walling, Choya K., 1970
Walling, Herbert M., 1970
Wallis, Robert, 1987
Walsh, D. E., 1950
Walsh, Donald, 1955
Walsh, Michael L. 1967
Walter, Robert O., 1969
Walters, D. A., 1957
Walters, Robert, 1985
Walton, T. T., 1923
Wamendorf, Mitch, 1978
Wanja, Joseph N., 1959
Ward, A. L. Jr., 1939
Ward, David E., 1985
Ward, E. B., 1953
Ward, Everett, 1962
Ward, J. C., 1927
Ward, James, 1986
Ward, M. M., 1960
Ware, F. S., 1944

Wariner, Richard, 1987
Warner, William A., 1970
Warren, Dickie K., 1951
Warren, L. L., 1951
Warren, M. D., 1951
Warren, Philip, 1990
Warren, R. L., 1942
Warsham, L., 1966
Washburn, P. J., 1921
Washington, Dawn, 1987
Washington, Gaylord, 1979
Waston, Mike, 1988
Water, J. C., 1903
Waters, Augustus L., 1970
Wathen, Ben R., 1972
Watkins, Bobby F., 1952
Watkins, C. E., 1916
Watkins, J. E., 1922
Watkins, Vernon E., 1972
Watley, J. D., 1937
Watson, Bradley, 1988
Watson, E. L., 1964
Watson, Ian, 1992
Watson, Mike, 1986
Watson, Raymond A., 1964
Watson, Robert N., 1970
Watson, Steve, 1971
Watson, Thomas W., 1964
Watts, Hubert B., 1951
Watts, M. A., 1958
Wayhle, Malcolm, 1975
Wearden, Paul, 1943
Weatherby, James L. Jr., 1960
Weatherford, John P. Jr., 1953
Weaver, Alfred, 1919
Weaver, Frederick P., 1973
Weaver, Gregory K., 1967
Weaver, H. R., 1925
Weaver, Michael E., 1968
Webb, J. F., 1938
Webb, Kenneth W., 1948
Webb, Morris S., 1959
Webb, R. M., 1951
Wechan, Jason, 1985
Weddle, M. N., 1959
Weed, Bobby P., 1954

Weeks, Wesley D., 1921
Weems, Jardon N., 1939
Weghorst, W. P., 1941
Wehner, B. T., 1936
Wehner, Byrom T., 1960
Wehner, Ernest L., 1937
Wehner, F. W. H. Jr., 1931
Wehner, H. H. Jr., 1935
Wehring, A. R., 1940
Wehrle, Larry J., 1936
Weiderstein, E. C., 1957
Weilert, Matthew, 1980
Weinert, C. H., 1944
Weinstein, S. B., 1964
Weir, Arthur T., 1950
Weir, Brian, 1986
Weir, G. S., 1942
Weir, Nathan, 1988
Weiss, C. L., 1962
Weiss, H. C. 1960
Welborn, Douglas, 1974
Welburn, William D., III, 1951
Welch, Mark, 1977
Welch, Robert L., 1941
Welhelm, C. A., 1954
Wellman, John, 1993
Wells, David, 1992
Wendtlandt, Walter G., 1946
Wentwoich, Karl, 1984
Wentworth, Jeffrey, 1958
Werchan, Jason, 1984
Werner, Elmer C., 1926
Wertz, Donald R., 1933
West, John E., 1953
West, M. L., 1961
West, O. I., 1962
West, T. B., 1924
Westbrook, Dan, 1989
Westbrook, Jack W., 1946
Westbrook, Richard C., 1964
Westbrook, Robert E., 1969
Wester, C. C., 1922
Wester, Lari M., 1953
Westmoreland, C. E., 1921
Westmoreland, J. R., 1927
Wetz, Ferman L., 1949

Weverka, T. L., 1922
Weyland, A. H., 1915
Weyland, Otto P., 1919
Wharton, R. H., 1941
Whatley, G. A., 1921
Wheeler, Carroll B., 1934
Wheeler, J. M., 1942
Wheeler, Jim E., 1946
Wheeler, Joseph, 1992
Wheeless, Tommy, 1948
Whilden, John, 1986
Whipple, D., 1951
Whitaker, Barron, 1979
White, C. C., 1916
White, Clinton D., 1954
White, David, 1974
White, David, 1985
White, David J., 1964
White, Doug, 1975
White, H. C., 1933
White, J. C., 1911
White, J. D., 1940
White, James, 1974
White, John D., 1959
White, John Thomas, 1970
White, L., 1966
White, Leroy, 1951
White, Neil, 1990
White, O. S., 1953
White, Pablo, 1993
White, Robert N., 1942
White, S. A., 1908
White, William F., 1947
Whiteaker, James E., III, 1966
Whitehead, Eric, 1988
Whitely, J. F., 1960
Whitemore, Paul, 1977
Whitley, Donald L., 1944
Whitman, R., 1966
Whitman, Worsham C., 1931
Whitten, Marion E., 1925
Whorton, R. N., 1939
Whyte, Carl B., 1946
Wickes, Henry G. Jr., 1947
Wideman, Scott, 1993
Widmer, Dennis A., 1962

Wiedenfeld, Jonathan, 1980
Wiederstein, Erwin C. Jr., 1959
Wier, G. S., 1938
Wier, Michael I., 1961
Wieting, James, 1938
Wight, R. E., 1957
Wigley, C. B., 1946
Wikes, Thomas, 1979
Wilbeck, James, 1965
Wilburn, E., 1968
Wilburn, T., 1918
Wilcox, Willie, 1975
Wilhelm, Thomas, 1983
Wilkerson, J. R., 1947
Wilkerson, Robert, 1965
Wilkes, Don E., 1958
Wilkes, Thomas, 1978
Wilkie, L. A., 1954
Wilkin, L., 1966
Wilkin, M. J., 1964
Wilkins, James R. S., 1971
Wilkins, K. T., 1964
Wilkinson, B., 1946
Wilkinson, David W., 1983
Wilkinson, Joseph L., 1968
Wilkinson, Sam L., 1927
Wilkinson, William, 1965
Wilks, Tom, 1980
Willaert, Albert L., 1952
Willaert, R. E., 1955
Willard, Douglas, 1984
Willason, W., 1968
Willett, E. R., 1921
Williams, Bill, 1980
Williams, C. B., 1946
Williams, C. D., 1942
Williams, C. W., 1950
Williams, Charles, 1980
Williams, Chip, 1988
Williams, Chris, 1983
Williams, Chris, 1993
Williams, Christian, 1988
Williams, Chuck, 1980
Williams, Clayton, 1986
Williams, Clayton W. Jr., 1950
Williams, D. D., 1953

Williams, D. G., 1937
Williams, D. H., 1961
Williams, D. O., 1942
Williams, David A., 1973
Williams, Donald C., 1969
Williams, Eric, 1993
Williams, George M. Jr., 1966
Williams, H. L., 1894
Williams, J. A., 1950
Williams, J. Duncan, 1970
Williams, J. O. Jr., 1946
Williams, J. S., 1916
Williams, James, 1975
Williams, James, 1980
Williams, Jason, 1991
Williams, John, 1971
Williams, John, 1973
Williams, John, III, 1967
Williams, Jonathan, 1989
Williams, Ken, 1941
Williams, L. A., 1950
Williams, L. D., 1895
Williams, Leland, 1964
Williams, M. Dan Jr., 1959
Williams, Michael, 1991
Williams, Montza, 1983
Williams, Pat, 1942
Williams, Robert D., 1949
Williams, R. K., 1941
Williams, S. M., 1912
Williams, Stanley, 1976
Williams, Stuart J., 1974
Williams, T. L., 1959
Williams, Tasha, 1993
Williams, Todd, 1984
Williams, W., 1966
Williams, William, 1980
Williamson, B. B., 1941
Williamson, D. P., 1960
Williamson, J. A., 1951
Williamson, J. Y., 1947
Williamson, Robert B., 1941
Williford, Connie, 1975
Williford, George, 1993
Williford, George H., III, 1970
Willis, Donald E., 1959

Willis, Giles W., III, 1979
Willis, Walter R., 1954
Willison, H. E., 1936
Willmann, James L., 1958
Willms, E. F., 1951
Willms, Walter R., 1957
Wills, Wesley, 1984
Willson, H. E., 1933
Wilmot, C. Scott, 1984
Wilson, Benjamin, 1993
Wilson, Brad, 1987
Wilson, Clarence A., 1933
Wilson, Douglas R., 1953
Wilson, E. L., 1950
Wilson, Francis W., 1932
Wilson, G., 1968
Wilson, G. O., 1925
Wilson, Gene M., 1945
Wilson, J. M., 1932
Wilson, Johnnie C., 1952
Wilson, Larry, 1981
Wilson, Martin L., 1986
Wilson, Michael, 1977
Wilson, Richard, 1988
Wilson, Robert, 1986
Wilson, Stephen F., 1968
Wilson, T. B., 1958
Wilson, W. D., 1907
Wilton, Bonsall S., 1968
Wiltse, M., 1958
Winburn, Lee, 1988
Windell, S., 1967
Winder, D. A., 1948
Winder, N. G., 1933
Windsor, Cecil O. Jr., 1962
Windsor, Marshall, 1979
Windsor, S., 1966
Winford, R., 1958
Winfrey, James E., 1961
Winfrey, John, 1966
Winn, Ronald, 1962
Winn, W. S., 1937
Winship, R. M., 1924
Winstein, G. D., 1935
Winston, Harry J., 1944
Winston, Jody, 1978

Winterrowd, Jack C. Jr., 1974
Wise, J. K., 1959
Wise, T. A., 1944
Wite, Harry, 1934
Witherspoon, B. W., 1925
Witkowski, Michael, 1980
Witt, Milton P. Jr., 1958
Witte, B. O., 1902
Witte, Herman B., 1926
Witte, W., 1894
Wittig, Stacy, 1986
Wittman, J. E., 1898
Wizig, B., 1936
Wlmer, J. F., 1945
Woffard, John W., 1972
Woffard, R. K., 1955
Wohflied, R. M., 1951
Wolfe, Ian, 1991
Wolff, William E., 1944
Wolford, J. L., 1936
Wolfschohl, Amber, 1993
Wolfskill, Lee, 1980
Wolfson, Daniel J., 1971
Womack, David, 1979
Womack, Richard H., 1974
Womble, Judson C., 1936
Wommack, Kevin D., 1973
Wong, R., 1966
Woo, Albert, 1980
Wood, Alan G., 1927
Wood, Charles R., 1921
Wood, David L., 1949
Wood, Glen, 1974
Wood, Matthew P., 1974
Wood, Samuel G., 1964
Wood, Todd, 1989
Woodall, B. F., 1932
Woodall, I. O., 1921
Woods, Damon C., 1906
Woods, Edgar, 1966
Woods, Fred Jr., 1939
Woods, J. K., 1894
Woods, Stuart, 1979
Woodward, W. W., 1961
Woolsey, R. T., 1920
Wooten, Walter, 1984

Work, Thierry, 1979
Worley, David B., 1985
Worley, Wilbur J., 1946
Worsham, Lushene M., 1962
Worsham, Stephen, 1981
Worth, Richard F., 1939
Worthely, N. R., 1951
Wray, Daryl, 1980
Wray, Lucian O., III, 1977
Wren, Herman, 1925
Wright, Billy, 1944
Wright, C., 1982
Wright, Donald, 1972
Wright, Eric, 1983
Wright, Harlan E., 1940
Wright, J., 1966
Wright, J. R., 1928
Wright, Lance R., 1973
Wright, Mark, 1973
Wright, Robert Jr., 1965
Wright, Robert K. Jr., 1958
Wright, Stephen E., 1973
Wright, Thomas R., 1972
Wright, Thomas W., 1961
Wrightson, Robert, 1988
Wyant, James, 1979
Wyatt, Charles E., 1947
Wyatt, Kenneth, 1986
Wyly, Grayson F., 1946

Ximenes, Andy, 1983

Yaklin, S., 1981
Yale, Charles, 1989
Yantiss, Edward H., 1985
Yarbrough, Ray E., 1969
Yeager, A. A., 1956
Yeager, J. R., 1950
Yeager, R. A., 1948
Yelverton, Guy, 1989
Yerigan, David, 1984
Yerigan, Richard Scott, 1981
Yett, R. P., 1923
Ylinen, Joh n A., 1973
Yoakum, Troy, 1986
Yoehle, H. J., 1950

York, Gregory, 1979
York, Norman, II, 1953
Youdal, Ellis, 1978
Youdal, Sam, 1980
Young, Bill, 1973
Young, Bobby, 1979
Young, D., 1958
Young, E. H., 1957
Young, F. W., 1952
Young, H., 1945
Young, J. A., 1956
Young, J. M., 1940
Young, John W., 1935
Young, L. H., 1944

Young, Robert D., 1970
Young, Robert W. Jr., 1972
Youngblood, J., 1964
Youngblood, J. R., 1957
Younger, B. C., 1953
Younger, W. C., 1954
Younger, W. S., 1908

Zak, A. J., 1951
Zedlitz, Alfred C., 1933
Zeitler, Carl Jr., 1954
Zetner, Thomas, 1943
Zerwekh, C. E., 1917
Zey, E. C., 1956

Zgainer, John, 1980
Ziegenhals, O. W., 1935
Zieschang, Wayne D., 1973
Zimmerman, Geoff, 1990
Zimmerman, Kenny, 1915
Zimmerman, P. E., 1922
Zinn, Bennie A., 1922
Zinn, W. R., 1925
Zipp, Thomas G., 1954
Zonana, Victor, 1977
Zotz, Lawrence P. Jr., 1973
Zotz, William T., 1972
Zuniga, Javier, 1989
Zwerneman, Robert C., 1971

This roster includes those men and women who have participated in the Aggie Band in the first 25 years of its second century—those entering the band during the 1994 to 2018 academic years. Unlike the previous roster, this one includes the class years of those Aggies who, like their predecessors, worked diligently to be known as the "Noble Men of Kyle." This list could not have been compiled without the input of the Aggie Band staff, current Aggie Band members, and the Texas Aggie Band Association, especially Chris Sullivan, Class of 1998, who gathered and confirmed massive amounts of data from a variety of sources and Michael Hudson, Class of 1997, for coming through with his class list at the last minute.

Class Years 1998–2022

Aaron, Daniel, 2013
Abaray, Steven, 2005
Abel, David, 2016
Abel, Joshua, 2000
Abell, Jacob, 2022
Abernathy, Jacob, 2011
Abernathy, Tom, 2012
Abinsay, Christian, 2019
Acosta, Brandon, 2021
Acosta, Gerson, 1997
Adame, Fernando, 2021
Adams, Andrew, 2006
Adams, Josh, 2006
Adams, K.K., 2009
Adams, Kenny, 2018
Adams, Kimberly, 2008

Afenkhena, Franklin, 2022
Agner, Andrew, 2020
Agold, Ella, 2017
Aguilar, Miguel, 2002
Ahart, Ryan, 2022
Ahn, Ju, 2019
Ahnberg, Kaylee, 2012
Aimone, Isabelle, 2022
Ainsworth, Taylor, 2006
Ainsworth, William, 2009
Alamia, Jeffrey, 2006
Alamia, Joseph, 2004
Alaniz, Juan, 2009
Alaniz, Phillip, 2004
Alarcon, Aurora, 2022
Albright, Derek, 2013
Alcorn, Austin, 2012
Alcozer, Dan, 2002
Aldrich, Ryan, 2001

Aldrich, Ryan, 2009
Alexander, Nicholas, 2017
Alexander, Simon, 2007
Alexander, Tyler, 2008
Alfano, David, 2016
Allen, Parker, 2014
Allgood, Eric, 2020
Almeida, Anthony, 2015
Alpert, Seth, 2002
Alsup, Todd, 2004
Alvarado, Isaac, 2004
Alvarez, Alfredo, 2021
Alvizo, Adrian, 1998
Amundson, Eric, 2009
Andersen-Matonic, Stephanie, 2013
Anderson, D., 2002
Anderson, D. J., 2017
Anderson, James, 2011

Anderson, Jason, 2018
Anderson, Josh, 2018
Anderson, Paul, 2001
Andreas, Joshua, 2003
Andrews, Alicia, 2012
Andrews-Moreno, Justin, 2022
Andrup, Ian, 2018
Angel, Michael, 2011
Anglin, Robert, 2012
Anitsakis, Jon, 2004
Anitsakis, Nicolas, 2001
Ankrum, Chris, 2004
Ansley, Shameika, 2009
Anthis, Keith, 2000
Anthony, Drake, 2015
Anthony, Maxwell, 2012
Anthony, Rachel, 2018
Applegate, Mike, 2008
Ardissono, Carl, 2016
Arguelles, Porfirio, 1998
Arkison, Erin, 2008
Arlitt, Travis, 1999
Armand, Jay, 2002
Armstrong, Jennifer, 2017
Arndt, Robert, 2007
Arnold, Brent, 2002
Arnold, Hayley, 2021
Arnold, Kelly, 1998
Arnold, Pierce, 2016
Arnold, Preston, 2015
Arquitola, Andrej, 2015
Arrington, Daniel, 2014
Arriola, Angelica, 2020
Arriola, Joey, 2018
Arriola, Maria, 2022
Astley, Kelson, 2011
Aston, Adam, 2000
Aston, Jason, 2012
Atkins, Brady, 2001
Atkinson, Aaron, 2014
Atkinson, Taylor, 2008
Atmar, Robert, 2008
Aulbaugh, Greg, 2011
Austin, Brian, 2018
Austin, James, 2021
Avery, Mack, 1997

Avila, Maria, 2015
Ayala, Carlos, 2007
Ayres, Jared, 2012
Azua, Marcos, 2005

Backof, Jonathan, 2009
Bacuyag, Donavan, 2009
Badrina, Eddy, 1998
Bailes, Corey, 2021
Bailey, Daniel, 2007
Bailey, Jena, 2013
Bailey, Jenson, 2017
Baird, Danny, 2012
Baird, Greg, 2002
Baird, Preston, 2022
Baker, Brian, 2000
Baker, Dori, 1997
Baker, Dustin, 2008
Baker, John, 1997
Baker, Nick, 2014
Baker, William, 1999
Balasko, Benjamin, 2003
Balasko, Clara, 2000
Baldree, Danny, 2005
Baldwin, Patrick, 2003
Baldwin, Ryan, 1999
Ball, Timothy, 2004
Ballard, Chrystel, 2009
Ballard, Myron, 2011
Baluyot, Xandrix, 2011
Banks, Michael, 2003
Banner, Craig, 2006
Barakat, Mark, 2019
Barber, Michael, 2004
Barbier, Michael, 2005
Barbier, Travis, 2007
Bardwell, James, 2016
Bardwell, Joel, 2021
Barenklau, Ryan, 2020
Barham, Grover, 2021
Barkley, Justin, 2011
Barna, Kelly, 2017
Barnard, Jeff, 2001
Barnes, Jason, 2005
Barnes, Justin, 2013
Barnes, Lincoln, 2009

Barnes, Rider, 2006
Barnett, Ryan, 2009
Barney, Katelyn, 2015
Barney, Kyla, 2018
Barnhart, Zachary, 2022
Baron, Kate, 1999
Barrera, Adrian, 2015
Barrera, Brianna, 2020
Barrett, Andrew, 2016
Barrientos, Anthony, 2013
Barrientos, Gerardo, 2009
Barron, Krystina, 2013
Barron, Kyle, 2005
Barrow, Justin, 2006
Bartee, Brandon, 2001
Barth, Craig, 1999
Bartle, Michael, 2004
Barton, J.P., 2013
Barton, Lowell, 2012
Barton, Randal, 2011
Barton, Ryan, 1998
Bashinski, Nathan, 2009
Baskin, Dustin, 2004
Bass, Justin, 2005
Bassham, Tony, 1997
Bauerschlag, Matt, 1999
Baugh, Robert, 2005
Baughman, Chauncer, 2014
Beagles, Payne, 2012
Beall, Colton, 2016
Beaman, Kyle, 2018
Bean, Crista, 2005
Bearden, Joshua, 2012
Beasley, Tim, 2001
Beatty, Samuel, 2020
Beazley, Ross, 2021
Beck, J., 2002
Becker, Phillip, III, 1997
Becktold, Ashley, 2017
Behrens, Samuel, 2000
Beimer, Scott, 2003
Beiseigel, Jon, 2012
Belden, Joseph, 2005
Belitzer, Abby, 2006
Bell, Erin, 2022
Bell, Grayson, 2016

Bell, Hayden, 2014
Bell, Jeremy, 2006
Bell, Matthew, 2007
Bell, William, 2021
Bell, Woody, 2002
Bellini, Chris, 2013
Beloney, Adam, 2003
Beltran, Wesley, 1999
Benac, David, 2012
Benjamin, Erica, 2013
Bennett, Katherine, 2015
Bennett, Key, 2015
Bennett, Shane, 2015
Benschoter, Henry, 2018
Benson, John, 2014
Bergeron, Thomas, 2022
Bergfeld, Bradley, 2012
Berggren, Franklin, 2001
Berry, Alden, 2017
Berry, David, 1999
Berry, Grey, 2015
Bert, Noah, 2021
Berzoza, Sammy, 2012
Best, Stephen, 2012
Bethel, Cindy, 2009
Beuerman, Thomas, 2007
Beuershausen, Chad, 1998
Beversdorf, Brian, 2000
Biberston, Ryan, 2015
Bible, Elizabeth, 1997
Bischak, Randall, 2013
Bishop, Erin, 2005
Bissett, Doug, 1999
Bissey, Bianca, 2014
Bittle, Austin, 2009
Bittle, Stewart, 2016
Black, Alexander, 2010
Black, Jessica, 2010
Black, Nick, 2017
Black, Paul, 2014
Blackburn, Hannah, 2011
Blackmar, Samantha, 2017
Blackwell, Layne, 2001
Blackwell, Payton, 2003
Blair, Mark, 2010
Blake, Cameron, 2017

Blake, Cameron, 2020
Blanchard, Michael, 2012
Blankenship, Daniel, 2012
Blankenship, James, 2009
Blankenship, Mark, 2000
Blanton, Chad, 2015
Bliss, Cody, 2019
Bliss, Robert, 2001
Blizzard, Joel, 1998
Bloxom, Lillian, 2022
Blum, Kevin, 2012
Blumenthal, Patrick, 2021
Boatright, Johnathan, 2003
Bobbitt, Kevin, 2001
Bodeker, Ross, 2017
Bodeker, Travis, 2002
Boeck, Kevin, 2010
Boese, Robert, 2011
Boettger, Robert, 2004
Bolf, Justin, 2018
Bolin, Brandon, 2003
Bomar, Amanda, 2017
Borden, Brett, 2000
Bordner, Cole, 2017
Borel, Matt, 2008
Bosquez, Kim, 2018
Bost, Trace, 2019
Bouma, Logan, 2017
Bounds, Christopher, 2005
Bowen, Alexis, 2017
Bowling, Boon, 2007
Boyd, Brady, 2010
Boyd, Matthew, 2005
Boyd, Patrick, 2004
Boyd, Steven, 2001
Boylan, Bryan, 2015
Bradford, Jason, 2000
Bradford, Jordan, 2020
Bradford, McKenna, 2012
Bradley, Jayme, 2005
Bradshaw, Amber, 2000
Brady, Kyle, 1999
Brady, Michael, 2015
Brady, Zach, 2010
Braley, Dawson, 2006
Brannen, Corey, 1999

Branyon, Rachel, 2017
Branyon, Thomas, 2015
Brashear, Bryan, 2009
Braswell, Ciaran, 2021
Bray, Aaron, 2004
Brazzell, Russell, 1998
Brechbuhl, Hans, 2021
Brewer, Raleigh, 2014
Brewer, Ross, 2017
Bridges, Tommy, 2002
Briggs, Jared, 2005
Brines, David, 1997
Brink, William, 2017
Brinkley, Erin, 2017
Bristo, Judd, 2001
Broadway , Corey , 2013
Brock, Katie, 2018
Brock, Lori, 2000
Broderick, Mark, 2006
Broderick, Matt, 1998
Bronaugh, Bert, 2010
Bronaugh, Brandon, 2013
Bronaugh, John, 2017
Brooks, Adam, 2004
Brooks, Victoria, 2010
Broussard, Aaron, 2011
Broussard, Adam, 2009
Brown, Ashton, 2008
Brown, Britney, 2004
Brown, Caleb, 2019
Brown, Chad, 1997
Brown, Chase, 1997
Brown, Daniel, 2007
Brown, Derek, 2005
Brown, Dylan, 2016
Brown, Eric, 2004
Brown, Jason, 2004
Brown, Josh, 2017
Brown, Justin, 2010
Brown, Michael, 1997
Brown, Sara, 2020
Brown, Travis, 2004
Browning, Thomas, 2021
Brownlee, Aaron, 2003
Brownlee, Chris, 2005
Brown-Pruitt, Christopher, 2015

Bruhn, Joshua, 2020
Bruner, Shaun, 2015
Brusenhan, Ross, 2022
Bryan, Hannah, 2013
Bryan, Klayton, 2021
Bryan, Riley, 2009
Bryant, John, 2005
Bryant, Thomas Jr., 1997
Brydie, Cory, 2007
Bubela, Larry, 1997
Buchanan, Shawn, 2022
Buettner, Jennifer, 1997
Buinn, Stephen, 1997
Bullard, Brandon, 2022
Bullen, Jeremy, 2017
Bullen, Jonathan, 2019
Bullington, Brett, 2017
Bullock, Kathryn, 2017
Burdette, Daniel, 1998
Burdick, Mason, 2016
Burdick, Travis, 2018
Burk, Cory, 1998
Burke, Zachary, 2012
Burkhalter, Isaac, 2014
Burley, Darien, 2022
Burlingame, Rob, 1999
Burnett, Jenifer, 2008
Burns, Kevin, 2000
Burrescia, John, 1999
Burt, Jonathan, 1999
Burton, Joseph, 2003
Bush, Andrew, 2016
Bush, Bradley, 2019
Bush, Jason, 2003
Busocker, Lauren, 2021
Butcher, Steven, 2011
Butler, Benjamin, 2017
Buttler, Jared, 1998
Byrne, Will, 2007

Caddenhead, Cole, 2018
Caguioa, Jerome, 1998
Cahill, Kyle, 2022
Calandria, Caitlin, 2020
Calberg, Sarah, 2005

Calderon, Alex, 2014
Calderon, Eric, 2009
Caldwell, Chris, 1999
Caldwell, Jeff, 2009
Callahan, Jeremy, 1998
Camarata, Joseph, 2015
Camarillo, Erik, 2013
Campbell, Erik, 2015
Campion, Leif, 2021
Campos, David, 2011
Campos, Jesse, 1997
Campos, Jorge, 2017
Campos, Richard, 2016
Campos, Tina, 2005
Canales, Bobby, 2005
Cantrell, Jonathan, 2020
Cantu, Aaron, 2012
Capehart, Carter, 2006
Capps, Mike, 2007
Captain, Caleb, 2018
Carapia, Tavo, 2015
Caraway, Cody, 2017
Caraway, Ross, 2000
Cardwell, Collan, 2019
Carjill, Natalie, 2020
Carlson, Conner, 2018
Carlson, Katherine, 1997
Carney, M., 2002
Carr, Brian, 2002
Carrasco, Clarissa, 2021
Carriker, Sara, 2015
Carrillo, Ashly, 2003
Carrillo, David, 2017
Carrillo, Reid, 2018
Carrol, Abbey, 2002
Carter, Brian, 2003
Carter, Chris, 1998
Carter, Keisha, 1998
Casarez, Julian, 2018
Casas, Ida, 1998
Casasnovas, Melanie, 2014
Casey, Christopher, 2006
Casey, Johnathan, 2006
Casey, Patrick, 2014
Cashen, Cordt, 1998

Cashion, Lee, 1998
Casso, John, 2022
Castaneda, Katherine, 2021
Castillo, Marissa, 2020
Castoreno, Jacob, 2010
Cate, Alexandre, 2019
Cavazos, Jayson, 2019
Caver, Josiah, 2019
Cawyer, Brad, 2003
Celaya, Enrique, 2017
Ceritelli, Michael, 1998
Cervantes, Anthony, 1999
Cervantes, Randy, 2004
Chamberlain, R., 2002
Chambers, Cody, 2018
Chamu, Steveng, 2016
Chance, Joshua, 2012
Chance, Ryan, 2008
Chapa, Joe, 2002
Chapman, Aaron, 2012
Chattaway, Stephen, 2006
Cheatham, Thomas, 2018
Chen, Cheri, 2009
Chen, Wyatt, 2017
Cheshier, Jim, 2004
Cheshire, Caelan, 2016
Chesney, Stephen, 2004
Chessher, Joshua, 2006
Chesshire, Kelton, 2022
Chico, Neil, 2001
Childers, Hailey, 2021
Childers, Jason, 1999
Childress, Chandler, 2019
Childs, Joshua, 2020
Childs, Sara, 2009
Chin, Andrew, 2018
Chipman, Chad, 2000
Chmielewski, Gabe, 2006
Chrismer, Timothy, 2008
Christian, MiKyle, 2020
Christie, John, 1999
Christopher, Benjamin, 2012
Chronister, Amy, 2018
Chumley, Kimberly, 1998
Cincotta, Tony, 2011

Cisneros, Eligio, 2020
Cisneros, Medrano, 2001
Citzler, Kyle, 2005
Clanton, Kristen, 2006
Clark, Brad, 2005
Clark, Elizabeth, 2017
Clark, Gabriel, 2012
Clark, Garrett, 2022
Clark, Rusty, 1998
Clark, Thomas, 2009
Clay, Taylor, 2011
Clayburn, Jesse, 2001
Clayton, Christina, 2013
Clayton, Tracy, 2004
Clayton, Trevor, 2002
Cleere, Jared, 2003
Clemenshaw, Andrew, 2019
Clemenshaw, Jared, 2022
Clemmons, Candace, 2020
Cline, Bob, 2013
Cline, Bryan, 2011
Clonts, Michael, 2001
Coatney, Joel, 2018
Cocetti, Zachary, 2017
Coe, Sara, 2022
Coggin, Kim, 2002
Colbert, Mike, 2001
Colby, Glen, 2017
Coleman, Adam, 2014
Coleman, Anton, 2006
Coleman, Matt, 2014
Collier, Courtney, 2001
Collins, Dorothy, 1999
Collins, Ian, 2022
Collins, Kyle, 2019
Colwell, Madeline, 2012
Comeaux, Jordan, 2005
Compton, Afton, 2022
Conger, Nathan, 1998
Conklin, Mason, 2020
Connally, Travis, 2002
Conner, Marina, 2020
Conrad, Richard, 2009
Conrad, Thad, 2007
Conrow, Marissa, 2013

Cook, Brittany, 2021
Cook, George, 2010
Cook, Sebastian, 2019
Coolidge, Greg, 2009
Coomes, Ryan, 2018
Coonrod, Xavier, 2021
Cooper, Cory, 2003
Cooper, Kyle, 2022
Cooper, Seth, 2010
Coovert, Eric, 2014
Copenhaver, Benson, 2005
Coppinger, Doug, 2003
Coppinger, Paul, 2000
Cornell, Katie, 2018
Cornell, Stephen, 2010
Coronilla, Alexis, 2021
Corrette, Kimberley, 2008
Corso, David, 2004
Cortez, Adalberto, 1998
Cortez, Alfredo, 2021
Costa, Naomi, 2006
Costilla, Marco, 2001
Cotton, Travis, 2017
Coull, Austin, 2019
Coursey, Jonathan, 2005
Covin, Marshal, 2018
Cowan, Roberto, 2011
Cowart, Matthew, 1999
Cowart, Randall, 2019
Cox, Austin, 2008
Cox, Courtney, 2009
Cox, Jonathan, 2002
Cox, Terra, 2013
Crady, James, 1998
Craft, John, 2015
Crain, Mike, 2005
Craven, Brooks, 2015
Crawford, Jacob, 2021
Creighton, Luke, 2001
Crenshaw, Richard, 2018
Crisp, Brian, 2004
Criswell, Matthew, 2000
Critchfield, Matt, 2011
Cropper, Chris, 2002
Crouch, Brendan, 2015

Croy, Melissa, 2007
Cruz, Cristina, 2012
Cummings, Brandon, 2007
Cummins, Timothy, 2016
Curtice, Drew, 2007
Cuttrell, Dakota, 2017

Dagley, Stephen, 2005
Dalton, Brandon, 2021
Daly, Daniel, 2002
Damin, Paul, 2000
Damin, Vince, 2003
Daniel, Andrew, 2018
Daniel, Andy, 1999
Daniels, Mercedes, 2018
Dannenbaum, Joe, 2007
Darby, Christopher, 2012
Darby, Todd, 2001
Darden, Dan, 2001
Darling, Justin, 2000
Darm, Jonathan, 2005
Darr, Justin, 2002
Daugherty, Edwin, 1999
Davenport, Troy, 2003
Davenport, Zeak, 2001
Davis, Brian, 2001
Davis, Clayton, 2020
Davis, Daniel, 2015
Davis, Gary, 2006
Davis, Jermaine, 2006
Davis, Matthew, 2021
Davis, Nathan, 2014
Davis, Robert, 2008
Dawkins, William, 2000
Dawson, Kevin, 2021
De Groh, Billy, 2015
De Jongh, Jacob, 2016
De La Cruz, Daniel, 2016
De La Fuente, Luis, 2021
de la Garza, Laura, 2010
Dean, Cassidy, 2012
DeAnda, Daniel, 2021
Dearing, Cody, 2009
Decker, James, 2010
Decker, Justin, 2005

Decker, Ryan, 2016
Decuire, Kody, 2022
Deeb, Thomas, 2022
DeFrance, Matt, 2015
Degollado, Enrique, 2021
Degrow, Keith, 2013
DeJesus, Anthony, 2018
DeLaFuente, Rafael, 2005
Delaney, Daniel, 2015
DeLay, Jeremy, 2004
DeLeon, Corina, 2021
Delgado, Hector, 2021
Delgado-Eberhart, Nito, 1998
Deman, Jacob, 2016
Demers, Dennis, 1999
DeMoor, Thomas, 2014
DeMuth, Hannah, 2020
Dendy, Austin, 2015
Dengler, Bryan, 2019
Dennis, Brittany, 2020
Dennis, Gary, 2005
Denslinger, Evan, 2017
DePalma, David, 2004
Derkowski, Brian, 2010
Derrington, Bill, 2000
Deschamps, Joe, 2015
DeVout, Jason, 2014
Dewese, Jeffrey, 2001
Diaz, Christian, 2018
Diaz, Haydee, 2019
Dibbley, Megan, 1999
Dickens, Taylor, 2014
Dickenson, Don, 1998
Dickeson, Jeffrey, 1999
Dicus, Robert, 2003
Dieterich, Brett, 1999
Dietrich, Calvin, 2017
Dittmar, John, 2007
Divita, Mark, 1998
Dixon, James, 2010
Dobiyanski, Brian, 2010
Dobiyanski, Cody, 2014
Dobiyanski, Vicki, 2003
Dock, Michael, 2012
Dodd, Chris, 2009

Dodd, Justin, 2003
Dominguez, Christopher, 2020
Dominguez, Clarissa, 2021
Dominguez, Mario, 2020
Dominy, Dean, 2002
Donaho, Brian, 2006
Donaldson, Luke, 2012
Dooley, Kolemann, 2021
Doranski, Michael, 2001
Dorough, Chris, 2002
Dorough, Justin, 2005
Dorsey, Steve, 2002
Douglas, Matthew, 2012
Douglass, Thad, 2016
Dousay, Kathryn, 2021
Dragisic, Paul, 2004
Drake, David, 2002
Driver, Jeff, 2007
Droemer, Aaron, 2007
DuBose, Daniel, 2010
DuBose, Taylor, 2022
Duck, James, 2006
Duffy, Shamus, 2020
Dugan, Ryan, 2004
Dugat, Will, 2007
Duigon, Luke, 2016
Duke, Jason, 2002
Dunbar, Jonathan, 2004
Duncan, Justin, 2016
Duncan, Michael, 2014
Dunham, Ragan, 1998
Dunk, Kyle, 2017
Dunk, Matthew, 2010
Dunne, Matthew, 2002
Duque, Lauriza, 2000
Durham, Jake, 2015
Durham, Jonathan, 2000
D'Urso, Simon, 2001
Duval, Stacy, 2004

Earle, Eric, 2014
Earnshaw, Ben, 2017
Earnshaw, Emily, 2013
Easley, Lucas, 2011
Eason, Elijah, 2022

Eastburn, David, 2000
Eastridge, Gabriella, 2013
Eblen, David, 1999
Echeveste, Nacho, 2018
Echeveste, Salvador, 2016
Edelman, Matt, 1997
Edgar, Michael, 2003
Edwards, Jane, 2016
Edwards, Kayla, 2015
Efeney, William, 2021
Egan, Rose, 2017
Eggenburger, Jason, 1999
Ehrman, Levi, 2022
Eickhoff, Jason, 2011
Eiland, Andrew, 2003
Ekelund, Scott, 2007
Eldridge, Samuel, 2010
Elliott, Lee, 2009
Elliott, Riley, 2015
Ellis, Landon, 2015
Ellis, Luke, 2012
Ellison, Jason, 1999
Elms, Ryan, 2015
Elmquist, Michael, 1997
Encinia, Edgar, 2020
Enderle, Jason, 2003
Engler, John, 1997
Epstein, Joel, 2021
Erickson, Timothy, 2012
Erikson, Keith, 2007
Erskin, Garrett, 2013
Erskine, Keith, 2002
Erwin, Jake, 2008
Esparza, Dalton, 2009
Esparza, Lianna, 2009
Esparza, Mando, 2000
Espinoza, Eric, 2013
Esquivel, Carlos, 2022
Esquivel, Nadia, 2019
Esselburn, Nathan, 2009
Estrada, Alain, 2018
Estrada, Jerome, 1999
Euker, Austin, 2019
Evans, Kris, 1999
Evans, Mackenzie, 2021

Evans, Steven, 2017
Evers, Lane, 2020
Evey, Chandler, 2017
Ewald, Evelyn, 2017

Fajfar, Kathryn, 2014
Falatko, Nick, 2018
Falla, Zachary, 2022
Fanick, Bryan, 2005
Fannin, Shane, 2001
Farber, Mike, 2003
Farmer, Connor, 2019
Farris, Lauren, 2012
Faterkowski, Kenneth, 1997
Faubion, Cody, 2008
Faughn, Brian, 2005
Faulkner, Brock, 2004
Faulkner, C.W., 2001
Fearn, Daniel, 1999
Fears, Adam, 2004
Feeny, Wesley, 2021
Feith, David, 2002
Feldman, Robert, 2005
Feliz, Bryan, 2019
Fellers, Boomer, 2009
Fellows, Bailey, 2010
Fergeson, Sabrina, 2007
Fernandez, Christopher, 2000
Ferris, Tanner, 2013
Ferron, James, 2011
Feuerbacher, David, 2020
Fiedler, Mason, 2022
Figueroa Alvarez, Pamela, 2015
Figun, Matthew, 2001
Fikes, Sarah, 2017
Findley, Michael, 1999
Finlayson, Ryan, 2015
Finney, Zachery, 2022
Fisher, Tom, 2005
Fitch, Sean, 2017
Fitch, Summer, 2003
Fitts, Eric, 2011
Fitzgerald, Lincoln, 2022
Flach, Ross, 2004
Flack, William, 2022

Flanagan, Cory, 2002
Flanagan, Sean, 2009
Flatt, Molly, 2021
Flatt, Tyler, 2018
Fleitman, Travis, 2014
Fleming, Alex, 2005
Fleming, Logan, 2013
Flores, Aaron, 2011
Flores, Alissa, 2022
Flores, Audie, 2018
Flores, Brandon, 2017
Flores, Chris, 1999
Flores, Jose, 2005
Flores, Manuel, 2020
Flores, Sergio, 1998
Flowers, Jessica, 2013
Fluker, Nathan, 2008
Focke, Joby, 1999
Foderetti, Michael, 2011
Fonseca, Edward, 2012
Ford, Cleve, 1997
Ford, Derek, 2005
Ford, Kimberly, 1997
Ford, Ryan, 1997
Ford, Stacey, 1999
Foreman, James, 2006
Foresman, Brandon, 2014
Forrester, Jason, 2011
Fountain, David, 2010
Fournier, Eddy, 2000
Fowler, Christian, 2016
Fox, , 2018
Fox, Anna, 2000
Fox, Rick, 2000
Franklin, Alexander, 2010
Franklin, Nathan, 2017
Frankson, Andrew, 2014
Frankson, John, 1999
Franz, David, 2000
Franz, Josh, 2018
Fraser, Aaron, 1998
Frazier, Cole, 2018
Freeman, Christopher, 2011
Freitag, Gretchen, 2011
French, Colton, 2016

French, Kyle, 2008
French, Sherri, 2004
Fresquez, Jarrod, 2005
Fricke, Aaron, 2000
Fritz, Josh, 2011
Fritzler, Jason, 2002
Frodyma, Misti, 1998
Froebel, Michael, 2013
Froelich, Cliff, 1998
Fry, Griffen, 2019
Fry, Peyton, 2016
Fryer, Richard, 2002
Frykholm, Samuel, 2018
Fuchs, Ginny, 1999
Fuentes, Juan, 2008
Fugitt, John, 1998
Fuller, Hugh Bob, 1998
Fullerton, Christopher, 2015
Fulton, Travis, 2016
Furr, James, 2003
Furtney, Sarah, 2005
Fuss, Allison, 2014
Fuss, Dalton, 2012
Fusselman, Clare, 2021

Gabelman, Cole, 2020
Gaeke, Brandon, 1998
Gaeke, Brent, 2000
Gage, Terry, 2005
Galindo, Matt, 2014
Galipp, David, 2009
Galloway, Marc, 2005
Galo, Isaiah, 2021
Galvan, William, 2016
Gamez, Stephen, 2020
Gandillon, Joe, 2005
Gandin, Mark, 2000
Ganotis, Melissa, 2011
Garcia, Abel, 2021
Garcia, Alan, 2012
Garcia, Andrew, 2019
Garcia, Carlos, 2018
Garcia, David, 2015
Garcia, Elijah, 2021
Garcia, Jordan, 2015

Garcia, Kimberley, 2011
Garcia, Kimberly, 2005
Garcia, Nancy, 2017
Garcia, Phil, 1999
Garcia, Robert, 1997
Garcia, Salvador, 2011
Garcia, Virjinia, 2013
Garmendez, Ruddy, 2022
Garner, David, 1998
Garner, Jon, 2003
Garrett, Matthew, 2019
Garrido, Christopher, 2021
Garza, Armando, 1997
Garza, Dick, 1998
Garza, Eddie, 2002
Garza, Frederic, 2000
Garza, James, 2000
Garza, Marc, 2000
Gaudlitz, Jeremy, 2019
Gavin, Aaron, 2021
Gawedzinski, David, 2021
Gay, Taylor, 2008
Gayre, Lauren, 2018
Gaytan, Rudy, 1997
Gebhardt, Daniel, 2006
Gebhardt, Geff, 2003
Geddes, William, 2016
Geer, Eber, 2005
Gendzwill, Jennifer, 2000
Gentes, Scott, 1997
George, William, 1999
Gerhart, Reed, 2014
Gerling, Brad, 2006
Germaine, Geoffrey, 2015
Gerwig, Mike, 2003
Gettemy, Daniel, 2012
Gibbs, Kevin, 2002
Gibson, Ian, 2012
Gibson, Jarett, 2020
Gibson, John, 2000
Gibson, Seth, 2002
Gibson, Zach, 2010
Giese, Samuel, 2019
Gilbert, Andrew, 2000
Gilbert, Jeremy, 2006
Gill, James, 2021

Gilleland, Daniel, 2008
Gillespie, Kevin, 2012
Gillman, Justin, 2017
Glaesmann-Till, Joshua, 2020
Glenn, Stuart, 1998
Glenn, Truman, 2000
Glick, Caden, 2022
Godwin, Mary, 2016
Godwin, Morgan, 2013
Goebel, Grant, 2019
Goertz, Aaron, 2007
Goff, Taylor, 2014
Goggin, David , 2002
Golden, Alexandra, 2012
Goldsmith, Adam, 2010
Goldstein, Kristina, 2015
Golub, Devon, 2011
Golub, Stephen, 2006
Gomez, Eduardo, 2009
Gomez, Eric, 2001
Gonzales, Andrew, 2007
Gonzales, Joel, 1998
Gonzales, John, 2005
Gonzales, Tony, 2014
Gonzalez, Alfredo, 2019
Gonzalez, Diana, 2016
Gonzalez, Eunice, 2016
Gonzalez, Fernando, 2002
Gonzalez, Frank, 2018
Gonzalez, Gilbert, 2005
Gonzalez, Jasmine, 2020
Gonzalez, Natalia, 2021
Gonzalez, Rosendo, 2015
Gonzalez, Timothy, 2006
Goodlin, Crystal, 2005
Goodson, Kyle, 2010
Goodson, Randy, 2018
Goodwin, Jake, 2014
Gordy, DeForest, 2017
Gorney, Adam, 1998
Gorney, Luke, 2001
Gorney, Michael, 2003
Goulas, Max, 2014
Gould, Thomas, 2014
Govea, Andrea, 2002
Govea, Michael, 2007

Graham, Courtney, 2015
Grant, Reed, 2014
Grantom, Ryan, 2015
Graves, Frank, 2017
Graves, Jacob, 2021
Graves, Josh, 2004
Gray, Andrew, 2004
Gray, Darius, 2008
Gray, Justin, 1998
Gray, Kendall, 2019
Gray, Lucas, 2020
Gray, Nicholas, 2017
Green, Brent, 2012
Green, Samuel, 2022
Greene, Bryan, 2010
Greenwald, John, 2016
Greenwald, Kevin, 2013
Greenwald, Maggie, 2019
Gremillion, Mark, 2005
Greunke, Garrett, 2002
Griffin, Brendan, 2021
Griffin, Eric, 1999
Griffin, Jason, 2001
Griffith, Connor, 2021
Grimberg, Jason, 2011
Grimes, Tim, 2000
Grobe, Melissa, 2003
Grounds, Tyler, 2016
Gruber, Jack, 2022
Guajardo, Tony, 2012
Guerra, Jacob, 2007
Guerra, Yvette, 2002
Guerrero, Alejandra, 2017
Guerrero, Robert, 2005
Guerrero, Yanelly, 2016
Guillory, Emmanual, 2006
Guillot, Stephen, 2003
Guinn, Stephen, 1997
Gunn, Dick, 1998
Gunn, Noble, 2006
Guo, Nikita, 2006
Gutierrez, Anthony, 2015
Gutierrez, Omar, 2001
Guzman, Itzel, 2022
Guzman, Jose, 2000
Guzman, Matthew, 1999

Haase, Dalton, 2015
Haber, Rex, 2004
Haby, Douglas, 2011
Hadley, Phil, 2000
Haefeli, Paul, 2012
Hagerty, Josephy, 1997
Hahn, John, 2005
Haines, Austin, 2014
Hainley, Catherine, 2004
Haire, Jerry, 2003
Haislet, John, 2004
Halcomb, Bryan, 2013
Hall, Christy, 2000
Hall, Jeremy, 2002
Hall, John, 2020
Hall, Justin, 2002
Hall, Patrick, 1998
Hall, Todd, 2002
Hall, Travis, 2006
Hall, Wesley, 2016
Hallam, Douglass, 2000
Halliburton, Alexander, 2019
Halling, Aaron, 2014
Halling, Lilliebeth, 2014
Halling, Pollyanna, 2014
Halling, Thomas, 2022
Hallmark, Adam, 2014
Hames, Jeffrey, 2022
Hamilton, Luke, 2004
Hamilton, Travis, 2020
Hamlin, William, 2012
Hamm, Lee, 2002
Hamm, Reed, 2005
Hammerstrom, Troy, 2005
Hamons, Andrew, 2022
Hance, David, 2018
Handley, Robert, 2011
Hankins, Steven, 2014
Hanks, Aaron, 2001
Hannemann, Don, 2004
Hannigan, Brendan, 1998
Hansen, Chris, 1997
Hanson, Kyle, 2007
Harber, Kevin, 2005
Hardaway, William, 2016
Hardin, Warren, 2007

Hardy, Katherine, 2010
Harmon, Joe, 2002
Harper, Andrew, 2000
Harper, Chris, 2007
Harper, Karlyn, 2010
Harper, Michael, 2014
Harper, Tim, 2004
Harrelson, Jacob, 2006
Harris, Bradley, 2008
Harris, Matthew, 2012
Harrison, Joel, 1998
Hart, Michael, 2004
Hartcraft, Parker, 2019
Hartigan, Campbell, 2022
Hartman, Karly, 2014
Hartmann, Bobby, 2014
Hartsfield, Jacob, 2010
Hartsfield, Rand, 2009
Hartsfield, Scott, 2014
Harvey, Kyle, 2011
Hassell, Aaron, 2002
Hatch, John, 2016
Hauck, Konrad, 2017
Havemann, Darrell, 2005
Havemann, Darren, 2001
Hawk, Stephen, 1998
Hawkins, Erin, 2008
Hayes, Brynn, 2008
Hayes, Michael, 1997
Hayman, Brandon, 2003
Hays, Casey, 2005
Hazel, Trevin, 2014
Heartwell, Derek, 2016
Heeter, Brandon, 1997
Hegefeld, Ross, 2004
Heggland, David, 2016
Heil, Brett, 2013
Heil, Nick, 2010
Heimann, William, 1997
Heisel, Ben, 2018
Heiser, Jason, 2000
Heitfeld, Chris, 2006
Helgren, Matthew, 2006
Helm, Steve, 2001
Henalsteen, Brian, 2005
Henderson, Amy, 2010

Henderson, Andrew, 2002
Henderson, Roy, 2006
Henkhaus, Robert, 2008
Henley, Matt, 2003
Henley, Stephen, 2001
Hennagan, Brandon, 2005
Henry, Bradley, 1999
Henry, Cory, 2007
Henry, Patrick, 2014
Hensel, Daniel, 2006
Henson, Chris, 2018
Henson, Garrett, 2004
Henson, Jacob, 2006
Herbst, Zachary, 2009
Hergert, Matthew, 2016
Heriford, Thomas, 2013
Hering, Steven, 2014
Hermosillo, M., 2002
Hernandez, Chuy, 2006
Hernandez, Danny, 2009
Hernandez, Ezekiel, 2019
Hernandez, Jaime, 2002
Hernandez, Leilani, 2010
Hernandez, Mark, 2017
Hernandez, Raf, 2004
Hernandez, Rene, 1999
Hernandez, Sam, 2004
Herod, Clint, 2005
Herrera, Jose, 2001
Herring, Blake, 2021
Herrington, Micah, 2002
Herron, Johnathon, 2012
Herzberg, Robert, 2017
Hess, Kyle, 2005
Hessler, Brian, 2014
Hevenor, Ben, 2015
Hewett, Joshua, 2014
Hicks, Emma, 2021
Hicks, Justin, 2010
Hicks, Terence, 2013
Hiebert, Spencer, 2016
Hiefner, Michael, 2017
Hignight, Micah, 2012
Hill, Alan, 1998
Hill, Alex, 2016
Hill, Benjamin, 2017

Hill, Donovan, 2014
Hillman, Christine, 2004
Hilscher, Austin, 2020
Hinds, Frank, 1997
Hinojosa, Juan, 2004
Hix, Joseph, 2010
Hixson, Adam, 2000
Hodges, Jaret, 2006
Hodges, Leah, 1999
Hodgson, Casey, 2015
Hoelscher, Danny, 2007
Hoelscher, Jacob, 2017
Hoffer, Joseph, 2001
Hoffman, Cason, 2016
Hoffman, Erik, 2014
Hoffman, Jessica, 2016
Hoffmann, Daniel, 2021
Hoffmann, Laura, 2016
Hoffmeister, Chris, 2000
Hogg, Jeff, 1999
Holand, Greg, 1997
Holcombe, Terry, 1999
Holder, Aaron, 2018
Holland, Bayley, 2021
Holloway, Ryan, 2004
Holly, Aric, 1999
Holmes, Jordan, 2015
Holmes, Riley, 2020
Holt, Kyle, 2000
Holzer, Howard, 2014
Holzer, Karl, 2017
Honeycutt, John, 2004
Hooker, Vivian, 2022
Hoover, Troy, 2021
Hopper, Brian, 2007
Hopson, Justin, 2002
Hornbuckle, Jack, 2001
Horne, Christopher, 2019
Horstmann, Robert, 2002
Horvitz, Aaron, 1997
Hostettler, Paul, 2006
Hounsel, Andrew, 2016
Houston, Jonathan, 2006
Houston, Sabrina, 2018
Houy, Fred, 2005
How, Emily, 2019

Howard, Alexandria, 2016
Howard, Aric, 2002
Howard, Ben, 1998
Howard, Christopher, 2007
Howard, Christopher, 2018
Howard, Jason, 2004
Howard, Jordan, 2012
Howell, Chauncy, 2004
Hubbard, Kassey, 2003
Huber, Parker, 2014
Hudgins, Tucker, 2021
Hudson, Matthew, 1997
Hudson, Michael, 1997
Huebner, Jonathan, 2010
Huebner, Thomas, 1999
Huebner, William, 2004
Hufford, Ryan, 2003
Hughes, Jeff, 2006
Hughes, Joshua, 2012
Hughes, Sean, 2017
Hughes, Stephen, 2012
Hughes, Thomas, 2015
Huhn, Barbara, 2001
Huhn, Michelle, 2003
Humpherys, Carol, 2004
Hunger, Ryan, 2015
Hungerford, David, 2009
Hunnicutt, Jonathan, 2006
Hunt, Alexander, 2015
Hunt, John, 1999
Hunter, Ernest, 2001
Hunter, Travis, 2017
Hunter, Wesley, 2000
Hurst, Adam, 2004
Huseman, Andy, 2006
Huseman, Jared, 2003
Hussain, Karim, 2017
Hutchison, Scott, 2004
Hutton, Ryan, 2008
Hyatt, Joshua, 2017
Hynes, Robert, 2000
Hynninen, Onni, 2001

Ibarra, Cipriano, 2020
Ibarra-Hunt, Jerry, 2008
Ickles, David, 1999

Iglesias, Jacob, 2019
Ilori, Nathaniel, 2019
Ilschner, Craig, 1999
Ilse, Scott, 2002
Immel, Alicia, 2015
Ingram, Tate, 2017
Ivey, Carl, 2017

Jackson, Caitlyn, 2020
Jackson, Christopher, 2020
Jackson, Derek, 2016
Jackson, Jessica, 2010
Jackson, Julius, 2003
Jackson, Nicholas, 2021
Jackson, Trevor, 2014
Jacobs, David, 2003
Jacobs, Matt, 2005
Jacobson, Luke, 2016
James, A., 2007
James, Ben, 2003
James, Cameron, 2010
James, Josh, 2009
James, Michael, 2016
James, Tamara, 1998
Jameson, Andrew, 2016
Janak, Bret, 2006
Janish, Gabriel, 2021
Jaramillo, Santiago, 2009
Jarzombek, Joseph, 2020
Jaska, Michael, 2014
Jaska, Pamela, 2010
Jaska, Paul, 2011
Jaska, Robert, 2016
Jawalka, Brian, 2004
Jay, Chris, 1997
Jay, Spencer, 2015
Jechow, Luke, 2008
Jeffers, Aubrianna, 2018
Jenkins, Adam, 2001
Jenkins, Crandall, 2015
Jenkins, Greg, 2014
Jenkins, Mary Ann, 2009
Jenson, James, 2017
Jesko, Markus, 2012
Jessup, Mark, 2012
Jetton, James, 2010

Ji, Hojun, 2016
Jimenez, Mario, 2015
Jimenez, Michael, 2010
Johannesen, Trace, 2000
Johnsen, Mark, 1999
Johnson, Brandon, 2021
Johnson, Brett, 1999
Johnson, C., 2003
Johnson, Charles, 2021
Johnson, Clay, 2019
Johnson, Jeff, 2003
Johnson, Jeffrey, 2012
Johnson, Levi, 1999
Johnson, Middleton, 2022
Johnson, Niyasha, 2022
Johnson, Sumner, 2019
Johnson, Tiffany, 2002
Johnston, Claire, 2021
Johnston, Curtis, 2011
Jones, Alex, 2003
Jones, Alex, 2018
Jones, Allen, 2002
Jones, Bryan, 2002
Jones, Caleb, 2014
Jones, CJ, 2014
Jones, Dalton, 2018
Jones, Hannah, 2010
Jones, Jacob, 2014
Jones, James, 1999
Jones, Justin, 2013
Jones, Kyle, 2008
Jones, Laura, 2010
Jones, Marcus, 2003
Jones, Matthew, 2012
Jones, Travis, 2011
Jordan, James, 2004
Jordan, Keltin, 2014
Joseph, Felton, 1999
Joseph, Wynton, 2012
Jouett, Jack, 2020
Judd, Connor, 2015

Kahl, Janell, 2009
Kahn, David, 2004
Kalinowski, Autumn, 2017
Kallina, Brian, 2014

Kam, Ryan, 2020
Kaminski, Andrew, 2020
Kapavik, Paul, 2010
Kapavik, Stephen, 2012
Kappelmann, Jonathan, 2017
Kasowski, Jacob, 2020
Kaus, Mitchell, 2020
Keese, Devin, 2018
Keiser, Scott, 2006
Keller, Joshua, 2019
Keller, Kyle, 1999
Kelley, Rodney, 1997
Kellum-Hudman, Danny, 2019
Kelly, Jason, 1998
Kelly, Kevin, 2000
Kelly, Patrick, 1997
Kelly, Steven, 2005
Kendall, Brian, 2006
Kenefic, Christopher, 2008
Kennedy, Clay, 1998
Kennedy, Eric, 1999
Kennedy, Korey, 2008
Kennedy, William, 2020
Kent, Bryan, 2011
Kent, Trevor, 2014
Keralis, Joel, 2009
Kern, Paula, 2011
Kessel, Kendall, 2009
Ketchen, William, III, 1997
Key, Janet, 2000
Khalid, Ameera, 2019
Kidd, Colton, 2009
Kidd, Max, 2007
Kidd, Tom, 1999
Kiley, Sarah, 2018
Kim, Tae, 2006
Kimes, Bradley, 2017
King, Amber, 2005
King, Ben, 2002
King, Dusty, 2006
King, James, 2006
King, Matthew, 2011
King, Will, 1997
Kinney, Natalie, 1998
Kinsel, Jeremy, 2001
Kirby, Jason, 2002

Kirby, Joshua, 2016
Kirk, Kelly, 2002
Kirkpatrick, Ben, 2001
Kirksey, Jonathan, 2005
Klein, Wyatt, 2018
Klett, Jason, 2008
Kline, Jeffery, 2011
Klinke, Jay, 2003
Kloesel, Chad, 2011
Knape, Aaron, 2001
Knape, Ryan, 2004
Knapp, Jeffrey, 2016
Knapp, Will, 2014
Kneupper, Justin, 1999
Knight, Justin, 2004
Knight, Kason, 2010
Knight, Kevin, 1999
Knight, Kyle, 2005
Kniss, Jason, 1998
Knolle, Mark, 1999
Knotts, Sam, 2007
Knowles, John, 2021
Knowlton, Andrew, 2018
Knox, Anna, 2019
Knox, Jessica, 2017
Koches, Brian, 1999
Kocian, Jeff, 2007
Koehn, Zachary, 2004
Koenig, Jay, 1998
Kohutek, Brian, 2004
Konderla, Jonathan, 2022
Korbacher, Kasey, 2015
Korioth, Sabrina, 2019
Kovatch, Jeff, 1999
Kowpak, Michael, 2014
Kraatz, Johnathan, 1997
Kramer, Chris, 2000
Krbec, Aidan, 2018
Krebs, David, 1998
Krebs, Douglas, 2002
Krebs, Kyle, 2013
Krebs, Marc, 1999
Kreiler, Cecilee, 2005
Krempel, Kelly, 2022
Krogel, Alex, 2015
Krogel, Nate, 2018

Krohmer, Gabriel, 2010
Kromer, Charlie, 2010
Kropp, Samantha, 2009
Krueger, Robert, 2009
Krueger, Tyler, 2012
Kruemcke, Roy, 2022
Krumrey, Jacob, 2022
Kuczkowski, Kathryn, 2022
Kuehner, Brian, 2008
Kujawski, Marcus, 2011
Kulkarni, Rachana, 2020
Kunisawa, Isaac, 2004
Kunisawa, Josh, 2004
Kutil, Charlie, 1998
Kwiatkowski, D.J., 2004
Kwiatkowski, Nicholas, 2006
Kwiatkowski, Sam, 2009
Kymes, Elizabeth, 2017

Labac, Greg, 2010
Labastida, Andrew, 2015
Labatt, Louis, 1997
Laengrich, Evan, 2022
LaGrone, Stuart, 2010
LaGrone, Thomas, 2015
Lair, Michael, 2001
Lair, Stephen, 1999
Laird, Jeff, 1997
Lake, Justin, 2000
Lamb, Steven, 2005
Lambeth, Aaron, 2005
Lamkin, Greg, 1999
Lamkin, Jeffrey, 2010
Lamkin, Mindy, 2009
Lander, Lawton, 2016
Lander, W. Hayden, 2017
Landgraf, Brooks, 2003
Landry, Drager, 2020
Landry, Mark, 2015
Laney, Michael, 2020
Lange, Matthew, 2017
Lanier, Brent, 2010
Lanoux, Riley, 2020
Lansdown, Trevor, 2007
Lantrip, Logan, 2013
Laporte, Justin, 2018

Lara, Esther, 2017
Laramore, Andrew, 2018
LaRocque, Kyle, 2004
Larsen, Travis, 2011
Larson, Nickolas, 2022
Lasater, Caleb, 2012
LaSeur, Stearns, 2006
Laster, Frederick, 2010
Lathem, Isaiah, 2021
Latiolais, Sarah, 2012
Laudermilk, Neal, 1997
Laughead, Jack, 2018
Laurel, Joshua, 2021
Lauritsen, Scott, 2018
Lavergne, Kevin, 1997
Lawson, Mike, 2003
Leach, Garrett, 2015
Leaveck, Katherine, 2004
Ledlow, Michael, 2012
Lee, Derrick, 2011
LeFlore Murphy, Symone,
    2020
LeFlore Murphy, Sydney, 2019
Leftwich, Charles, 2007
LeGros, Mark, 2017
LeGros, Renee, 2020
Leija, Amanda, 2004
Lemond, Andrew, 2010
Lenaway, Bradley, 2019
Leonard, Josh, 2006
Leonard, Kevin, 2009
Leos, Garrett, 2020
Lescallett, Megan, 2009
Leslie, Blake, 2003
Leutermann, Karl, 2016
Leutermann, Maximilian, 2012
Leveridge, Autumn, 1998
Lewis, Andrew, 2012
Lewis, Jake, 2020
Lewis, Michael, 2004
Lewis, Tyler, 2011
Lewis, Will, 2014
Lietzau, Rae, 2011
Liffrig, Nicholas, 2012
Lillis, Chris, 2009
Lilly, Daniel, 2002

Lim, Andrew, 2020
Lin, Michael, 2011
Lindsey, Kyle, 2001
Lindstrom, Jonathan, 2003
Linger, Steven, 2001
Linn, John, 2004
Lipinski, Andrew, 2015
Listi, Andrew, 2017
Listi, Michael, 2014
Listi, Nicholas, 2006
Litteken, Brad, 2001
Little, John, 2017
Little, Taelor, 2012
Littlejohn, Jeffrey, 2018
Littleton, Bradely, 1997
Lloyd, Jason, 2010
Lloyd, Jonathan, 2000
Locascio, Matthew, 2016
Lockard, Jim, 1998
Locke, Jacob, 2019
Locke, Robert, 2016
Lockett, Shane, 2017
Lockhart, Jeffrey, 2001
Lockhart, Ransom, 2013
Logan, Chase, 2011
Long, Jack, 2017
Long, Lacy, 2006
Long, Marshall, 2011
Long, Sara, 2013
Longoria, Alvaro, 2000
Longwell, Charles, 2011
Loomis, Justin, 2007
Lopes, Jacqueline, 2009
Lopez, Alejandro, 2016
Lopez, Cameron, 2021
Lopez, Denilzon, 2022
Lopez, Laura, 2017
Lopez, Mateo, 2014
Loria, Jennifer, 2008
Lovelady, Kevin, 2002
Loveless, Erin, 2006
Loy, Jordan, 2014
Lozano, Mario, 2000
Lucas, Cullan, 2011
Lucas, Paul, 2004
Lucas, Thomas, 2005

Luce, Donovan, 2022
Ludwigsen, Sarah, 2006
Luecke, Amber, 2010
Lugo, David, 2009
Lutz, Ben, 2021
Ly, Bryan, 2022
Lynn, Vaughan, 2017
Lyon, Tyler, 2022
Lyons, David, 2011
Lyons, Tristan, 2019
Lytle, Maura, 2016

Mabe, Christopher, 2013
MacFarlane, John, 2019
Macha, Amber, 2019
Macias, Carlos, 2010
Macias, Richard, 2017
Macicek, David, 2004
Macicek, Mark, 2000
Macicek, Michael, 1997
Mack, Gerald, 2010
Maddux, Kaylee, 2016
Maddux, Robert, 2017
Madsen, Jillian, 2010
Maginness, Mike, 2000
Mahalingham, Aubrey, 2022
Mahler, Jacob, 2022
Mahlstedt, Erik, 1998
Mahoney, Mike, 2012
Maida, Jon, 2007
Majerczyk, Eddie, 2003
Makusky, Madeline, 2021
Malcolm, Emily, 2022
Maldonado, David, 2019
Maldonado, Francisco, 1999
Maldonado, Jesus, 2018
Maldonado, Lorenzo, 2018
Malin, Michael, 2014
Malkasian, Matthew, 1998
Malone, Michael, 1998
Maltsberger, Mark, 1997
Mambretti, Andrew, 2008
Mandola, Michael, 2000
Maney, John, 2009
Mann, Andrew, 2013
Mann, Miranda, 2020

Manning, Samantha, 2008
Manos, Carlos, 2016
Maraist, Evan, 2019
Marek, Conner, 2018
Marek, Cullen, 2021
Margrave, Ian, 2008
Margulieux, Lauren, 2011
Markos, Chris, 2004
Marks, Brian, 1999
Marquette, Frank, 2013
Marroquin, Osmar, 2016
Marsden, Devin, 2006
Marsh, Mendy, 2000
Marshall, Brandon, 2004
Marshall, Daniel, 2004
Marshall, Zack, 2002
Martin, Austin, 2014
Martin, Brad, 2006
Martin, Chris, 2015
Martin, Christopher, 2018
Martin, James, 2000
Martin, Josh, 1998
Martin, Karen, 2020
Martin, Nicholas, 2020
Martin, Nicole, 2004
Martin, Reagan, 2013
Martindale, Jacob, 2017
Martinez, Adrian, 2021
Martinez, Alondra, 2022
Martinez, Dean, 1999
Martinez, Francisco, 2011
Martinez, George, 2004
Martinez, Jesse, 2015
Martinez, Jessica, 2019
Martinez, Jovan, 2010
Martinez, Julia, 2000
Martinez, Mike, 1997
Martinez, Mikey, 2015
Martinez, Roberto, 2019
Martinez, Rogelio, 2016
Martinez, Rudy, 1999
Martinez, Scott, 2001
Martinez, Stephen, 2017
Martinez, Travis, 2012
Martinez, Urbane, 2014
Martinez-Linares, Clarissa, 2018

Martinez-Makowski, Matthew,
  2020
Martins, Tiago, 2002
Marubio, L., 2003
Marvin, Sophia, 2019
Massengale, Meagen, 2011
Massey, Cory, 2012
Massey, Laura, 2006
Masters, Tay, 2008
Mattair, Stephanie, 2009
Mattei, Evan, 2005
Matthews, Nathan, 2012
Matthews, Pat, 2004
Maulden, K., 2006
Maury, Matt, 2003
Maxwell, Kyle, 2003
May, Aaron, 2002
May, Christopher, 2006
May, Matthew, 2009
May, Shelby, 2020
Mayeaux, Derreck, 2021
Mayeaux, Garrett, 2017
Mayer, Elliot, 2021
Maze, Shawn, 1997
McAnulty, Jordan, 2020
McBrayer, James, 2002
McBrayer, John, 1998
McBryde, Erin, 2022
McCall, Ethan, 2021
McCall, Ross, 2003
McCasland, Connor, 2015
McClain, Harrison, 2019
McClelland, Rob, 2004
McClendon, Carter, 2022
McClendon, Jayson, 2002
McClendon, Travis, 2017
McClenny, Levi, 2014
McClung, Meredith, 2000
McClure, Daniel, 2008
McClure, Matt, 2016
McCoy, Jason, 2009
McCullough, Ryan, 2014
McDaniel, Scott, 2003
McDonald, Gabe, 2018
McDonald, Jayson, 1997
McDonald, Samuel, 2018

McDonald, Spencer, 2015
McDougald, Hannah, 2021
McEwin, Aaron, 2006
McGehee, Jacqueline, 2006
McGehee, Paul, 2009
McGough, Lance, 2001
McGowan, David, 2000
McGrath, Brian, 2002
McGuffey, Jeremy, 2004
McKenzie, Eric, 1997
McKenzie, Nancy, 2001
McKinney, Chris, 2006
McKinney, Matt, 2007
McLauchlan, Joseph, 2021
McLean, Connor, 2017
McLemore, David, 2008
McLeod, Andrew, 2018
McLeod, Ian, 2006
McLeod, Joshua, 2006
McMahan, Ross, 2019
McMillan, Alexander, 2020
McMillan, Timothy, 2015
McMullen, Alexander, 2011
McMurray, Doug, 2002
McNair, Jerry, 2018
McPhee, Alison, 2011
McReynolds, Ezekiel, 2017
Meador, Jacob, 2016
Medellin, Christian, 2020
Medford, Michael, 1997
Medley, Ethan, 2022
Medlin, Alex, 2018
Medlock, Kyle, 2021
Meeks, Hayden, 2017
Mehrer, John, 2003
Meier, Travis, 2008
Melancon, Ross, 2003
Melnyk, Walter, 1998
Mena, Merlinda, 2017
Mendelsohn, Douglas, 2019
Mendez, Daniel, 2004
Mendiola, Jacob, 2020
Meneghetti, Michael, 2022
Menke, Mills, 2004
Meriwether, Cale, 2007
Merki, Mark, 2015

Messer, Billy Bob, 2007
Metz, Lawrence, 2004
Metz, Travis, 2008
Meuret, Jackson, 2019
Meyer, Ryall, 2005
Michael, Garrett, 2019
Michals, Shelby, 2012
Midkiff, Luke, 2014
Migl, Christopher, 2000
Migliaccio, Louis, 1997
Miles, Austin, 2010
Millard, Adam, 2012
Millard, Alex, 2012
Miller, Andrew, 2005
Miller, Dub, 1997
Miller, Erik, 2012
Miller, Grant, 2003
Miller, Kevin, 2016
Miller, Lance, 2003
Miller, Mason, 2022
Miller, Paul, 2010
Miller, Paxton, 2007
Miller, Tanner, 2008
Miller, Travis, 2014
Miller, William, 1997
Mills, Abby, 2007
Mills, Kenneth, 2003
Milton, Michael, 2020
Miralrio, David, 2019
Misamore, Brian, 2000
Mitchell, Amy, 2004
Mitchell, Brandon, 2002
Mitchell, Brent, 2000
Mitchell, Jonathan, 2019
Mitchell, Steven, 2005
Mize, Andrew, 2007
Mnench, Michael, 2002
Moak, Evan, 2010
Moczygemba, Kelly Sue, 2012
Moersen, Cristina, 2012
Moffett, Sam, 2006
Mohn, Sarah, 2008
Mohr, William, 2021
Mokry, BJ, 2004
Molden, Mark, 2017
Molden, Matthew, 2019

Molina, Nadia, 2004
Molinar, George, 1998
Monk, Cheryl, 2009
Montes, Celia, 2003
Montgomery, Hunter, 2017
Montoya, Dianna, 2001
Mooney, Matt, 2000
Moonjian, Pete, 2007
Moore, Austin, 2012
Moore, David, 2002
Moore, David, 2020
Moore, Jacob, 2016
Moore, Michael, 2022
Moore, Ryke, 2018
Moore, Tonya, 2006
Moorman, Steven, 2017
Morado, Rick, 2015
Morales, Leticia, 2019
Morales, Stephanie, 2011
Moran, Christopher, 2003
Moran, Dan, 2003
Moran, Daniel, 1998
Moran, David, 2005
Moran, Erin, 1999
Morefield, David, 2000
Morehead, Albert, 2009
Moreno, A., 2002
Moreno, John, 2016
Morgan, Aaron, 2013
Morgan, Chris, 1997
Morgan, Thomas, 2019
Morris, Chris, 2018
Morris, Jonathan, 2005
Morris, Kayla, 2000
Morris, Scott, 2008
Morrison, Jon-Michael, 2008
Morrison, Matthew, 2003
Moss, Kevin, 2014
Moultrie, Tai, 2003
Moyer, David, 2007
Mueller, Aaron, 2001
Mueller, Andrew, 2019
Mueller, Brendan, 2012
Mueller, R., 2002
Muema, Beatrice, 2021
Muir, Joseph, 2021

Mullins, Scott, 1998
Munns, Austin, 2016
Munns, Catherine, 2011
Munns, Kevin, 2009
Munoz, Carlos, 2015
Munoz, Kelsey, 2011
Muse, Catherine, 2011
Muske, Bryan, 1999
Musquiz, Mark, 2011
Muzyka, Debbie, 2002
Myers, Hazel, 2017
Myers, Travis, 2012

Nabors, Jeffrey, 2010
Naiser, Jayson, 2005
Nalley, Joel, 2005
Nallie, Gregory, 2016
Namendorf, Robert, 2008
Naradovy, Bryan, 2007
Narcisse, Marcus, 2010
Nash, James, 2017
Nash, Travis, 2005
Nash, Tucker, 2016
Natho, Clayton, 2005
Natishak, Joseph, 2017
Nauck, Cullen, 2015
Nauert, Geoffrey, 2013
Nava, Ricardo, 2014
Neal, Zachary, 2021
Neeley, Perry, 1997
Neeson, Nicholas, 2019
Negrete, Erick, 2021
Neiman, David, 2005
Nelson, Andy, 2002
Nelson, Caleb, 2000
Nelson, Christopher, 2019
Nelson, Cole, 2015
Nelson, Craig, 2005
Nesline, Lucian, 1999
Netardus, Luke, 2008
Neuenschwander, Jace, 1999
Neuenschwander, Joel, 1997
Newberry, Matt, 2006
Newman, Joseph, 2015
Newman, Tim, 2005
Newsom, Alexandria, 2019

Newton, Justin, 2016
Newton, Nathan, 2015
Nichols, Darrell, 2014
Nichols, Kayla, 2016
Niekamp, Amanda, 2002
Niemiec, Nick, 2015
Nieto, Sara, 2003
Niewierski, Kyle, 2020
Nolen, Paige, 2002
Noll, Mario, 2013
Noriega, Jose, 2021
Norrell, Mary, 2019
Norris, Chase, 2022
Norris, Peter, 2000
Norton, Madison, 2018
Noska, Nicholas, 2021
Novikoff, Cameron, 2015
Novosad, Blake, 2009
Nuhn, Ben, 2009
Null, Kurtis, 2016
Nunn, Christopher, 2021

Obi, Gregory, 2017
Ocasio, Will, 2012
Ochoa, Samuel, 2021
O'Connor, Justin, 2016
Odlozil, Mason, 2012
Odom, Buck, 1998
O'Flaherty, Trevor, 2010
Ogg, Jeremy, 2005
Ogier, Caleb, 2019
O'Gorman, Will, 2010
Ojo, Tolulope, 2021
Olbrich, Anneliese, 2021
Oldham, Caleb, 2006
Olivarez, Katarina, 2009
Olivarez, Mario, 2009
Oliver, Brian, 2004
Oliver, Glenn, 2015
Oliver, Matthew, 2000
Oliver, Nathan, 1998
Olmos, Emily, 2017
Olsen, Chad, 2002
Olson, Andrew, 1998
Olson, Christopher, 2020
Olson, Miata, 2016

Olvera, Leslie, 2014
O'Muirgheasa, Mairtin, 2003
O'Neal, Chris, 2006
O'Neal, Miles, 2019
Onstott, Jarrod, 2019
Opipare, Louis, 2002
Orillac, Rene, 2006
Ornelas, Cesar, 2018
Orr, Ashley, 2019
Orsted, John, 2004
Ortega, Heather, 2013
Ortegon, Juan, 2001
Ortiz, Samuel, 2021
Osborn, Toby, 2003
Ostberg, Joshua, 2019
Osterhold, Robert, 2018
Ott, Catherine, 2019
Oudie, Samantha, 2015
Ouellette, Derrick, 2001
Oviedo-Gomez, Analisa, 2020
Owens, Brandt, 2006

Pace, James, 2006
Padilla, Richard, 2017
Page, Jonathan, 2004
Page, Kathryn, 2006
Palacio, Joe, 2019
Palin, Ashley, 2010
Palmer, Jacob, 2012
Paniagua, Asael, 2002
Panneton, Bradley, 2018
Pantleo, Benjamin, 2020
Papandrea, Matthew, 2019
Parchman, Marshall, 2006
Park, Daniel, 2003
Park, John Claude, 2017
Parker, Bryan, 1998
Parker, Kayla, 2022
Parker, Scott, 1998
Parker, Zack, 2002
Parkman, Austin, 2020
Parks, Jared, 2006
Parrish, David, 2017
Parrish, Samuel, 2020
Parsley, Kristen, 2010
Parsons, Kyle, 2009

Parsons, Mark, 2003
Partlow, Justin, 2007
Partlow, Robert, 2005
Partridge, Michael, 2000
Passmore, James, 2022
Patterson, Laura, 2013
Patton, Ethan, 2008
Patton, Tyler, 2014
Paul, Chris, 2003
Paul, David, 2013
Pawlak, Daryl, 1999
Payne, Jeremy, 2006
Payne, Jeremy, 2014
Payne, Will, 2010
Pearce, Allan, 2014
Pearce, Derek, 2020
Pearce, Doc, 2004
Peck, Brian, 2017
Peck, Coleman, 2013
Pedroza, Mariana, 2020
Peel, Robert, 2012
Pelayo, Olivia, 2009
Pelayo, Sarah, 2011
Pena, Alexander, 2019
Pena, Elaina, 2010
Pena, Lorissa, 2012
Pence, Taylor, 2017
Penington, Christian, 2019
Penney, Erin, 2013
Penrod, Sean, 2000
Perez, Aaron, 2017
Perez, Christopher, 2009
Perez, Mari, 2009
Perkins, Jeff, 2013
Perkins, Justin, 2002
Perlman, Brian, 2013
Perry, Hayden, 2016
Perry, Jonathan, 2017
Peters, Anthony, 2007
Peters, Bryan, 1998
Peters, Trent, 2017
Petersen, Sarah, 2018
Peterson, Hanslin, 2002
Peterson, Jennyth, 1997
Petkovsek, Kyle, 2004
Pett, Tyr, 2022

Peyton, Reid, 2006
Pfeil, Sarah, 2015
Philips, Joshua, 2005
Philley, Andrew, 2004
Philley, Coleman, 2007
Philley, Jacob, 2004
Phillips, Aaron, 2000
Phillips, Bryan, 2002
Phillips, Chris, 2008
Phillips, Daniel, 2022
Phillips, Denise, 2003
Phillips, Jordan, 2020
Phillips, Kaisey, 2013
Phillips, Nate, 2000
Phillips, Rachel, 2009
Piazza, Mike, 2004
Pick, Ethan, 2020
Pilgrim, Brent, 1999
Pineda, Jose, 2020
Pineda, Luis, 2021
Pistor, Jacob, 2001
Pitcher, Andrew, 2011
Pitcher, David, 2009
Piwonka, Nathan, 2001
Pizzitola, Aaron, 2001
Plant, Jacob, 2014
Ploss, Chris, 2006
Pluff, John, 1998
Plummer, Kristin, 2003
Pluta, Timothy, 2011
Poehl, Mark, 2013
Pompa, Luis, 2016
Pompa, Michael, 2016
Poore, A. J., 2015
Pope, Jared, 2016
Pope, Jason, 1999
Popp, Andrew, 2009
Popp, Matt, 2006
Popp, Philip, 2011
Porter, Jason, 2016
Post, Vincent, 2022
Poteet, Alexandria, 2019
Poteet, Bryton, 2016
Potter, Brian, 2000
Poulsen, Jake, 2008
Pounders, Erin, 2003

Powell, Cody, 2008
Powell, Ernest, 2021
Powell, Nathan, 2019
Powell, Ryan, 2005
Powers, Alexis, 2019
Powers, Shelby, 2018
Poznanski, Nick, 2006
Pradel, Jonathan, 2022
Prado, Andrew, 2011
Prather, Michael, 2010
Pratt, Thomas, 2001
Prescher, Walter, 1998
Price, Cecylee, 1999
Price, Elizabeth, 2019
Price, John, 2015
Price, Ross, 2008
Price, Seth, 2012
Priego, Manuel, 2015
Primeaux, Jesse, 2007
Prince, Kyle, 2013
Prince, Ben, 2004
Privett, Grayson, 2022
Pruden, James, 2011
Prudhome, Parker, 2022
Prukop, Brian, 2001
Pruneda, Joshua, 2013
Przybyla, William, 2015
Puda, Josh, 2000
Pulvino, John, 2007
Purdy, Thomas, 2000
Putz, Bobby, 2014
Putz, John, 2000
Putz, Samuel, 2022

Qiang, Steven, 2022
Quesada, Andrew, 2015
Quintana, David, 1998
Quintero, Eddie, 2013

Raddatz, Karen, 2000
Raine, Travis, 2005
Rainey, Jayton, 2015
Rains, Billy, 2015
Rambo, Charles, 2010
Ramey, Walter, 2016
Ramirez Rubio, Fernando, 2017

Ramirez, Carlos, 2000
Ramirez, Erick, 2020
Ramirez, Hersaim, 2015
Ramirez, J.R., 2001
Ramirez, Miriam, 2009
Ramirez, Rebecca, 2020
Ramirez, Rodolfo, 2021
Ramos, Alexandria, 2008
Ramos, Joshua, 2021
Ramos-Williams, Christian, 2021
Randle, Tatiana, 2017
Range, Clayton, 2003
Rast, Ty, 2021
Rathke, Benjamin, 2017
Rathke, Bryan, 2011
Ratliff, Ryan, 1998
Ray, Carter, 2014
Rayfield, Robbie, 2010
Raymond, Chris, 2003
Read, Corey, 2017
Ream, Alden, 2019
Redding, Gregory, 1999
Redding, Ryan, 2013
Reed, Aaron, 1998
Reed, Connor, 2019
Reed, Kendall, 2015
Reed, Nathan, 1998
Reed, Tyler, 2009
Reeves, Brad, 2008
Reeves, Reagan, 2021
Reich, Joey, 2020
Reichel, William, 2015
Reid, Joshua, 2012
Reinecke, Kevin, 1998
Rek, Jon, 2007
Remmers, David, 2010
Rendon, Alfredo, 2022
Renfro-Pihut, Terry, 2016
Reola, Joshua, 2002
Resendez, David, 2017
Resendez, Jacob, 2017
Restivo, Andy, 2008
Restivo, Anthony, 2011
Reyes, Ben, 1999
Reyes, Jonathan, 2000

Reyes, Orlando, 2007
Reynolds, Kyle, 2018
Reynolds, Matt, 2004
Reynolds, Ryan, 2002
Reynolds, Shawn, 1998
Reynolds, William, 2020
Rhea, Chris, 2005
Rhodes, Dustin, 2011
Rhodes, Edward, 2002
Rhodes, Laura, 2021
Rice, Caitlin, 2018
Rice, Michael, 2007
Richard, Dennis, 2014
Richards, Jason, 2002
Richards, Lance, 2000
Richards, Travis, 2005
Richardson, Joe, 2019
Richardson, Matthew, 2006
Richardson, Rob, 1998
Richardson, Zachary, 2018
Richbourg, John, 2011
Richter, Danielle, 2015
Rico, Gabriella, 2021
Rico, Madeleine, 2021
Riesterer, Karl, 2021
Rigelsky, Jay, 2002
Riggs, Abbey, 2021
Riggs, Benjamin, 2020
Riggs, Lucas, 2019
Riggs, Robert, 1997
Riley, Abigail, 2022
Riley, Blake, 2012
Riley, Chip, 1998
Riley, Connor, 2020
Rios, Gabe, 2007
Rios, Gabriel, 1999
Rios, Paola, 2009
Ripkowski, Kenneth, 2000
Rippe, Chris, 1999
Riske, Ronald, 2000
Riske, Walt, 2005
Ritch, Zachary, 2020
Ritchie, Rex, 2016
Rivard, Chris, 1998
Rivas, Martin, 2019
Rivera, Edwin, 2007

Roach, Jonathan, 2000
Roach, Riley, 2010
Robbins, Colby, 2001
Roberson, Travis, 2017
Roberson, Tyler, 2017
Roberts, Elizabeth, 2002
Roberts, Rebekah, 2010
Roberts, Thomas, 2003
Robertson, Karissa, 2015
Robertson, Zane, 2009
Robinson, Jillian, 2006
Robinson, Sam, 1998
Robles, Amy, 2016
Rockwell, Kenny, 1999
Rodgers, Bryan, 1999
Rodriguez, Carlos, 2001
Rodriguez, Dan, 1999
Rodriguez, Evelyn, 2020
Rodriguez, Fernando, 2016
Rodriguez, Gonzalo, 2015
Rodriguez, J.J., 2014
Rodriguez, James, 1997
Rodriguez, Javi, 2012
Rodriguez, Jeremy, 2014
Rodriguez, Reuben, 2007
Rodriguez, Rudy, 2013
Rodriguez, Rusty, 1999
Rodriguez, Victoria, 2022
Rogers, Ayanna, 2022
Rogers, Christopher, 2008
Rogers, Kyle, 2010
Rohach, Alex, 2006
Roland, Je'Neal, 2009
Roland, Thomas, 2006
Rollins, Matthew, 2017
Roman, Thelma, 2001
Romero, Ceasar, 2009
Rooks, David, 2003
Rosas, Alondra, 2020
Rose, Cody, 2010
Rose, John, 2017
Rose, Sam, 2018
Ross, Matthew, 2001
Ross, Shaun, 2000
Rossi, Nathan, 2022
Rossi, Nicholas, 2020

Rothmann, Karla, 2022
Rothmann, Kristi, 2019
Routh, R., 2002
Rowe, Zachary, 2010
Rowland, Matt, 2011
Rowlette, Kacie, 2013
Roy, Aaron, 2004
Ruddick, Samuel, 2002
Rudolf, Rebecca, 2015
Rudy, Christopher, 2002
Ruffino, Angela, 2015
Ruiz, Efrain, 2018
Rusek, Michael, 1998
Rush, Benjamin, 2010
Rush, Scott, 1997
Russell, Abigale, 2022
Russell, Kelsey, 2014
Russell, Matthan, 2008
Russell, Matthew, 2006
Russell, Richard, 2011
Russell, Ryan, 2022
Rutan, Marcus, 2001
Rutherford, Charlie, 2007
Ryan, Colby, 2014
Ryan, Matthew, 2022
Ryan, Robert, 2021
Rydman, Ryan, 2011

Saadeh, Launa, 1998
Saathoff, Kyle, 2018
Sacher, Eric, 2000
Sackett, Chris, 2009
Saenz, Elise, 2009
Sajdak, Kyle, 2008
Sajewski, J. J., 2004
Sajewski, Leigh, 2011
Salas, Christopher, 2018
Salazar, Aaron, 2002
Salch, Ryan, 2008
Saldana, Angelica, 2004
Saldivar, Kathlynn, 2021
Salge, Bryan, 2005
Salinas, Servando, 2016
Sallee, Henry, 2009
Salmeron, Mateo, 2021
Saloma, Mikel, 1998

Salter, Nicholas, 2021
Sanchez, Angela, 2007
Sanchez, Briana, 2017
Sanchez, David, 2001
Sanchez, Jose , 2019
Sandfort, Stephen, 1999
Sandoval, Jennifer, 2013
Santana, Eric, 2015
Santiago Salazar, Juan, 2021
Santiago, Johnny, 2019
Santillan, Melissa, 2017
Sartain, Jay, 2000
Sartor, Chris, 1997
Sathe, Ritwik, 2021
Satterthwaite, Ryan, 1997
Satterwhite, Jason, 2001
Saulino, Peter, 2010
Scarborough, Cody, 2015
Schaap, Jody, 2000
Schenk, Leisha, 2011
Scherz, Aaron, 2000
Schiel, Lewis, 2003
Schiffner, Ryan, 2003
Schimank, Colton, 2015
Schindler, Christopher, 2001
Schindler, Jonathan, 2005
Schipul, Stockton, 2018
Schladt, Jason, 2010
Schlather, Collin, 2022
Schlattner, Jonathan, 2008
Schlebach, Alex, 2012
Schlueter, Jonathan, 1999
Schlueter, Josh, 2005
Schmidt, Bradley, 2001
Schneider, Chip, 1999
Schneider, Jacob, 2013
Schneider, Joshua, 2005
Schneider, Peter, 2014
Schneider, Phillip, 2011
Schneider, Thomas, 2012
Schoeffler, Kristofer, 2003
Schoelzel, Christopher, 2022
Schoonover, Ashley, 2009
Schuck, Joseph, 2017
Schuelke, Derek, 2004
Schuster, Justin, 2016

Schwarz, Nathan, 2009
Sciandra, James, 2012
Scoggins, Chris, 1999
Scott, Bryan, 2014
Scott, Daniel, 2007
Scott, Jonathan, 1999
Scott, Julia, 1998
Scott, M., 2002
Scott, Murray, 1999
Scott, Patrick, 2003
Scott, Stephen, 2010
Sears, Conneley, 2017
Seeger, Garrett, 2021
Seek, Daniel, 2019
Segner, Craig, 2005
Segovia, Jose, 2007
Seitz, Steven, 2005
Sellers, Jennifer, 2004
Selzer, Asa, 2003
Semper, James, 2018
Seng, Hong, 2000
Senor, Christopher, 2019
Serur, Chad, 1998
Seward, Ben, 2004
Sexton, Kat, 2015
Sexton, Susan, 2012
Seybold, Ryan, 2010
Seydler, Albert, 2009
Shackelford, Trenton, 2017
Sharp, Stephen, 2016
Shaver, Dustin, 2017
Shaver, Dylan, 2017
Shaw, Steven, 2011
Shearod, Shawn, 2013
Shelton, Blake, 2012
Shene, James, 2005
Shepherd, Jennifer, 2020
Sherman, William, 2003
Sherrill, Anthony, 2003
Shields, Lee, 1997
Shifflett, James, 2018
Shillings, Phillip, 2006
Shin, Alex, 2006
Shirley, J., 2003
Shofner, Nicholas, 2020
Shupak, Brandon, 2005

Shupak, Shane, 2003
Siefkin, Andy, 2001
Siefkin, Katherine, 1998
Sikel, Chris, 2007
Simmang, Austin, 2018
Simmons, Jeffery, 2004
Simms, Bobby, 2004
Simms, Jed, 2020
Simon, Josh, 2016
Simpson, Bryan, 2000
Simpson, Jared, 1999
Simpson, Neal, 2002
Sims, Alexandra, 2015
Sinclair, George, 2015
Sisco, Hayley, 2020
Sites, Catherine, 2017
Sittig, Ashton, 2021
Skidmore, Jason, 2009
Skinner, Rachel, 2013
Slack, John, 2000
Slattery, Stuart, 2011
Slezia, Ryan, 2008
Sloan, Grayson, 2005
Smart, Laura, 2015
Smith, Aaron, 2001
Smith, Barrett, 2013
Smith, Brad, 2005
Smith, Brian, 2013
Smith, Cullen, 2015
Smith, Erica, 1999
Smith, Ethan, 2020
Smith, Jordan, 2021
Smith, Kade, 2022
Smith, Kelly, 2006
Smith, Matthew, 2017
Smith, Michael, 2002
Smith, Patrick, 2009
Smith, Ryan, 1997
Smith, Ryan, 2015
Smith, Sarah, 2002
Smith, Shauntelle, 2007
Smith, Shelby, 2014
Smith, Steven, 2002
Smith, Wyatt, 2003
Sneed, Landon, 2014
Snider, Aubrey, 2008

Snider, Jennifer, 2006
Snow, Nate, 2007
Snyder, Sheldon, 2017
Sohne, Michelle, 2017
Sokol, Jeremy, 2005
Solis, Marsie, 2008
Solop, Harper, 2011
Somers, William, 2009
Sones, Joshua, 2012
Sonnen, Jarrett, 2000
Sorenson, Daniel, 2001
Sower, Jonathan, 2011
Spangler, Michael, 2017
Speakmon, Derek, 2000
Speasmaker, Latham, 2018
Spence, David, 1997
Spence, Kevin, 2000
Spence, Robert, 2007
Spence, Von, 2005
Spies, Patrick, 2000
Springer, Jacob, 2012
Springer, Sean, 2009
Springer, Stephen, 1999
Spurlock, Jennifer, 2001
Spurlock, Jeremy, 2005
Stacey, Hannah, 2018
Stacey, John, 2021
Stamm, Brett, 2000
Stanchos, Jennifer, 2001
Stancik, Kyle, 2016
Stanford, Jeff, 1999
Stanish, Benjamin, 2020
Stanislav, Derec, 2011
Stanley, Jackson, 2022
Stapleton, Ray, 2005
Starck, Matt, 1998
Starr, Adam, 2005
Starr, Clay, 1999
Statesir, Laura, 2002
Steele, Courtney, 2016
Stegall, Samuel, 2018
Steiger, Carl, 1998
Steinhauser, Alex, 2021
Stephens, Mark, 2012
Sterle, Megan, 2009
Sterling, Philip, 2001

Steskens, Patrick, 2017
Stetina, Alyson, 2013
Stetina, Danelle, 2005
Steubing, Michelle, 2011
Stewart, Caleb, 2017
Stiles, Zachary, 2008
Stilwell, Jackson, 2022
Stipek, Mitchel, 2016
Stobie, Michael, 2002
Stodola, Anna, 2017
Stone, Nathan, 2015
Stone, Richard, 2011
Stoudt, Alexa, 2016
Stoudt, Dustin, 2011
Stout, C., 2003
Stout, Darren, 2012
Stout, Wilton, 2013
Stowe, Essence, 2015
Stricklin, Taylor, 2016
Stringer, Connor, 2017
Stringer, Kyle, 2014
Stringer, Malcom, 2011
Striplin, Jennifer, 2014
Strock, Chris, 2015
Stroo, Joshua, 2022
Stroud, Tristan, 2018
Stroup, Jonathan, 2009
Struzick, Danny, 2005
Struzick, Robert, 2011
Stuckey, Daniel, 2000
Stuckey, Matthew, 2002
Stump, Elliot, 2009
Stump, Tabitha, 1999
Sturdivant, Preston, 2015
Sturm, Samuel, 2015
Sublette, John, 2001
Sullivan, Christopher, 1998
Sullivan, Jonathan, 2009
Sullivan, Larry, 2012
Sultenfuss, Daniel, 2002
Sultenfuss, Mark, 1999
Sumerlin, Christopher, 2008
Supak, Cameron, 2012
Sustaita, Wyatt, 2017
Sutherlin, Aaron, 2001
Sutton, Matthew, 1998

Swain, Daniel, 1998
Swanzy, Jesse, 2008
Swartz, Matthew, 2015
Sweat, Gregory, 2000
Swendig, Kyle, 2007
Swift, Scott, 2008
Swiney, Joseph, 2019
Swisher, Jonathan, 2004
Symm, Daniel, 2002

Taft, Timothy, 1998
Talkington, Rachel, 2022
Talley, Carson, 2011
Tamayo, Katelynn, 2011
Tames, Joey, 2017
Tamplen, Alan, 2013
Tanner, Daniel, 1998
Tanner, Eric, 1998
Tanner, Shane, 1997
Tash, Justin, 2015
Tate, Brad, 1999
Taylor, Aaron, 1999
Taylor, Andrew, 2016
Taylor, Cade, 2010
Taylor, Cory, 2012
Taylor, Diana, 2006
Taylor, Jacob, 2022
Taylor, Kyle, 2008
Taylor, Patrick, 2011
Taylor, Zach, 2001
Tedesco, Marcel, 2016
Teinert, Alton, 2022
Teltschik, Aaron, 1998
Tenbrink, Ian, 2015
Thacker, Josh, 2005
Thames, Dale, 2011
Theiss, Paul, 2017
Thelen, Jack, 1999
Thelen, Mary, 2008
Thomas, Jordan, 2010
Thomas, Jesse, 1997
Thomas, Kelly, 2009
Thomas, Kirk, 2011
Thomas, Wyatt, 2018
Thompson, Benjamin, 2011
Thompson, Greg, 1999

Thompson, Jesse, 2012
Thompson, Lee, 2010
Thompson, Ryan, 2009
Thompson, Steve, 2004
Thomson, Allen, 2000
Thomson, Patrick, 2003
Thornton, Duncan, 2017
Thornton, Evan, 2014
Thornton, Jaret, 2020
Thuss, Daniel, 1999
Tice, Landon, 2019
Tighe, Mitch, 2016
Tillman, Michael, 1999
Tillotson, Kyle, 2011
Timmermann, Robert, 2009
Timmons, Connor, 2022
Timmreck, Albert, 2006
Timmreck, Ashley, 2006
Timmreck, Stephen, 2009
Tinajero, Salvador, 2016
Tipley, Geoff, 2006
Tobias, Adam, 2004
Tobitt, Victoria, 2017
Todd, Aaron, 2019
Toetter, Edward, 2012
Tolar, David, 1998
Tomlin, Brian, 2017
Toone, Roy, 2001
Toronjo, William, 2022
Torres, Adan, 2011
Torres, Ben, 2009
Torres, Cristina, 2019
Torres, Cruz, 2003
Torres, David, 2003
Torres, Ehren, 2011
Torres, Gabie, 2012
Torres, Juan, 2005
Torres, Mason, 2011
Torrez, Kathryn, 2016
Toth, Mitchell, 2019
Trahan, Adam, 2016
Travis, Eric, 1998
Trawick, Aimee, 2011
Traylor, Amy, 2008
Trchalek, Daniel, 2019
Trejo, Eric, 2021

Trenchard, Andrew, 2003
Trenchard, Charlie, 2006
Trentham, Jessica, 2015
Treude, Jacob, 2017
Trevino, Christine, 2011
Trevino, Claudio, 2019
Trevino, Nicholas, 2021
Trevino, Nick, 2018
Trichel, Grant, 2021
Tripp, Tara, 1998
Tripson, Tiffany, 2005
Trujillo, Zachary, 2017
Truong, Andrew, 2019
Tschirhart, Allen, 2016
Tschirhart, Michael, 2008
Tschirhart, Ryan, 2016
Tucker, Andy, 2000
Tucker, Jenna, 2008
Tucker, Michael, 2014
Tucker, Tyler, 2017
Tucker, Zach, 2009
Tuley, Hayden, 2011
Tullis, Stephanie, 2001
Tumulty, Travis, 2007
Turk, Jeremy, 2005
Turner, Jett, 2019
Turner, Lucas, 2012
Turner, Stephanie, 2012
Turney, Jason, 2010
Tutt, Adam, 2004
Tyndall, George, 2014

Udovich, Sam, 1999
Ulrich, Caitlyn, 2020
Upright, Rory, 2009
Urbanosky, Jon, 2009
Urbanowich, Michael, 2010
Usher, Kevin, 2004

Vacek, Elizabeth, 2006
Vaculik, Stewart, 2001
Vader, Clayton, 1999
Vader, Kevin, 1997
Valadez, Steve, 2000
Valderrama, Gabriel, 2000
Valdez, Brandon, 2022

Valdez, Edwin, 2015
Valdez, Michael, 2008
Valdez, Ruben, 2008
Valdivia, Peter, 2009
Valenciano, Marcos, 1998
Valenta, Cameron, 2014
Valentine, Buddy, 2006
Vallejo, Mark, 2014
Van Sciver, Matt, 2007
Vanbuskirk, Brian, 1997
Vance, Kerri, 2006
Vander Straten, Teagan, 2019
Vander Sys, Michael, 2008
Vargas, Matthew, 2009
Vargo, Leonard, 2022
Vargo, Matthew, 1998
Varman, Alex, 2012
Varnell, B., 2007
Varner, Joel, 2009
Vasser, Anthony, 2002
Vasvani, Nikunj, 2016
Vaughan, Amber, 2000
Vaughan, Jenna, 2008
Vazquez, Victor, 2016
Veach, David, 1998
Vedda, Joseph, 2002
Vega, Adriana, 2012
Vega, Pedro, 2009
Velasquez, Gabe, 2015
Venable, Justin, 2017
Vendt, Paul, 2008
Venesky, Michael, 2014
Venghaus, Leslie, 2002
Vera, James, 2015
Vermedahl, Nathan, 1998
Vernor, Charles, 2008
Vierling, Ted, 1997
Villalobos, Christina, 2003
Villalovoz, Michael, 2001
Villarreal, Carlos, 1999
Villarreal, Gabe, 2000
Villegas Juarez, Gerardo, 2016
Visel, Matthew, 2012
Voelkel, Beau, 1999
Voelkel, Trevor, 2002
Vogel, Andrew, 2017

Voges, Corbin, 2019
Voinis, Michael, 1997
Vu, Aaron, 2018
Vu, Eliza, 2019
Vu, Thai, 2018

Wade, Darla, 2005
Walden, Rebecca, 2012
Waldrep, Jordan, 1998
Wales, Derek, 2019
Walker, Adam, 2019
Walker, Connor, 2022
Walker, Jonny, 2004
Walker, Jonathan, 2010
Walker, Kyle, 2012
Walker, Travis, 2014
Walker, Zachary, 2012
Wallace, Cody, 2018
Wallace, Danny, 2003
Wallace, Jacob, 2019
Wallace, Johnathon, 2011
Wallace, Kathy, 2005
Wallace, Katy, 2018
Wallace, Paul, 2010
Wallek, Megan, 2004
Wallis, Matt, 2015
Walters, Chad, 2006
Walther, Philip, 2012
Walton, Cynthia, 2002
Waninger, Evan, 2017
Wann, David, 2001
Ward, Cody, 2014
Ward, Jordan, 2005
Warren, Justin, 2000
Washburn, Zachery, 2000
Washington, Dezlun, 2015
Wasko, Kenneth, 2001
Waterman, Joshua, 2018
Watson, Christopher, 2019
Watson, Gabriella, 2018
Watson, Matt, 2000
Watson, Ruben, 2011
Watters, Tyler, 2007
Waun, Michael, 2001
Way, Charles, 1998
Weast, Kevin, 2016

Weaver, Bobby, 2019
Weaver, Carl, 2003
Weaver, Danielle, 2006
Weaver, Scott, 2016
Weaver, Todd, 2021
Webb, Eric, 2002
Webb, J. D., 2009
Webb, Matthew, 2014
Webster, Reid, 2018
Wedelich, Jackson, 2020
Weerts, Trevor, 2008
Wehmann, David, 2012
Weidenbach, Bryan, 1998
Weiner, Benjamin, 2008
Weiner, William, 2011
Weinzettle, Caleb, 2015
Weinzettle, Cameron, 2008
Weisberg, Chris, 2018
Weisberg, Robert, 2016
Weiss, Evan, 2017
Welch, Phillip, 2005
Weldon, Aaron, 2003
Welling, Glenn, 1998
Wellman, David, 1997
Wells, John, 2007
Wells, Matthew, 2004
Welsh, Logan, 2022
Welty, Austin, 2011
Wenk, T. J., 2004
Wenmohs, Chip, 2002
Wentworth, Jason, 2004
Wenzel, Michael, 2017
Wenzel, Stephen, 2015
Wessels, Neil, 2009
West, Casey, 1998
Westbrook, Adam, 2017
Weston, Josh, 2012
Weyer, Amanda, 2017
Whatley, Colton, 2015
Wheeler, Andy, 1999
Wheeler, Jennifer, 2011
Wheeler, Kevin, 2013
Whigham, Matt, 2009
White, Bret, 2002
White, Chris, 2005
White, David, 2005

White, Garrett, 2020
White, Jefferson, 2017
White, Matt, 2008
White, Parker, 2015
Whitely, Rocky, 2005
Whiting, Samuel, 2020
Whitley, Andrew, 2000
Whittington, Forrest, 2010
Wiatrek, Nathaniel, 2017
Wideman, Scott, 1997
Wiedenfeld, Herman, 2007
Wierzbicki, Melissa, 1999
Wierzowiecki, John, 2002
Wiese, Wes, 2002
Wiggs, Kyle, 2017
Wilcox, Conner, 2021
Wilcox, Stephen, 2004
Wilcoxson, Brandon, 2011
Wiley, Hank, 2000
Wiley, Steven, 1997
Wilfong, Kevin, 2016
Wilkes, Jordan, 2013
Will, Robert, 2008
Willcox, Jason, 2001
Williams, Chris, 1997
Williams, David, 2015
Williams, Garrett, 2013
Williams, John, 2006
Williams, Joshua, 2022
Williams, Ryan, 2001
Williams, Shanae, 2004
Williams, Steven, 2003
Williams, Steven, 2004
Williams, Tasha, 1997
Williams, Zachary, 2020
Williamson, Andy, 2004
Williamson, David, 2012
Williamson, John, 2006
Williamson, Mark, 2017
Williamson, Sarah, 2009
Williford, George, 1997
Williford, Kyle, 2001
Willimann, Kristof, 2018
Willis, Aaron, 2016

Willis, John, 2018
Willis, Paula, 2014
Willis, Rachel, 2011
Wilson, Cassandra, 2012
Wilson, Greg, 2017
Wilson, Katelyn, 2012
Wilson, Keith, 1999
Wilson, Lyndon, 2022
Wilson, Matt, 2001
Wilson, Taylor, 2021
Wilson, Timothy, 2004
Wilson, Zachary, 2019
Windham, Lee, 2002
Windham, Matthew, 2013
Winn, Wayne, 2004
Wishert, Elizabeth, 2016
Withrow, Frances, 2012
Witten, Abigail, 2021
Wittie, Todd, 2008
Wittner, Matthew, 2010
Wofford, Brandon, 2021
Wolf, Bob, 1999
Wolf, Marc, 2000
Wolfer, Cole, 2018
Wolff, Chris, 2018
Wolff, Nicholas, 2020
Wood, Ben, 2009
Wood, Chris, 2016
Wood, Frank, 2020
Woodard, Katie, 2010
Woods, Vince, 1999
Woppman, Alexa, 2020
Works, Cody, 2010
Worley, Brayden, 2021
Wozny, Nicholas, 2000
Wright, Brenna, 2006
Wright, Daniel, 2001
Wright, Derek, 2001
Wright, Lesley, 2009
Wright, Matthew, 2012
Wright, Zach, 2005
Wurzbach, Christopher, 2012
Wurzbach, Matthew, 2008

Wylie, Matthew, 2000
Wynn, Sarah, 2017
Wyrick, Amanda, 2001

Yarbrough, Elton, 2005
Yates, Brian, 1999
Ybanez, Caleb, 2022
Yen, Albert, 2012
Yim, Sabrina, 2020
Yocum, Benjiman, 2013
Yoder, Clay, 2016
Yohi, Jean-Luc, 2020
Yosko, Braden, 2021
Young, Ben, 1998
Young, Bianca, 2015
Young, Michael, 2007
Young, Michael, 2012
Younggren, Tracy, 1999

Zabcik, Bethany, 2006
Zachariades, Catherine, 2002
Zaharoff, Austin, 2021
Zaharoff, Patrick, 2010
Zahn, Chip, 2001
Zahn, Matthew, 2010
Zajaczkowski, Greg, 2003
Zalmanek, Mandy, 2020
Zamora, Rudy, 1999
Zapatero, Alejandro, 2015
Zavala, Monica, 2011
Zeitler, Ryan, 2001
Zenn, Jasmine, 2019
Zesch, Zach, 2007
Zeutschel, Ryan, 2019
Zevenbergen, Reid, 2007
Zikias, Travis, 2014
Zimmermann, J.R., 2016
Zirges, Kothe, 2005
Zoch, Daniel, 2019
Zoch, Philip, 1999
Zoellner, McKinley, 2021
Zorn, A.J., 2005
Zorn, Will, 2009

Notes

Chapter 1. Joseph Holick and the Early Bandmasters

1. John Holick, interview with Donald B. Powell and Mary Jo Powell, March 17, 1993.

2. John E. West, Texas A&M University news release, College Station, Texas, February 11, 1966.

3. Holick, interview.

4. Holick, interview.

5. Bill J. Leftwich, *The Corps at Aggieland* (Dallas: Taylor Publishing, 1976), 39.

6. Walter H. Bradford, "Aggie Fashion: More Than a Century of Cadet Uniforms," excerpts from an unpublished manuscript, 1993.

7. Leftwich, *Corps at Aggieland*, 39.

8. Leftwich, 39–40.

9. David Brooks Cofer, *Fragments of Early History of Texas A. and M. College* (College Station: Association of Former Students of Texas A. and M. College, 1953), 15.

10. Ossie Greene, interview with Donald B. Powell, San Angelo, Texas, April 21, 1993.

11. Steve Fullhart, interview with KBTX-TV, aired October 28, 2006.

12. Holick, interview.

13. Leftwich, *Corps at Aggieland*, 40.

14. Leftwich, *Corps at Aggieland*, 40–41.

15. Tom Mulvany, "Band, War Hymn Share Aggie Fame," *Houston Chronicle*, March 24, 1963.

16. Holick, interview.

17. Henry C. Dethloff, *A Centennial History of Texas A&M University, 1876–1976* (College Station: Texas A&M University Press, 1975), 183.

Chapter 2. The Tradition Begins

1. Leftwich, *Corps at Aggieland*, 41–42.

2. B. Kennerly, "They're Working to Beat the Band," *Texas Aggie*, December 1952.

3. "Recognition for Col. Richard Dunn," *Texas Aggie*, November 1980, 6–7.

4. *Longhorn* (College Station: Agricultural and Mechanical College of Texas).

5. Bradford, "Aggie Fashion."

6. Bradford, "Aggie Fashion."

7. "New Band Uniform Given Approval by Junior Class," *Battalion*, May 20, 1931, 2.

8. Bradford, "Aggie Fashion."

9. Earl Patterson, interview with Robert Lang, Houston, Texas, March 15, 1993.

10. Leftwich, *Corps at Aggieland*, 42–44.

11. Leftwich, 42–44.

12. *Texas A&M University 1993 Football Media Guide*, 156.

13. Leftwich, *Corps at Aggieland*, 44.

14. "Recognition for Col. Richard Dunn," 7.

15. Unpublished correspondence files, Richard Dunn, Texas Aggie Band Association, College Station.

16. "Recognition for Col. Richard Dunn," 7.

17. *Battalion*, February 11, 1931.

18. *Longhorn*, 17.

19. *Battalion*, January 19, 1943.

20. *Battalion*, October 23, 1943.

21. *Battalion*, November 21, 1942.

22. *Longhorn*, 62.

23. *Battalion*, November 21, 1942.

24. E. Elkins, interview with Donald B. Powell, College Station, Texas, May 24, 1993.

Chapter 3. The Military Precision

1. Joe Buser, "Best Band in the Land," *Texas Aggie*, November 1966, 4.

2. Clipping dated January 7, 1946, source unknown, Mrs. E. V. (Belle) Adams's scrapbook.

3. Holick, interview.

4. Buser, "Best Band in the Land," 4.

5. Mrs. E. V. (Belle) Adams, interview with John E. West, Bryan, Texas, April 4, 1993.

6. Leftwich, *Corps at Aggieland*, 44–45.

7. Buser, "Best Band in the Land," 4.

8. Mrs. Adams, interview.

9. Edward V. Adams Jr., interview with John E. West, Bryan, Texas, April 4, 1993.

10. Undated clipping, source unknown, Mrs. Adams's scrapbook.

11. "Aggie Band at Pre-War Strength," September 14, 1946, source unknown, Mrs. Adams's scrapbook; *Battalion*, October 7, 1949.

12. Leftwich, *Corps of Aggieland*, 45.

13. "How Band Stunts Develop," *Battalion*, October 23, 1951.

14. Leftwich, *Corps of Aggieland*, 45.

15. Joe Buser, *Big! Brassy! Beautiful!*, vol. 2, *The Texas Aggie Band in Stereo*, album notes, 1970.

16. "How Band Stunts Develop"; "Achievement Award Winners Honored at Sbisa Banquet," *Battalion*, February 26, 1948.

17. *Longhorn*, 359–60.

18. John E. West, interview with Donald B. Powell, College Station, Texas, May 17, 1993.

19. Mrs. Adams, interview.

20. West, interview.

21. West, interview.

22. Buser, *Big! Brassy! Beautiful!* album notes; Jay O. Brewer, interview with Donald B. Powell, College Station, Texas, June 4, 1993.

23. Edward V. Adams Jr., interview; Buser, *Big! Brassy! Beautiful!* album notes.

24. West, interview.

25. Buser, *Big! Brassy! Beautiful!* album notes.

26. Buser, *Big! Brassy! Beautiful!* album notes; West, interview.

27. Bradford, "Aggie Fashion."

28. "Precision Marching and Military Airs Spread Fame of Aggie Band, College Station," clipping, source and date unknown, Mrs. Adams's scrapbook.

29. West, interview.

30. John E. West, personal files, Bryan, Texas.

31. "The 'Colonel' Steps Down," *Texas Aggie*, September 1973, 14.

32. "Rather Burn Than Switch," clipping, source and date unknown, c. 1967, Mrs. Adams's scrapbook.

33. Martin Dreyer, "Aggieland's Last Salute for Col. Adams—Leader of the Best Band in the Land," *Texas Magazine* of the *Houston Chronicle*, May 6, 1973, 20–32.

34. Memo from publicity director, University of Southern California, September 20, 1955, Mrs. Adams's scrapbook.

35. West, interview.

36. Dreyer, "Aggieland's Last Salute for Col. Adams," 24.

37. Buser, *Big! Brassy! Beautiful!* album notes.

38. West, interview.

39. West, interview.

40. West, interview.

41. West, interview.

42. Brewer, interview.

43. "Aggie Album Premier Set for Guion Tonight," *Battalion*, February 19, 1951.

44. Photograph caption, *Texas Aggie*, January 1971.

45. West, interview.

46. John West, "Fine New Home for the Fightin' Texas Aggie Band," *Texas Aggie*, October 1970, 14–16.

47. West, interview.

48. Jerry Gray, "Colonel Ends 27 Years," *Bryan–College Station Eagle*, April 15, 1973.

49. John West, "Aggie Band Halts War Hymn in Salute to Col. Adams," *Texas Aggie*, October 1982, 6.

50. Donald B. Powell, personal recollections.

Chapter 4. The Big Bold Sound

1. Joe T. Haney, interview with Donald B. Powell and Mary Jo Powell, Bryan, Texas, March 30, 1993.

2. Haney, interview.

3. Haney, interview.

4. "Aggie Band Won't Change," *Texas Aggie*, September 1973, 15.

5. Haney, interview.

6. John West, "Bugles Flash in Autumn Air, 267 Men Step Forth as One . . . ," *Bryan–College Station Eagle*, October 27, 1961.

7. Correspondence files, Texas Aggie Band Association, November 20, 1979.

8. Correspondence files, Texas Aggie Band Association, December 11, 1979.

9. "Instant Footnotes in A&M History," *Houston Chronicle*, date unknown, Jay Brewer's scrapbook.

10. "Instant Footnotes in A&M History."

11. "First Woman Earns Seniority in Aggie Band," *Bryan–College Station Eagle*, August 27, 1988, A4.

12. Jay Brewer, interview with Donald B. Powell and Mary Jo Powell, College Station, Texas, March 29, 1993.

13. Haney, interview.

14. Haney, interview.

15. Haney, interview.

16. Donald B. Powell, personal observation.

17. John E. West, personal files, Bryan, Texas.

18. "Band Is Just Human—Haney," *Houston Post*, October 25, 1981.

19. "Just What Happened?," *Bryan–College Station Eagle*, October 25, 1981.

20. Haney, interview.

21. Haney, interview; Jay Brewer, email to Mary Jo Powell, July 23, 2018.

22. Haney, interview.

23. "Wikipedia: Kyle Field," Wikimedia Foundation, last modified January 22, 2019, https://en.wikipedia.org/wiki/Kyle_Field.

24. Brewer, interview.

25. Brewer, interview.

26. Haney, interview.

27. Haney, interview.

28. "First Woman Earns Seniority in Aggie Band," A4.

29. Dorothy Hopkins, interview with Donald B. Powell and Mary Jo Powell, College Station, Texas, June 11, 1993.

30. "First Women Earns Seniority in Aggie Band," A4.

Chapter 5. The Legend Continues

1. Ray E. Toler, interview with Mark Slavit, KRCG-TV, Columbia, Missouri, September 18, 1992.

2. Ray E. Toler, interview with Donald B. Powell and Mary Jo Powell, College Station, Texas, March 15, 1993; telephone interview with Mary Jo Powell, College Station, Texas, June 7, 2018. All subsequent quotations from Toler are taken from one of these two interviews.

3. Haney, interview.

4. Brewer, interview.

5. Timothy Rhea résumé, courtesy of Ray E. Toler.

6. Hopkins, interview.

7. Hopkins, interview.

8. Brewer, interview.

9. Jay Brewer, email to Mary Jo Powell, July 28, 2018.

10. Brewer, interview. All subsequent quotations from Brewer are taken from this interview.

11. Various media accounts, including the *Bryan–College Station Eagle*, the *Battalion*, the *Houston Chronicle*, the *Dallas Morning News*, the *Texas Aggie*, and television stations including KBTX-TV, Bryan–College Station, Texas, and others.

12. Donald B. Powell, personal recollections.

13. West, interview.

14. Brewer, interview.

15. Brewer, interview.

16. Robert Lang, interview with Donald B. Powell, College Station, Texas, June 7, 1993.

17. Brewer, interview.

18. Edwin Cooper, remarks at Adams's retirement dinner, April 13, 1971.

19. Texas Aggie Band Association permanent files, now stored with the records of the Texas A&M Corps of Cadets Association, Bryan, Texas.

20. Donald B. Powell, recollections.

21. Mary Jo Powell, personal recollections and notes.

22. Jordan Overturf, "Aggie Jack Jernigan, Who Had a Heart Attack at Kyle Field in 1994, Dies at age 80," *Bryan–College Station Eagle*, January 7, 2015, and obituary.

Chapter 6. The Expanding Music Program

1. Timothy Rhea, written interview with Mary Jo Powell, February 15, 2018. All subsequent quotations from Rhea are taken from this interview.

2. "Wikipedia: Timothy Rhea," Wikimedia Founda-
tion, accessed June 30, 2018, https://en.wikipedia.org/wiki/Timothy_Rhea; American Bandmasters Association, accessed June 30, 2018, http://www.americanbandmasters.org/.

3. Texas A&M University fact sheet for the University Bands Program, Department of Music Activities, https://musa.tamu.edu/university-bands/.

4. American Bandmasters Association, http://www.americanbandmasters.org/.

5. Texas A&M University fact sheet for the John D. White '70–Robert L. Walker '58 Music Activities Center, Department of Music Activities, http://musa.tamu.edu.

6. Donald B. Powell, "The Board of Regents of The Texas A&M University System," biography of John D. White, http://www.tamus.edu.

7. Michael Ayo, "Texas A&M Fundraiser Bob Walker Retiring after 46 Years," *Bryan–College Station Eagle*, July 13, 2014.

Chapter 7. "On the Road Again . . ."

1. Bruce Bockhorn, personal conversations with Donald B. Powell and/or Mary Jo Powell, 2003 to the present.

2. Bockhorn statistics, provided to Mary Jo Powell, May 2018.

3. "Wikipedia: Southwest Conference," Wikimedia Foundation, last modified January 16, 2019, https://en.wikipedia.org/wiki/Southwest_Conference.

4. "Wikipedia: Big 12 Conference," Wikimedia Foundation, last modified February 28, 2019, https://en.wikipedia.org/wiki/Big_12_Conference.

5. Mary Jo Powell, personal observation.

6. "Wikipedia: Southeastern Conference," Wikimedia Foundation, last modified March 7, 2019, https://en.wikipedia.org/wiki/Southeastern_Conference.

7. Robert C. Barker, correspondence with Mary Jo Powell, July 27, 2018.

8. Texas Aggie Band Association files.

9. Rod Zent, multiple conversations with Donald B. Powell.

10. Donald B. Powell, verbal reflections.

11. Bockhorn statistics.

12. "Texas Aggie Band Show," RDM Pros, accessed July 17, 2018, http://www.rdmpros.com/tabs.

Chapter 8. The Definitive Aggie Bandsman

1. Jay O. Brewer biography on the Texas A&M University Bands web page https://www.musa.tamu.edu/university-bands/.

2. Jay O. Brewer, interview with Mary Jo Powell, July 2, 2018.

3. Brewer, interview.

4. Brewer, interview. All subsequent quotations from Brewer are taken from this interview.